NEXT WAR

INDIA • PAKISTAN • CHINA

Attention Authors

'We Convert Fighters into Writers'. That's the motto of Manas Publications since more than four decades. Our message to the world is that India can win the battle not only by the bullet but also by the pen. There is no dearth of intellectuals in our country, but their knowledge is confined to them only. No sincere effort has been made by any other publisher to channelise their knowledge in national interest. That is why the talent of a large number of intellectuals remains latent. An author transforms his knowledge into a manuscript, and it is our job to spread his/her knowledge by converting it into a beautiful book. For over four decades, Manas has been motivating the intellectuals by publishing their manuscripts and would like to publish your manuscript too. If you or your colleagues have any manuscript ready for publication or are working on it, kindly contact us with detailed synopsis and list of contents. We will transform your work into a valuable publication. If you wish, we can also suggest you the suitable subjects for writing the books related to your area of expertise. Manas is known for its publishing quality and commitments. We take utmost care in production and give wide publicity to the book as well as its author through our national and international distribution network.

NEXT WAR

INDIA • PAKISTAN • CHINA

Dr NC Asthana, IPS

Manas Publications
(We Convert Fighters into Writers)
New Delhi - 110 002 (INDIA)

MANAS PUBLICATIONS
(We Convert Fighters into Writers)
(Publishers, Library Suppliers, Importers & Exporters)
4402/5-A, Ansari Road (Opp. HDFC Bank)
Darya Ganj, New Delhi - 110 002 (India)
Phones: Off.: 011-23260783, 23265523, Res.: 011-23842660
E-mail: manaspublications@gmail.com
manaspublications@yahoo.com
Website: www.manaspublications.in

ISBN 978-81-7049-525-3

₹ 995.00

Designed at
Manas Publications

Printed in India at
R.K. Printers, Delhi
and published by Mrs Suman Lata for
Manas Publications, 4402/5-A,
Ansari Road (Opp HDFC Bank),
Darya Ganj, New Delhi - 110 002 (INDIA)

Preface

Why I wrote this book and why you need to read this book? The reason is simple. I wrote this book because such a comprehensive book was sorely, desperately needed. In my considered opinion, in India, the subject of defence has been deliberately mystified and made obscure. I have determined that a common problem with authors coming from the background of defence forces has been that they find it very difficult to rise above the myopic view of their organization and the petty organizational concerns and hence are unable to take a holistic view of the matter. The problem with the 'academic' authors associated with various think-tanks etc has been that, overcome by the desire to sound knowledgeable and earn academic respectability, they tend to become verbose and, in the process, obfuscate the real issue.

You need to read this book because wars concern us all and they will have a profound impact on the lives of everybody—they entail the potential of causing great destruction as well as giving everlasting national pride. Peace, peaceful coexistence, development, bilateral trade, prosperity, and strong economy, etc are all good and desirable; but, as history stands witness, wars have been fought at the cost of all these because, in the lives of nations, there are issues much higher than material comforts and progress. According to Juliet Kaarbo and James Lee Ray (*Global Politics*, Wadsworth, Boston, 2011, p 183), mankind has spent a total of only 292 years without war in more than five-and-a-half millennia of civilized existence. As the human race has progressed, wars are becoming deadlier. Over 150 million people have perished in all kinds of wars so far. However, nearly 96% of them have been killed in the past 400 years only. Thus none of us can afford not to be interested in war. **The fate of the nations is still decided by their wars and it will continue to be so in the foreseeable future also**.

Nations will be prepared to suffer a great deal for the sake of those issues, irrespective of whether they are resolved or not. Wars do not always resolve issues; it has not, however, prevented nations from going to war. Going to war becomes imperative when reason does not work anymore and there is no way but to pick up arms. It is a human necessity for situations where you cannot make a compromise. **A just war is, in fact, better than an unjust peace**.

No race can afford to decry war as immoral, because then each and every prize of victory too, in which all races have exulted and have taken pride, would automatically become immoral. Tell me of a nation which does not take pride in the military victories it has had? Nations could perhaps apologize for war crimes or atrocities committed during wars; they never apologize for wars per se or for the carnage and mayhem caused in a war.

Since the coming of the nuclear age, it has often been argued that an all-out war has become rationally unthinkable or economically impossible. I strongly maintain that this notion is not only untrue in this age, but has been repeatedly belied in all the ages when the invention of some deadly weapons had made them appear like the ultimate weapons in that era. In fact, such a notion is based on the false premise that whatever is very horrible, cannot happen. **The truth is that even a nuclear war can take place and, if we have to survive that and emerge victorious, we must be prepared for that**. This book will tell you how.

Since the complex issues pertaining to defence and wars have been deliberately made obscure, loaded with unnecessary jargon and confined to in-house journals of the think-tanks or TV debates of a few people, they neither involve the people at large nor educate them. Thus the people, in whose name billions upon billions of the taxpayers' hard-earned money are spent, have no idea at all of how we are going about the whole business of defence and wars. The future of 1.33 billion people cannot be allowed to be mortgaged in the hands of a few people with vested interests and dubious credentials.

As a concerned citizen of this country, I consider it my moral duty that I must make the people of this country really understand this complex subject. This book demystifies the subject and opens up the vital subject of national security from external aggression to public discussion and debate. Modern warfare is such a complex subject that unless it is understood in a comprehensive manner, one is likely to be grossly mistaken in his beliefs and inferences. Verbosity in TV studios, oratorical skills, histrionics, heroic gestures, booming voice with theatrical modulations, and poetic lines do not win wars for the nation. **This book will take you out of the fantasy land of wars in TV studios and the sheer verbosity of the so-called academicians**.

It is foolish to assume that future military crises on the subcontinent would follow the same script as in the past conflicts. **One of the most fundamental mistakes which military planners are apt to commit is that they think that the next war will also be essentially like the last war**. Nothing could be farther from the truth. Many nations, over the centuries, have suffered horribly as a result of their commanders thinking like that. The French strategy in the Second World War became a prisoner of its own Maginot Line. The USAF had a cakewalk in Afghanistan with practically no opposition from the ground or air. It would not be so elsewhere. We fought the 1971 war essentially like the battles of the Second World War, not even like battles in the Korean and the Vietnam Wars. The experience of the 1971 war and the lessons drawn from that, or from any subsequent military exercise conducted basically along that line, will not be of any help in the next war. It is true that the hardware has changed greatly since then; however, as long as the mindset remains the same, the exercises would not help.

India's position is complicated by two things. The first is that a nuclear-armed Pakistan would not let itself be subjected to a decisive defeat of the 1971 type at any cost. The second is that the Chinese not only have a much higher overall military potential than us, they are ruthless in the execution of their designs as well—more importantly, if push comes to shove, they would not be deterred by what the USA says or does. Hence we have no option but to have a serious relook at the way we approach our defence concerns. We also need to appreciate that the relative strengths of two nations are not determined by the size of their armies alone or the number of weapon systems they possess.

The analysis which is presented in this book is vital because it strikes a balance between strategic planners of a school that derives its precepts and lessons from historical experience, and the planners of a school and that is mesmerized by the products of technology. Since the Second World War, it has been found that both are imperfect and a hybrid, more inclusive modelling is necessary.

Being in government service means that I have not commented on any matter of government policy. **This book therefore focuses on India as a nation—what our imperatives must be if we have to survive as a nation and emerge victorious in a war; that should be the concern of every citizen—armies win battles, it's nations that win wars; strong armies do not**

win wars; strong nations do. Conversely, if the nations are not strong, they will not be able to win wars, though their armies might win some battles. That's where the real military crisis of India lies. Strong nations require, above all, strong people and a strong national character—something that we lack miserably and must develop before it is too late.

Given the way the scene around us is unfolding, war is a real possibility. As this book goes to press, India has, for the first time mounted surgical strikes on terrorist 'launch pads' across the LOC in the wake of the terrorist attack on the 12th Infantry Brigade HQ in Uri in September 2016. Tensions between India and Pakistan are at an all-time high.

This treatise provides a rare insight into the subject of defence and wars, and extremely authoritative knowledge that is extremely hard to get except from a million sources. Most people have only notions of war derived from TV or films—they are as wrong as they could be. **This book busts all the myths associated with the business of wars**. It is for the first time that absolutely authoritative knowledge has been presented about what real wars comprise and how the popular notions are so unrealistic and so very wrong. **As a responsible citizen, it is your duty to be well-informed so that your reactions to any development on matters related to national security are guided by reason and not by emotions**. Whether you are a lay man, a student, a homemaker, a media person, a policy-maker, or a man in the armed forces, the rare knowledge contained within the pages of this book will set you free from the tyranny of the ignorant.

New Delhi, 2016

Dr NC Asthana

Declaration: In terms of Rule 6 of the All India Service (Conduct) Rules, 1968, I hereby declare that the views and opinions expressed in the book are my own, and not those of the Government of India. That the views and opinions expressed are my own means that they are my personal intellectual creations and are not endorsed in any way by the Government of India or the official position held by me. It is further certified that, in terms of Rule 7 of the All India Service (Conduct) Rules, 1968, there is nothing in the book which has the effect of an adverse criticism of any current or recent policy or action of the Central Government or a State Government; or which is capable of embarrassing the relations between the Central Government and any State Government; or which is capable of embarrassing the relations between the Central Government and the government of any foreign State.

Contents

CHAPTER 1

War Clouds over India, Pakistan and China

INDIA-PAKISTAN FACE-OFF: HURDLES IN THE PATH OF NORMALIZATION

THE ISSUE OF KASHMIR, BALOCHISTAN AND GILGIT-BALTISTAN

India and Pakistan do seem to agree on the objective of a normalized relationship as it would be in the interest of both, but they disagree deeply on how to get there. The differences are sort of fundamental and mutual suspicion runs deep. The mutual suspicions has taken such roots in the collective subconscious that the moods of the public in both the countries can be swung diametrically almost overnight by suitable manipulation of their minds by the media.

While there are several irritants between India and Pakistan, Kashmir is like a festering wound that has refused to heal in nearly seven decades. India, through a Resolution in the Parliament (February 22, 1994), has reiterated that Kashmir is and shall be an integral part of India and any attempts to separate it from the rest of the country will be resisted by all necessary means. India further demands that Pakistan must vacate the areas of the Indian State of Jammu and Kashmir, which they have occupied through aggression in 1947. Pakistan, on the other hand, views it differently and maintains that enduring peace in the region will not be possible without what they describe as a just resolution of the Kashmir dispute. This resolution, in their opinion, must be in line with the aspirations of its people and in accordance with UN resolutions that call for a plebiscite in J&K. They accuse India of subjecting the Kashmiri people to human rights violations and atrocities. So crucial is the issue of Kashmir to Pakistan that, in mid-2015, the Pakistani Army Chief Raheel Sharif described it on two occasions as the **"unfinished agenda of the Partition in the subcontinent."**

Both countries wish to resolve the Kashmir problem. But while India insists on bilateral talks; Pakistan wants it tripartite, with the Kashmiri secessionists included in the talks. India says that it is a matter between India and Pakistan only and there is no place for a third party like the Hurriyat/APHC (All Party Hurriyat Conference) in it. In Indian view, there is no way the secessionists can be included in the talks because that would make them into de facto 'legitimate stakeholders' in the Kashmir problem. Pakistan, on the other hand, insists that they indeed are legitimate stakeholders. India says that after 1972 and the signing of the Simla Agreement by the then Prime Ministers of India and Pakistan, there are only two stakeholders on the issue of Jammu and Kashmir—the Union of India and the Islamic Republic of Pakistan. India adds that this is a principle which is the bedrock of Indo-Pak bilateral relations and that this was reaffirmed in the Lahore Declaration of 1999 between Prime Ministers Nawaz Sharif and Atal Bihari Vajpayee also.

Pakistan, on its part has been accusing India of fomenting trouble in Balochistan and covertly supporting insurgency there.

In June 2015, India accused Pakistan of 'forcible and illegal occupation' of Gilgit-Baltistan in the wake of the polls in Gilgit-Baltistan (a part of the princely state of Kashmir before 1947) which was described by India as Islamabad's "attempt to camouflage its forçible and illegal occupation of the region." Pakistani foreign office spokesperson Qazi Khalilullah accused

India of maintaining "its illegal hold on Jammu and Kashmir by suppressing Kashmiri Muslims and holding sham elections at gunpoint."

THE ISSUE OF PAKISTAN SUPPORTING TRANS-BORDER TERRORISM

Terrorist organizations like Lashkar-e-Taiyyibah (LeT), Jaish-e-Muhammad (JeM), and a battery of other outfits continue to function in Pakistan under various aliases and their leaders roam free pretending to be social workers. India has consistently stressed to its interlocutors the need for Pakistan to fulfil is oft-repeated assurances, given to India at the highest level, that territory under its control would not be allowed to be used for anti-India activities in any manner. By the time of writing this book in late 2016, there had been no impact.

In fact, following two deadly attacks on the installations/ camps of the Indian armed forces in 2016 (first at the Pathankot Air Force Station on January 2, 2016 in which 7 personnel were martyred; and the second in Uri near the LOC at the 12th Infantry Brigade HQ on September 18, 2016 in which 19 personnel were martyred), the Indian Government, for the first time in 28 years, mounted a surgical strike across the LOC in Bhimber, Hotspring, Kel and Lipa sectors with its Special Forces on terrorist 'launching pads' and killed some 35-40 terrorists.

COMPLICATIONS INDUCED BY CONVENTIONAL ASYMMETRY AND LACK OF STRATEGIC DEPTH

The pronounced asymmetry in conventional forces is a factor that complicates the dynamics of India-Pakistan relationship. The lack of strategic depth in Pakistan is another very important factor. Inferiority in conventional forces means that Pakistan cannot take on India in a conventional war of a decent duration; lack of strategic depth means that the Pak army cannot afford to retreat substantially and trade space for achieving a favourable position to strike back. Both make Pakistan deeply apprehensive and jittery.

On the other hand, Pakistan's having allowed **strategic access to China** through Pakistan-Occupied Kashmir is viewed very seriously in India. China is linking Kashgar in China-held Sinkiang (Xinjiang) to Gwadar in Balochistan, via POK and Gilgit-Baltistan replete with rails, roads and pipelines etc. The proposed $46 billion project has serious implications for the security of India.

LIKELY FLASH POINTS

All these accusations and counter-accusations take place all the time in the backdrop of utterly juvenile rhetoric in the media and amongst the people on both sides of the border—ranging from refusal to play cricket with each other; promises to hold talks at various levels and then calling them off in the middle of the night; frequent ceasefire violations and casualties on both sides including those of civilians; and jingoistic slogan-shouting in the media; to threats of use of nuclear weapons.

It is not really possible to predict the flash points with accuracy because of the unpredictability of the **pressure of the public opinion**. Now public opinion, fickle though it may be, is never wanting in intensity. And how public opinion is made? There are many ways in which it is made but these days undoubtedly the most powerful means is the electronic media. Its immense influence comes from the fact that most of the people lack both knowledge and critical faculties to form an opinion of their own. They want someone else to apply his mind and hand them an opinion. This is what the media does. Depending on his sensitivities and latent proclivities, the viewer latches on to some opinion.

Should they desire, the media can whip up passions—should they not desire, they can tell people to relax at home and watch the Indian Premier League cricket matches. The media could demand the nation to go to war on any issue—a terrorist attack; the issue of terrorist camps across the border; attack on Indian missions aboard; dispute over water; some incursion somewhere; or even some little misunderstanding over a military exercise. Nothing prevents the media from speaking the language of George Bush and his successors—they could sugar-coat a war as 'interventions on purely humanitarian ground' also. Even as a sober leadership could responsibly act with restraint, the media could very well turn everything into an issue of the honour of the nation—replete with visuals of emotionally charged moments like coffins draped in the Tricolour; young kids saluting dead fathers; widows wailing and angry outbursts of relatives.

The popular reaction to any terrorist activity is shaped primarily by the media, that is, how they perceive it—the public swallows it hook, line and sinker. The colour of their reaction is based on various factors such as the number of casualties; the daring involved in the attack; the nature of the target struck, such as whether it was a military target, a public place or a place of worship etc; whether the terrorists were able to escape successfully after the attack; whether the attackers had palpably infiltrated from the other side of the border/LOC; the nature of the weapons used; the degree of brutality shown (such as in the beheading of some Indian soldiers); and so on. In nutshell, the reaction of a terrorist attack depends on how sensational it is perceived to be by the media.

Similar reactions are found in respect of instances of ceasefire violations also. The reactions are understandably jingoistic but often border on the irrational. Some of them go the extent of demanding that India should nuke Pakistan so as to 'solve' the Pakistan problem forever. The situation in Pakistan is essentially the same. It becomes a major challenge for any government not to come under the pressure of the frenzy generated by the media and still be guided by saner principles of diplomacy and international relations.

Still, in spite of all these unpredictable factors, with the backdrop of popular fulminations in both the countries over the decades as a pointer, it can be reasonably concluded that escalation to war is possible under the situations described below. Please take note of the word escalation. This is to underline the fact that wars take place due to purely political reasons also. For example, we went to war in 1971 for political reasons of what was happening in the then East Pakistan. Precipitating causes mean that they constitute situations which can lead to a war even if sufficient political reasons for going to war cannot be found at that moment, or the political situation is not volatile enough. However, given the inherently illogical behaviour of humans, the list cannot be exhaustive.

1. Repeat of a Kargil-like venture.
2. A repeat of an obnoxious attack like the 26/11 or the Parliament attack. The target could be any important city or Srinagar.
3. India's 'hot pursuit' of terrorists and surgical strikes rather deep into Pak territory by its air force or Special Forces.
4. Indian drone attack or air attack on terrorist targets in Pak territory.
5. A military misadventure at a local level by either side (such as unusual shelling in a place like Siachen or a diversionary attack sort of thing at some infiltration point to facilitate infiltration) but in an important place and which is likely to be misinterpreted as a prelude to a regular attack. In this connection, I must

mention that retired army officers like Afsir Karim have been demanding such weapon systems "that will cause unbearably heavy casualties on Pakistani forces deployed on the LOC/border. The new techniques and weapon systems should be such that they would penetrate the enemy's concrete overhead shelters over their bunkers and communication trenches to expose Pakistani troops to lethal firing. The new weapon systems should be able to cause very heavy casualties, cut off lines of retreat and destroy logistic support bases in the immediate vicinity of the offending Pakistani posts, also jam their rear and forward communication systems. It will be necessary to isolate and destroy Pakistani forward posts and forward logistic support bases fully." Well, well!

6. A repeat of an incident like beheading of Indian soldiers of a patrol party after incursion into Indian territory.
7. Terrorists shooting down some civilian or military aircraft.
8. Terrorist attack on some important military base like the Badamibagh Cantt, Srinagar using non-line-of-sight weapons like 81 mm or heavier mortars or improvised/factory-made rockets in which the attackers are not to be seen and hence it is not possible to engage them.
9. Misinterpretation of a military exercise in times of existing tension.
10. Shooting down of some military aircraft by the air force or ground fire of the other country alleging that it had intruded into their territory with hostile intentions.
11. A cyber attack which creates situations similar to the instance of damage caused to uranium centrifuges or even shutdown of nuclear facilities (for example, the

damage caused to Iran by the US through the Stuxnet virus); widespread disruption of mobile phone services; and malfunctions in power plants etc which are likely to interpreted as State-sponsored and not accidental or the result of some lone hacker's job.

12. Attack on civilian aircraft (like Air India Flight 182 Kanishka or Pan Am Flight 103 Lockerbie bombings) in which the perpetrators are strongly suspected or proved to have originated from Pakistan.
13. Pakistan accusing India of things similar to the above in respect of say Balochistan.
14. Border skirmishes spiralling out of control due to failure of control over local commanders.
15. Attack on Indian naval or air force facilities by terrorists.
16. Terrorist attack on strategic assets like offshore oil rigs or gas pipelines.

There have been a series of Confidence-Building Measures (CBMs). Slow but steady negotiations have aimed at addressing some contentious issues such as Siachen, Sir Creek, Baglihar, Tulbul navigation project, drug trafficking, organized crime, prisoners, roadblocks to trade, and transit routes. While significant achievements have been made on certain issues, there are vital issues over which no agreements have been reached. As such, realism seems to indicate that "and never the twain shall meet". You must have frequently come across the words called 'comfort level in the relations' in the media. However, 'comfort level in the relations' is no guarantee that there would never be any war. Mutual economic dependence level might have increased, trade volume might be going up, even joint military exercises could have started—it does not mean that the countries cannot go to war or would not go to war.

THE COMPLEX MECHANICS OF INDO-CHINA RELATIONSHIP

HOW DOES IT DIFFER FROM THE RELATIONSHIP WITH PAKISTAN?

India and China have a relationship which can, at this moment, be described as 'uncomfortable'. It is materially different from their relationship with Pakistan. The difference in the way we approach China originates from the humiliating defeat of 1962. The Chinese did not as much test the might of the Indian military machine in 1962, as they tested India as a nation—how they respond to military aggression. The 1962 war exposed all that is weak and feeble with India as a nation. It is not really that important as to how the Indian Army had performed in 1962—what we must remember is how the Indian nation performed in 1962. Fact is, the entire nation buckled and let us not cheat ourselves about it. We were shocked, horrified, scandalized, petrified, stunned, dazed, and traumatized beyond measure. Remember, how we started collecting blankets in the public to send them to the troops on the freezing border. Women started donating their jewellery. Young men started donating blood. None of these had any effect on the battles; they could not have. Yet they signified one thing—that we were both sad and shocked. The defeat still haunts India—the ghost of 1962 could never be exorcised from the collective Indian psyche.

India has acrimonious relationship with Pakistan too. However, India has, in the past been victorious over Pakistan. Hence there is no psychological barrier in, at least theoretically adopting the 'forget it' route. China had not only defeated India, it still maintains the arrogant stance of a superior power too. This is what distinguishes Indo-China relationship from Indo-Pak relationship. India would find it extremely difficult to adopt the 'forget it' route with China. As such, in public perception and in public statements (as against in covert diplomacy), intransigence dominates the mechanics of the relationship between the two countries.

India's problems with China are two-fold—first, it is the problem between India and China; second, China knows it too well that it can profitably meddle in a possible Indo-Pak conflict.

THE PERMANENT IRRITANTS AND CURRENT TRENDS

China and India share a border 2,175 miles (3,500 km) long. China has illegally occupied a huge chunk of Indian Territory. It also keeps on provoking India by frequent military incursions into the Indian territory and by its statements regarding Arunachal Pradesh—it had the audacity of objecting to the visit of the Indian Prime Minister to Arunachal Pradesh, and its practice of issuing stapled visas. The permanent irritants from the point of view of both the countries are:

- the Indian territory which China forcibly occupied in 1962;
- China's claim on Arunachal Pradesh. There is considerable public pressure in China to recover what they call 'Southern Tibet' (Zang Nan in Chinese)—that is, the PRC's name for India's Arunachal Pradesh;
- India's allegation that China is arming Pakistan, including the latter's nuclear and missile programme;
- the Dalai Lama and the Tibetan government-in-exile in India; and
- India's stance on the issue of the South China Sea and its military and economic activities there.

Realistically speaking, the issues are not likely to be resolved easily because no nation is going to back out. The current state of affairs between India and China is that war may not be inevitable but peace cannot be taken for granted either. Without any direct military confrontation, the tension between Asia's two giants is ratcheting up. At least on the face of it, both the nations are seeking to undo a mistake committed by history, and that is not possible by conventional negotiations unless there is paradigm shift. It's a kind of historic scar that impedes normalization of relations. At present, the position is that:

- China and India's sustained economic growth fuels their increasing geopolitical and military influence.
- Despite their developmental similarities, China and India's bilateral strategic rivalry means that they have competing priorities on most major global issues.
- The two rising powers broadly agree on matters relating to the international economic system, energy security, and the environment.
- Sino-Indian differences are considerable on issues relating to the non-proliferation system, Asian security, regional stability in Southern Asia, and security in the maritime commons, space, and cyberspace.

Though a lot had been done during the Sino-Indian official border talks, with number of border-related CSBMs (Confidence and Security Building Measures) put in place, the border issue remains mired in various bilateral and domestic compulsions and contradictions on both sides. As both China and India continue to boost their respective military capabilities on the border, it adds to mutual suspicion. China has methodically developed its infrastructure along the disputed border, littering the barren terrain with highways and railways capable of moving large numbers of goods and troops. In other words, they know their basics and understand the importance of logistics.

Then there are geopolitical considerations too. There are two geo-political entities: the first is the 'Periphery' and the second is 'Eurasia'. The Periphery is a collective term for those nations which are either geographically located on the margins of the Eurasian landmass or altogether geographically outside of the Eurasian landmass. Aside from the US, the EU, and Japan, the Periphery includes Australia, Canada, South Korea, Singapore, and Israel. Both India and China are demographic dinosaurs and are competing between themselves and with the status quo Peripheral powers for resources. China believes that in Indian perception, it is far easier to reduce the effect of global resource competitions by working to emaciate China rather than competing with the Periphery. **In Chinese perception, New Delhi has tilted clearly in favour of the Periphery**.

THE COMPLICATING FACTORS

The broad framework mentioned above is rendered more complex by the following considerations.

China's Desire to Dominate

China's main expansion has been towards Central Asia and the South China Sea, whereas India's strategic window is towards the Indian and Arabian Seas. The direct line of contact—the Himalayas—forms a natural barrier and does not lend itself to large scale military confrontation. A simplistic view would suggest that in that case, India and China could exist and grow independently. But China's basic desire is to seek influence and global status. All Chinese actions, namely, the building of the port of Gwadar at the mouth of the Persian Gulf and providing road link to it; the Zangmu dam on the river Brahmaputra (also called the Tsangpo in Tibet); and erection of military infrastructure in Tibet, etc. Are seen as manifestations of the desire to dominate.

Trade and Trade Rivalry

China is India's second largest trading partner, but India represents only 1% of China's global trade. India runs a growing trade deficit with China, and Indians are worried that Chinese goods will undermine domestic manufacturing. The quest for raw materials is a key driver behind both States' global ambitions, and hence a source of global rivalry. The scope for these two countries to develop peacefully and fulfil their national interests without entering into competition is getting smaller due to internal social pressures and rising nationalism. The question is, can increased trade be of any help in averting a war? I do not think so. Trade may be important but there are always issues bigger than trade. (For a detailed analysis of this issue, please see my treatise *Strategic Thought and the Art of War*.)

Role of the USA

In case, they tilt towards India, the US Navy would quietly leverage the sea power of its closest allies—India in the Indian Ocean and Japan in the Western Pacific—to set limits on China's expansion. Beijing would, however, react sharply to any 'restriction' by the US and Russia, respectively in Taiwan Straits and Ussuri river border. The Americans have kept other possibilities also in mind. To obstruct the alliance of Russia, Iran and China, in 2004 they had intensified the venture of using India as a Eurasian wedge or counter-weight to China. The US aim is to eventually undermine the coalition between Russia, China and Iran by using India or alternatively to use India as a spearhead against the Chinese.

Quadrilateral Coalition and Ring of Containment

The Chinese believe that India has been involved in the framework of military cooperation with the Periphery, aimed at

China. Under this framework, India has joined Japan, the US, and Australia in forming a de facto 'Quadrilateral Coalition' to neutralize China through the establishment of a ring of containment that could see a naval blockade form in the event of a war around the borders of China.

Triangular Relationships and American-Indian-Israeli Axis

In Chinese perception, India's ties with America and Israel are viewed as a real strategic 'American-Indian-Israeli Axis'. Triangular relationships have become a key element in the security dynamic of South Asia. This was illustrated by the US-India agreement on civil nuclear cooperation, which immediately led to a new agreement between China and Pakistan. It is also seen in the case of Myanmar. Myanmar is of particular significance to China, given China's present dependency on the vulnerable Malacca straits for access to the westward sea lines of communication. China has been engaged in an active policy of economic assistance, including planned construction of transit routes across Myanmar territory and ports on the Bay of Bengal.

Irresponsible Behaviour of the Media and the Academia

Given the fact that when it comes to acts of provocation, China does not seem to care two hoots about the nuclear power of India, every single Chinese act against India becomes an act of insult. The media and the self-styled academia lace it liberally with *masala* and sensational speculations. According to *The Economic Times* of July 13, 2009, in 'Nervous China may attack India by 2012: Expert', Bharat Verma, editor of the *Indian Defence Review* had claimed that a leading defence expert had projected that China will attack India by 2012 to divert the attention of its own people from 'unprecedented' internal dissent, growing unemployment and financial problems that are threatening the hold of Communists in that country. Well, 2012 came and went quietly—there was no attack. So much so for the self-styled defence experts of India.

China's Grand Strategy

Most Indians do not realize that India serves a larger purpose for China's grand strategic objectives. Humiliating India in a war of whatever type and duration would be a potent signal to the USA that the world is now to be divided into two empires: America's Western empire and China's Eastern one, and that each should respect the other's domain. China's collective psyche has still not recovered from the 'humiliation' the Middle Kingdom had suffered at the hands of the Europeans in the 19th century and the Japanese in the early 20th century. The Dragon is just biding its time and building up its strength to recover its lost hegemonic glory.

Muscle Flexing by Incursions

Border tensions between China and India flared after India claimed that a contingent of 30 to 50 PLA soldiers had crossed about 12 miles beyond the Line of Actual Control between the two countries on April 15, 2012 and stayed there for three weeks. There was another standoff between Indian and Chinese troops in close proximity to each other and the Line of Actual Control between Jammu and Kashmir's Ladakh region and Aksai Chin in April-May 2013 when a platoon-sized contingent of the Chinese PLA set up a camp in Raki Nula, 30 km south of Daulat Beg Oldi in the Depsang Plain. The Chinese agreed to withdraw their troops in exchange for an Indian agreement to demolish several 'live-in bunkers' 250 km to the south in the disputed Chumar sector. Yet another standoff took place in September 2014 when some Chinese workers crossed over with equipment to build a road up 5 km deep inside Indian Territory. The two armies were locked in a stare-down at Chumar in Ladakh since September 11, which clouded Chinese President Xi Jinping's three-day India visit too. For days, over 1,000 soldiers of the Chinese PLA and 1,500 Indian Army personnel were engaged in an eyeball-to-eyeball confrontation in the area.

CHAPTER 2

Strategic Peculiarities, Problems and Advantages of the Three Countries

INDIA'S STRATEGIC PROBLEMS

HOSTILE NEIGHBOURS AND VULNERABLE BORDERS

The fundamental strategic problem of India is that it is surrounded on its two sides by major hostile neighbours, both of whom happen to be nuclear powers. Incidentally, almost of its entire land border is vulnerable to hostile elements. Not only that, its oceanic border is also open to hostile naval presence. As such, it can be said that there is hardly any inch of the boundaries of India which are not prone to misadventures of the enemies. Not many nations find themselves in such an unenviable situation. This places obviously heavy demands on resources.

LIMITS TO THE TECHNOLOGY THAT CAN BE PURCHASED

The US will be selling more and more weapon systems to India in due course. They would, however, not sell just about anything which India is capable of purchasing or demands. They are likely to hold back certain weapon systems because, if supplied, they will have adverse effect on regional stability, crisis and arms race stability, and deterrence stability. In short, they would not like the power balance in the subcontinent to be disturbed by technological asymmetry.

For example, the following types of weapon systems appear to be potentially destabilizing. Possession of these conventional weapons could result in dramatic shift in the balance. The Joint Standoff Weapon could facilitate precision strikes without requiring manned platforms to cross into Pakistani airspace. This could be used for attacking terrorist camps or even cities and military installations. Second, advanced cluster munitions are designed as an area weapon capable of defeating combat vehicles, including main battle tanks. Such munitions have the potential to dramatically improve the efficacy of a single sortie against ground targets, with the potential to quickly disrupt the balance in ground forces. Thus Pakistan, which hopes to put up a respectable fight in a ground war, will stand to get denied even that opportunity. The third is missile defence technology. Needless to say, this will have great destabilizing effect. It will incentivize the production of even greater fissile material by Pakistan, will incentivize greater production and use of cruise missiles, and could incentivize Pakistan to use nuclear weapons earlier and in greater numbers in a crisis. The fourth is next-generation fighters which could bring about a generational gap between the fighters of the two sides.

HOW OTHER NATIONS COULD FIGHT WARS OF ATTRITION?

India is a large nation with great reserves of manpower and resources. From this, most people would gain an impression that India could fight a long conventional war of attrition. The fact is otherwise. A nation's capacity to fight for long and suffer the ravages of war does not depend on its manpower and resources. It has more to do with the mental make-up of the people of the nation. I will illustrate the point with some examples. The main contestants in the Second World War, namely, Germany, France and England were all rather small nations in comparison to India. German had a population of 69.3 million; France had a population of 41.68 million; and England had a population of 47.76 million—in comparison,

India had a population of 377.8 million. Yet these small nations were able to pay a heavy cost in terms of the lives lost. German sacrificed about 5.7 million people (soldiers and civilians both) in killed in the war, that is, about 8.23% of its total population. France and England, even though they emerged victorious, sacrificed about 6,00,000 and 4,50,900 people each. The number of injured is usually three to four times the number of persons injured. Japan had a population of 71.38 million and their estimated casualties range from 2.5 million to 3.1 million. Estimates of Soviet Union's casualties range from 26 to 27 million out of a population of 188.8 million. Casualties did not deter any of them.

And they were badly ravaged too. The number of people rendered homeless as a result of the bombings, even if they survived it, was much greater. Whole books have been written on the extent of destruction caused. In Germany alone in the strategic bombing campaign, nearly 1.6 million tonnes of bombs were dropped by the RAF and the USAF together in about 3,65,000 sorties besides the 0.9 million tonnes of bombs dropped otherwise. Industries were almost completely wrecked. By the end of the war, the tonnage capability of the German railroad system had been reduced by 85%. Their overall fuel production had gone down by 88%. But they fought on. England was as badly battered in the Second World War as it could be. Durig the Battle of Britain itself, in just 9 months, the Luftwaffe dropped about 46,000 tonnes of high explosive bombs and 1,10,000 tonnes of incendiary bombs, which destroyed about 2,50,000 homes, and damaged 20,00,000 others and resulted in about 55,000 civilian casualties including about 23,000 in dead. Yet the tenacious British hung on.

The horrors of the Vietnam War were infinitely greater. Americans dropped about 7.08 million tonnes of bombs during the Vietnam War—compare it with their total of 2.06 million tonnes in the entire Second World War in all theatres combined. The North Vietnamese suffered about 1.03 million casualties of which civilians contributed about 57%, making it fundamentally different from the Second World War where casualties of the combatant soldiers were usually much higher than that of the civilian non-combatants. And this was suffered by a nation which had a population of just 15.9 million in 1960.

WHY INDIA CANNOT FIGHT WARS OF ATTRITION?

Character of the People and the Media

That these nations could withstand such frightful losses and yet fight for years owes itself primarily to the character of their people. Given the sort of people Indians are, it is rather unlikely that the people of this nation would permit a long-drawn out war of attrition to take place. The ability to suffer and yet fight for long has more to do with the type of people they are than with the capacity of the nation to fight the war. The Iran-Iraq War lasted some eight years because the people of both the countries were prepared for it. That the war was regional made no difference to their resolve to continue fighting. The Indian people are psychologically not equipped to suffer the privations of a long-drawn war even as the Indian war machinery and economy could theoretically be capable of sustaining it.

There are good reasons to believe that the people of India will mount pressures on the ruling dispensation to end the war somehow. In this effort, they will be duly supported by the Indian media which has become a victim of its own rhetoric. The Indian media, in its unabashed, unashamed pursuit of sensationalism and jingoism, has divorced reality-check a long time back. The channels are so used to screaming that in a few short days Indian forces will steamroller the opposition and triumphantly march into enemy territory on the strength of the great imported weapon systems they have and the superior fighting quality of the Indian soldiers; they would suffer a huge loss of face if the war were to get drawn out. Hence they too will acquire a vested interest in lobbying for a rather quick end to war—it is not at all difficult to mould the public opinion any time, particularly in a country where printed word is regarded as truth and imagery on TV screens is regarded as the ultimate truth.

Susceptibility to American Pressure

India and Pakistan, if not China, are quite susceptible to international (read primarily American) pressure. The Americans have their own reasons to not allow a long conflict albeit conventional. It is not that they are bothered about the destruction and human suffering caused by the war. Can the Americans say so? They are responsible for the deaths of about half to one million European civilians and about half a million to 0.8 million Japanese civilians in the Second World War, and about 0.6 million Vietnamese civilians during the Vietnam War. The destruction caused in these wars and the Korean War was horrendous. We also know the destruction they unleashed in the two Gulf Wars and in Afghanistan which, as they themselves love to describe, had bombed back to the Stone Age. They were militarily involved in Grenada, Beirut, Libya, Panama, Somalia, Haiti, and Yugoslavia. Of all the people in the world, the Americans are historically the least averse to war.

The simple fact is that a long-drawn out war may hurt their business interests in the countries involved. Secondly, if they do not intervene, they will think that they are losing their position as the self-appointed guardian of the world. Thirdly, it does not serve their purpose if some regional disputes are permanently solved either by good sense or by 'ultima ratio regum'. Disputes must continue to simmer; negotiations and talks must go on endlessly. Then only the Big Brother can play its role of the more senior, more responsible member of the world community.

PAKISTAN'S STRATEGIC DILEMMAS

LACK OF STRATEGIC DEPTH

Pakistan's fundamental military problem is that it lacks strategic depth. Pakistan averages only 300 miles in width. This leaves little scope for generals to plan strategies in which they could conduct controlled retreats in which they could, like the Red Army in the Second World War facing the Wehrmacht's relentless onslaught, trade space for getting opportune moment and place to make pitched defence or mount a counter-offensive.

That limits the strategic options of the Pak military severely. They cannot fight a defensive war. They do not have that luxury. Pakistan cannot afford to remain on the strategic or even on the tactical defensive as both situations would be disastrous. To complicate matters further, it does not possess the relative conventional military strength necessary for adoption of an outright offensive posture against India. Then what could it do? Devising a suitable military strategy under such constraints is a general's nightmare.

IMBALANCE IN CONVENTIONAL ARMAMENTS AND LIMITATIONS IN ACQUISITION OF NEW WEAPON SYSTEMS

India enjoys a large and still further growing conventional military superiority over Pakistan. Can Pakistan bridge that gap? Unlikely, Pakistan cannot afford the money needed to bridge that yawning gap even if they were to find suppliers—and given the way they are likely to get isolated in the world community, suppliers are not too many. Their long honeymoon with the USA is coming to an end and China seems to be the only hope till such time that Russia grows beyond selling helicopters and conducting joint exercises. And China has its limitations. The Al Khalid main battle tank and the JF-17 Thunder multi-role fighter, made with Chinese collaboration/joint venture cannot make up for all the other equipment which the Pakistan military needs.

POOR INDIGENOUS DEFENCE INDUSTRIAL BASE

This problem is common to India and Pakistan. Pakistan now depends heavily in China for assistance in defence production whether in design or in the so-called 'joint development'; India purchases from all over the world, but mainly from Russia (all sorts of primary weapon systems like fighters, and tanks, etc), Israel (all sorts of secondary systems like radars, electro-optical sights, and UAVs, etc), France (submarines and now the Rafale), Germany (engines and transmission for the Arjun tanks) and the US (heavy transport aircrafts). Both countries thus happen to be primarily importers and not producers of major weapon systems—at best, systems are assembled or produced on someone else's design and machines. Imports take time; they are not guaranteed either. Nothing is available off-the-shelf. Above all, wars consume materials on an unprecedented scale. One who produces his own weapon systems has an obvious advantage in a crisis. Others are left scurrying around when the supplies run low.

England was a small nation but when the need arose, its industrial base also rose to the occasion and produced war materials on a phenomenal scale. The British defence industry went on to produce 14,929 heavy bombers; 14,385 medium bombers; 5,648 light bombers; 48,581 fighters; 9,808 naval aircrafts; and 8,063 other operational aircrafts—a total of 1,01,414 aircrafts. They produced 34,962 bombers against 18,499 bombers of Germany—a factor critical in the strategic bombing of Germany. They also produced a total of 14,483 tanks during the Second World War. The industries of India and Pakistan are simply unable to contemplate anything of this sort.

THE LIMITED UTILITY OF THE STRATEGY OF INSTIGATING INSURGENCY

Pakistan has made a serious miscalculation in respect of their thinking about the strategic effect of instigating insurgency. Since 1947, they seem to feel that if they encouraged insurgency in Kashmir, it would grow exponentially and eventually create a 'climate of collapse'—and then it would automatically secede from India without a war. Obviously, they never factored in the sheer size of India (resulting in a high 'moment of inertia') and India's ability to absorb both casualties amongst the security forces and also the extremely heavy expenditure on counterinsurgency in spite of a poor handling of the insurgency. The expected 'climate of collapse' could never set in. They tried the same thing in the 1965 war and then again in 1999 for the Kargil war. It did not work even once. In spite of three failed examples, they refuse to understand the truth.

Pakistan's support to insurgency in Kashmir has indeed led to the bogging down of huge numbers of Indian security forces in counterinsurgency operations besides a massive expenditure on keeping the forces there as well as in keeping the state economically afloat. But India can afford both and has been doing that for 28 years now. **Pakistan had presumed that their support to insurgency would inflict the classical 'death by a thousand cuts'. Yes, they did inflict the thousand cuts, but**

India did not die—as simple as that. The Pakistanis failed to take into account the capacity of India to take punishments. Moreover, on a political level also, extending support to insurgency and terrorism did not help the cause of Pakistan in any way—if anything, it weakened it, projecting Pakistan as the exporter of terrorism.

CHINA'S STRATEGIC ADVANTAGES AND DISADVANTAGES

MASSIVE DEFENCE INDUSTRIAL BASE

Amongst India, Pakistan and China, the latter is technologically the most advanced. Their overall military potential is also the greatest. It has the distinction of being the only country of the three which is totally independent in its armament supply because it designs and produces them indigenously. They are also the only country amongst the three with thermonuclear warheads in megatonne size and proper SLBMs.

A country's military potential must be viewed against the backdrop of its military ethos, its determination to win, its ability to take and absorb 'punishment', and the ingenuity/innovativeness of its military leadership also. Today's Chinese leadership is obstinate, headstrong and confident of its prowess. As against Pakistan, China has great strategic depth. Though the Himalayan range ensures that a land invasion is not possible from this side, the strategic depth also translates into their ability to absorb several nuclear strikes.

LINKS FROM CHENGDU TO THE EAST AND TO TIBET

On the Eastern landward side, China is constructing road and other communication links from Chengdu to Mandalay and thence southwards to Rangoon. Proposed and funded by China, ostensibly to reduce transportation costs and improve access to its hinterland, these road-cum-river linkages also permit rapid deployment of troops from Chengdu, the headquarters of the PLA's Chengdu Military Region, which also encompasses Tibet. Talking of Tibet, it is already proposed to extend the Chengdu-Lhasa railway all the way to Kathmandu. Reports indicate that China's Tibet region now possesses a good military road network running parallel to the Indo-Tibet border.

I do not find any reason to lend any credence to the surmise that in a broader, drawn-out war, the Tibet rail and road links could be interdicted by India and the Tibetan population could be inflamed to expel the Chinese from their land. From a military point of view, this is almost improbable.

FORWARD AIRFIELDS AND MISSILE SITES

Tibet is also known to have numerous India specific missile sites with most parts of India within range of their warheads. The string of forward airfields also now make it possible for PLAAF aircraft to conduct sorties into Northern India, with almost all northern and Eastern airbases of India being within their striking range.

CHINA'S RELATIONSHIP WITH SRI LANKA

Sri Lanka figures prominently in the Chinese strategic planning against India. One may call it by any name—String of Pearls, encirclement, envelopment and entanglement, whatever. India has a huge historical advantage in its relationship with Sri Lanka. But the fundamental problem of Sri Lanka is that no leader in Sri Lanka can afford to be seen as 'taking orders from Delhi'.

Infrastructure projects in which China has invested include the $361 million Phase-I of the Hambantota deep-sea port, the $1.4 billion port city on reclaimed land off Colombo, a

$500 million China-owned container terminal at Colombo port, a $455 million coal power plant, highways and expressways, and a theatre. Rajapaksa had reciprocated by enthusiastically endorsing China's Maritime Silk Route (MSR) Project, a vital strategic initiative for China in the Indian Ocean, and China's growing military presence in Sri Lanka—a Chinese warship and submarine docked at Colombo port in 2014, in spite of Indian reservations. The MSR is a vital strategic project for China in the Indian Ocean, and will increase China's presence in South Asian shipping routes. Hambantota is the perfect location to meet the strategic objectives of the MSR.

CHINA'S RELATIONSHIP WITH NEPAL AND MYANMAR

Nepal is the ideal buffer between the two giants—India and China. As such, Nepal is strategically valuable to both the nations and they must jostle for supremacy there. **Controlling Nepal would bring China right on the shoulders of India—a clear strategic advantage.** Their infrastructural developments in Nepal, combined with the build-up of military capabilities in Tibet, will enable the People's Liberation Army to deploy rapidly on to India's borders. Moreover, Nepal, being the southern gateway to Tibet, like Italy to Europe, is the soft underbelly of China. It has to be kept under watch and control.

The Chinese know that, as in Kashmir, India would not let the North-East go, come what may. India can afford to deploy troops on a massive scale there and also spend a hell of a lot of money over the decades. This means that the realistically-inclined Chinese would not waste their energies trying to set the North-East ablaze or hope that the insurgencies could make parts of the North-East secede from India. They would just keep it smouldering. They would arm the insurgent groups and let them do what best they can do. Their strategic interests would be served better by seeking maritime help from Myanmar in Chinese submarine and surface craft operating from a string of ports along the Myanmar coast (Chinese firms have constructed or modernised ports at Sittwe, Kyuakpu, Mergui and Hainggyi islands of Myanmar) and guided by the electronic eavesdropping from the Great Coco monitoring station or engineering occasional friction in Indo-Myanmar relations.

DISADVANTAGE CHINA: CHINA'S CHICKEN'S NECK

Quite like India's Chicken's Neck in the Siliguri Corridor, China too has a Chicken's Neck in Pakistan's Gilgit-Baltistan Hunza-Nagar district. The major connection between Pakistan and China is through the narrow area of the Khunjerab Pass, along the Karakoram Highway, which winds through Karakoram Pass. From a Chinese perspective therefore, China must ensure that her access to Karakoram Pass remains firmly in either her hands or in Pakistan's. **If Pakistan is decimated, or is in danger of losing control of this critical mountain Pass, China would most certainly enter the war with all weapons at her disposal. In a way, their entire future with Pakistan depends on this Pass; render it unusable by a nuclear strike (or some other means) and all those billions which China has invested in Pakistan in the CPEC, Gwadar and elsewhere would be wasted**.

CHAPTER 3

Comparative Study of the Armed Forces of the Three Countries

COMMAND AND ORGANIZATIONAL STRUCTURE OF THE INDIAN ARMY

The Indian Army operates six tactical commands: Central Command at Lucknow; Eastern Command at Calcutta; Northern Command at Udhampur; Southern Command at Pune; South-Western Command at Jaipur; and Western Command at Chandimandir. A command generally consists of two or more corps. The Training Command is at Shimla.

A corps is an army field formation responsible for a zone within a command theatre. There are three types of corps in the Indian Army: Strike, Holding and Mixed. A Mountain Strike Corps is being raised. The cutting edge of the Indian Army is cantered around the Strike Corps—each built around one armoured division and two infantry divisions, probably with more mechanized brigades than basic infantry formations. The Holding Corps are not as well supplied with support elements like engineers and the CADA (Corps of Air Defence Artillery) and do not possess armoured formations larger than brigades and the armoured regiments attached to the infantry regiments.

India's infantry divisions are divided into plains and mountains formations which, as their names suggest are trained and equipped to fight in different geographic environments. The mountain divisions are primarily earmarked for use against China, though they could be converted for use on the plains after re-equipping them. A typical infantry division comprises three infantry brigades, an artillery brigade and an armoured regiment. Support elements include an engineer regiment, a signal regiment and an air observation post flight, in addition to medical, transport, supply and repair units. Mountain divisions lack the armoured regiment and tend to have smaller calibre artillery. They also have more engineering and support/logistics elements than plains formations. The RAPID (Reorganized Army Plains Infantry Division) is a unique Indian creation and is specifically designed for the south Asian battlefield. The basic RAPID has one mechanized infantry and two standard infantry brigades. The RAPID provides the Holding Corps with an extremely flexible unit that dramatically enhances their ability to withstand offensive operations by armour. Moreover, the RAPID possesses sufficient armoured/mechanized infantry assets to conduct reasonably significant offensive operations. The RAPID is also claimed to be adaptable to NBC warfare.

The Indian Army has strength of over a million troops and fields 37 divisions including 4 RAPID divisions, 18 infantry divisions, 10 mountain divisions, 3 armoured divisions and 2 artillery divisions. In addition to the brigades in various army divisions, the Indian Army also has 5 Independent armoured brigades, 15 Independent artillery brigades, 7 Independent infantry brigades, 1 Independent parachute brigade, 3 Independent air defence brigades, 2 Independent air defence groups and 4 Independent engineer brigades. These Independent brigades operate directly under the Corps Commander (GOC Corps).

The Indian Army has four engineer brigades and 14 Army Aviation Corps Helicopter Units. A separate Corps of Air Defence Artillery (CADA) operates six air defence brigades and two surface-to-air missile groups. The mainstay of the CADA was the Russian SAM SA-6.

COMMAND AND ORGANIZATIONAL STRUCTURE OF THE PAKISTANI ARMY

The Pakistani army operates three commands, Northern, Central and Southern. The Pakistani army is also believed to have the same three types of corps: Strike, Holding and Mixed. The Army Air Defence Command is another Corps of Pakistan army which plays the role of anti-aircraft artillery whereas army aviation corps provides air support to Pakistan army. Now there is greater emphasis on ground air-defence (AD) by surface-to-air missiles (such as the Swedish RBS70 and US Stinger) and extensive gun systems, intended to be deployed rapidly during obstacle crossings and break-out. The Army Strategic Forces Command is responsible for training, deployment and activation of Pakistan's nuclear missiles.

In the 1990s, the Pak army created a strong centralized corps of reserves for its formations to support its combat doctrine of Riposte. The Army Reserve North (ARN) and Army Reserve South (ARS) are an approximate equivalent to the Indian Strike Corps in terms of size and composition.

Currently, the Pakistani army has 29 Divisions including 20 infantry divisions, 2 armoured divisions, 2 mechanized divisions, 2 air defence divisions, 2 strategic divisions and 1 artillery division. In addition to the brigades in various army divisions, the Pakistani army also has 7 independent armoured brigades, 5 independent artillery brigades, 3 independent infantry brigades, and 3 anti-tank brigades.

THE PEOPLE'S LIBERATION ARMY

ORGANIZATION AND STRUCTURE

The PLA comprises five main service branches consisting of the PLA Ground Force, PLA Navy (PLAN), PLA Air Force

(PLAAF), Second Artillery Corps (Strategic Nuclear or Missile Force), and the PLA Reserve Force. The State military system upholds the principle of the Communist Party's absolute leadership over the armed forces. The PLA is formally under the command of the Central Military Commission of the Party. Troops around the country are stationed in seven military regions and in more than 20 military districts. They are: Shenyang Military Region; Beijing Military Region; Lanzhou Military Region; Jinan Military Region; Nanjing Military Region; Guangzhou Military Region; and Chengdu Military Region. The Chengdu Military Region covers most of the border with India and the forces there are of interest to us.

THE PARADIGM SHIFTED FROM QUANTITY TO QUALITY

The Chinese army was historically criticized for having mainly numbers; men who were poorly equipped and poorly trained—the military doctrine was criticized for its readiness to achieve an objective by the sheer force of numbers irrespective of the casualties. In other words, it was criticized for emphasizing quantity over quality. Establishment of a professional military force equipped with modern weapons and doctrine capable of taking on sophisticated armies was the last of the Four Modernizations announced by Zhou Enlai and supported by Deng Xiaoping. As a result considerable demobilization took place over the years. This was followed by 'Revolution in Military Affairs' (RMA) being made part of the official national military strategy in 1993 in order to modernize the Chinese armed forces (emphasizing information technology; electronic and information warfare; long-range precision strikes in future warfare; integrated battlefield information networks featuring local/wide-area networks (LAN/WAN); satellite communications; unmanned aerial vehicle (UAV)-based surveillance and reconnaissance systems; and mobile command and control centres). The PLA is now just 2.3 million strong with 1.3 million in the Ground Force.

THE PLA GROUND FORCE

The Ground Force consists of 18 Group Armies, which are corps-size combined arms units containing contain 9 armoured divisions, 3 mechanized infantry divisions, 24 motorized infantry divisions, 15 infantry divisions, two amphibious assault divisions, one mechanized infantry brigade, 22 motorized infantry brigades, 12 armoured brigades, 7 artillery divisions, 14 artillery brigades, 19 anti-aircraft artillery missile brigades, and 10 army aviation (helicopter) regiments (two training). At least 40% of PLA divisions and brigades are now mechanized or armoured, almost double the percentage before the reduction.

THE INDIAN AIR FORCE

THE IAF COMMANDS AND BASES

According to the globalsecurity.org and the Wikipedia, the IAF operates over sixty airbases belonging to four Air Commands (Western, Central, Southern, and South Western), with more being built or planned. Western Air Command (16 bases from Punjab to Uttar Pradesh) and South Western Air Command (12 bases) control air operations in proximity to Pakistan. Of these, the airfields at Adampur, Ambala, Chandigarh, Halwara, Hindan, Jaisalmer, Jamnagar, Jodhpur and Pathankot are located within 300 km of the Pakistan border—with obvious advantages and disadvantages both. Other Scuth Western Air Command main operating bases are at Barmer, Bhuj, Nalia, and Poona with forward airbases at Ahmedabad, Nal, Suratgarh and Uttarlai. The Eastern Air Command operates 15 airbases in Eastern and North-Eastern India.

AIRCRAFTS WITH THE IAF

According to open sources such as the Wikipedia, the IAF has 242 Su-30MKI, 2 HAL Tejas, 69 MiG-29, 50 Mirage-2000,

245 MiG-21, 145 Jaguars, and some MiG-27 which are not retired by 2016—a total of somewhere around 753-800 fixed-wing combat aircrafts of which 363 are in the top bracket. The media maintains that the IAF has 32 squadrons against an authorization of 42. They also have some 20 Mi-35 attack helicopters.

The Sukhoi Su-30MKI is the IAF's primary air superiority fighter with the capability to conduct strike missions. The Mikoyan MiG-29 known as Baaz is the IAF's dedicated air superiority fighter and forms the second line of defence for the IAF after the Sukhoi Su-30MKI. The Dassault Mirage-2000, known as Vajra in Indian service, is the IAF's primary multi-role fighter. The old, venerable Mikoyan-Gurevich MiG-21 Bison serves as an Interceptor aircraft in the IAF—everybody knows its problems. It will eventually be replacesd by the indigenously built HAL Tejas.

After the Rafale arrives, reportedly the first by 2019 and all the 36 in next six years by 2022, it will be the most modern multi-role combat aircraft in the IAF. Media reports suggest that the Rafale can be used for delivery of nuclear weapons, a role which presently the Mirage-2000 does. However, it is not clear as to why we still need to load nuclear 'gravity bombs' on to aircrafts when we have so many missiles capable of carrying 500 kg to 1,000 kg payload, and when missiles are more reliable means of delivering nukes? I do not know whether it has something to do with any problem pertaining to miniaturization of the bombs to make them warheads fit for the missiles?

THE PAKISTAN AIR FORCE

THE PAF COMMANDS AND BASES

The PAF operates from the following bases: Mushaf (Sargodha); Masroor (Karachi); Rafiqui (Shorkot); Peshawar;

Samungli (Quetta); Mianwali; Minhas (Kamra); Chaklala (Rawalpindi); Faisal (Karachi); Pakistan Air Force Academy (Risalpur); and Shahbaz (Jacobabad) belonging to three Air Commands (Northern, Central, and Southern).

THE PAF'S AIRCRAFTS

According to open sources such as the Wikipedia, the PAF has 76 F-16, 250 JF-17 Thunder (joint development with China—performance similar to the US F-16), 80 Mirage-III, 85 Mirage-V, and 193 Chengdu F-7 aircrafts (Chinese-built—quite similar to the MiG-21). The Mirages are 1968 and 1973 vintage respectively. They are said to have been extensively upgraded but we do not know how useful or reliable they are. Thus, of the newer variety they have only 326 aircrafts; if we include the Mirages then they too notch up to 684 aircrafts. They have nothing in the calibre of the Su-30, MiG-29, and Mirage-2000.

The most capable fighter in PAF service is still the F-16 Fighting Falcon. This is followed by the JF-17 Thunder a new fighter jointly developed by China and Pakistan. The Chengdu F-7 is an air defence fighter. The PAF was supposed to purchase a number of the Chinese Chengdu FC-20, an advanced PAF-specific variant of the Chengdu J-10 (design similar to the Israeli Lavi) some time back but the delivery schedule is not yet clear.

Pakistan has paid considerable attention to SAMs, obviously with the intention to offset its numerical inferiority. Their SAMs include the MBDA Spada-2000 besides older systems.

THE CHINESE AIR FORCE: MODERNIZATION AND INDIGENIZATION

The People's Liberation Army Air Force (PLAAF) operates over 150 airbases in its seven Military Regions. Even now, in spite of the stress at modernization, it is keeping about 2,100 combat aircrafts. Of these, the modern aircrafts are 73 Su-30MKK, 24 Su-35S, 75 Su-27, 24 Shenyang J-16 (similar in performance to the F-15E Strike Eagle), 205 Shenyang J-11 (similar to the Su-27), and 240 J-10 (similar to Israeli Lavi, and F-16)—that is, about 641 top-notch aircrafts. They have some 1,040 older aircrafts including 192 Shenyang J-8 (interceptor based on the MiG-21) 728 J-7 (almost reverse engineered MiG-21), and 120 Nanchang Q-5 (ground attack aircraft based on the MiG-19) also besides several other types.

The bomber wing still depends on the 120 Xian H-6S which, in turn, are derived from the venerable Soviet Tu-16 of 1950s vintage, but can carry ALCMs. They also have 120 Xian JH-7 supersonic fighter-bombers, touted as a nuclear strike bomber.

Fifth generation aircrafts under development include the stealth fighter Chengdu J-20, the Shenyang J-XX stealth fighter (both supposed to be somewhat similar to the F-22 Raptor), and multi-role fighter Shenyang J-31.

In connection with a possible Chinese attempt on Arunachal Pradesh discussed later in the book, I have mentioned that their air transport and particularly heli-drop capabilities will be critical. The Chinese have developed the Xian Y-20 which has been inducted in July 2016 only and is similar to the famous C-17 Globemaster—a highly commendable effort, even if the designs were allegedly stolen. Unfortunately, they have only 2 of these as yet. The Shaanxi Y-9 is similar to the C-130J Super Hercules but they have only 7 of these. They have 16 Ilyushin Il-76 also. The bulk of the transport wing consists of 78 Shaanxi Y-8 which is similar to the Antonov An-12; 43 Xian Y-7 which is similar to the An-24; and 9 Xian MA60 which is a ruggedized STOL version of the An-24. They do not have any helicopter in the class of Chinook or the Merlin. They depend on 10 Mi-17, 6 Eurocopter AS332

Super Puma, 34 Changhe Z-8 (based on SA321 Super Frelon), and 1 Changhe Z-18 (medium transport).

Their KJ-200 or Y-8 Balance Beam is and airborne early warning aircraft, the radar of which is similar to the Swedish Saab Erieye AESA.

Since the Chinese make their own aircrafts, this gives them a huge advantage over India.

THE INDIAN NAVY

The Indian Navy operates three commands, namely, Western Naval Command at Bombay; Eastern Naval Command at Visakhapatnam; and Southern Naval Command at Cochin. There is also the Andaman and Nicobar Command, a joint navy, army and air force command set up in the Andaman and Nicobar Islands in 2001.

The Indian Navy currently operates, according to public domain sources like the Wikipedia, around 295 ships of various types and 251 aircrafts. It has over 79,000 personnel. The combat ships include 2 aircraft carriers, 10 destroyers, 14 frigates, 24 corvettes, 14 submarines, 25 patrol vessels, 6 mine countermeasure vessels, 1 amphibious transport dock (INS Jalashwa from the USA—cannot be used for offensive operations under the agreement, unless permitted by the USA), 9 landing ship tanks, and 4 replenishment oilers.

AIRCRAFT CARRIERS

The INS Viraat (originally Royal Navy's Centaur-class HMS Hermes, a 28,700 tonne STOVL carrier commissioned in 1959) is in the process of being decommissioned. The INS Vikramaditya (formerly Admiral Gorshkov, a modified Kiev-class aircraft carrier built in 1978-1982 at Black Sea Shipyard, Mykolaiv, Ukraine) had a short and troubled life in the Russian

Navy. It had undergone major repairs and was eventually decommissioned in 1996. After extensive repairs and upgrades for years, she was commissioned in November 2013. The ship has a STOBAR (Short Takeoff But Arrested Recovery) configuration, with a 14.3° ski-jump on the bow and three arrestor wires on the stern of the angled deck. This allows the operation of the MiG-29K aircraft—a total of up to 34-36 aircrafts including 26 MiG-29K and 10 helicopters. The MiG-29K is an advanced, all weather multi-role fighter capable of undertaking both the fleet air defence, low level strike and anti-shipping roles. The primary ASW (Anti-Submarine Warfare) platform is the venerable Westland Sea King or the Kamov Ka-28, while AEW (Airborne Early Warning) is undertaken by the Kamov Ka-31. The INS Vikrant (formerly called ADS-air defence ship and IAC-indigenous aircraft carrier) is being built at Cochin Shipyard and scheduled to enter service in 2018. It will be a 40,000 tonne ship. It will also be a STOBAR configuration. It is expected to take up to 30 MiG-29K/naval variant of Tejas and 10 helicopters.

DIESEL-ELECTRIC SUBMARINES

The Indian Navy operates a fleet of 13 diesel-electric attack submarines of the Sindhughosh- and Shishumar-classes. Ten submarines were of the Sindhughosh-class; four are of the Shishumar-class—you may recall, one of the Sindhughosh-class, the Sindhurakshak had sank in 2013 in an on-board explosion. The Sindhughosh-class is a variant of the Russian Kilo-class (3,076 tonnes) built under a contract between Rosvooruzhenie and India. The Shishumar-class subs are a lengthier and heavier Indian variant of the German HDW Type 209 submarine (designated Type 1500 by HDW) at 1,850 tonnes. The first two vessels were built at HDW, while the remainder was built at Mazagon Dock Limited (MDL) under a technology transfer agreement.

India has started construction of six Scorpene-class submarines with MESMA (Module d'Energie Sous-Marine Autonome) air-independent propulsion at the Mazagon Dock since 2009. It is developed by the French DCN and the Spanish company Navantia and now by DCNS. The Scorpene subs vary from 1,575 tonnes to 2,000 tonnes. INS Kalvari will be the first sub to become operational.

NUCLEAR SUBMARINES

According to the BBC, *India Today* and a Russian website (en.rian.ru/military_news) one Akula-II class sub called INS Chakra is there with India on a ten-year lease and it was commissioned in April 2012. According to Airmech.in the Indian Navy had sponsored the building of (since 1993) and sea trials of the submarine provided it was given to the Indian Navy on lease for 10 years. It was launched as K-152 Nerpa in October 2008 and entered service with the Russian Navy in late 2009. The submarine was leased to the Indian Navy in 2011. This is a SSN of 8,140 tonne surface and 12,770 tonnes submerged displacement sub. Media reports suggest that it is armed with four 533 mm torpedo tubes and four 650 mm torpedo tubes. Apparently, there are no SLBMs but it is capable of taking the Klub-S family of tactical missiles.

The Indians had earlier operated a Russian Charlie-class nuclear submarine (christened INS Chakra only) during 1988 to 1991. It was supposed to have six SS-N-7 Starbright anti-ship missiles.

India's first SSBN INS Arihant, a 6,000 tonne sub is under construction under the Advanced Technology Vessel (ATV) project at the Ship Building Centre at Visakhapatnam. It is likely to be armed with 12 K-15 Sagarika SLBMs (750 km with 1,000 kg payload and 1,900 km with 180 kg payload) or 4 K-4

SLBMs (some 3,500 km range) and six 21 inch torpedo tubes.

DESTROYERS

The Indian Navy has 10 destroyers; three of the Delhi-class (6,700 tonnes—built at Mazagon Dock); five of the Rajput-class (4,974 tonnes—built in the Soviet Union on the Kashin-class destroyers); and two of the Kolkata-class (7,500 tonnes—built at Mazagon Dock).

FRIGATES

The 14 guided-missile frigates currently in service are three Shivalik-class (presumably stealth features, 6,200 tonnes—India), six Talwar-class (4,035 tonnes—Russian), three Brahmaputra-class (3,850 tonnes—India) and two Godavari-class (3,850 tonnes—India).

NAVAL AIR ARM

I have mentioned the carrier-based aircrafts and helicopters earlier. Boeing P-8 Poseidon (4 in service and 4 in process of acquisition) conducts anti-submarine warfare (ASW), anti-surface warfare (ASUW), and shipping interdiction, along with an electronic signals intelligence (ELINT). This was Boeing's first military sale to India. The Ilyushin Il-38 is a maritime patrol aircraft and anti-submarine warfare aircraft designed in the Soviet Union from the Ilyushin Il-18 turboprop transport. We also have the Tu-142, a maritime reconnaissance and anti-submarine warfare (ASW) aircraft derived from the venerable Tu-95 turboprop strategic bomber. We are given to understand that the Tu-22M supersonic, variable-sweep wing strategic bomber has been phased out.

The UAV arm consists of around 30 UAVs like Heron and Searcher-IIs that are operated from ships and shore for better surveillance.

THE CHINESE NAVY

Currently the second largest navy in the world after the United States, the PLA Navy's 485 ships include 1 aircraft carrier, 27 destroyers, 47 frigates, 27 corvettes, 70 submarines, 109 missile boats, 94 submarine chasers, 29 mine countermeasure vessels, 4 amphibious transport docks, 32 landing ship tanks, and 11 replenishment ships. The naval air arm has about 700 aircrafts.

DIESEL-ELECTRIC SUBMARINES

The PLAN currently operates 57 five different classes of conventional submarines. They are: Type 039A submarine (NATO designation Yuan-class-15 in active service. 5 more under construction); Type 039 submarine (NATO designation Song-class-13 in active service); Kilo-class submarine (NATO designation Kilo-class-12 in active service); and Type 035 submarine (NATO designation Ming-class-17 in active service).

The Ming-class 035, first commissioned in 1974 could be considered as China's first indigenously-designed submarine. The Kilo-class is, of course, of Soviet origin. The Song-class design became operational from 1999. It features Western influences with a German propulsion system, seven blade skewed propeller and noise-reduction rubber tiles. The Song presents a major milestone to indigenous submarine designs, being comparable in capabilities to contemporary Western submarines. The Yuan-class appeared in 2005. The hull seems to have Russian influences (as it is similar to the Kilo). The Yuan has an AIP (Air Independent Propulsion) system to achieve maximum quiet operational capabilities. The Yuan came as a surprise to US military intelligence, as the submarine's existence was entirely unknown until images on the Internet emerged.

China is reported to be pursuing the option of purchasing the more advanced Russian Amur-class SSK.

NUCLEAR ATTACK SUBMARINES (SSNS)

The PLAN currently has two types of nuclear-powered attack submarines in service: Type 093 submarine (NATO designation Shang-class, 2 in active service and 4 more to enter service); Type 091 submarine (NATO designation Han-class, 3 in active service); and Type 095 submarine (NATO designation unknown, 1 completed to enter service and an unknown number planned).

NUCLEAR BALLISTIC MISSILES SUBMARINES (SSBNS)

The PLAN currently operates two classes of ballistic missile submarines, with a further class under development: Type 094 submarine (NATO designation Jin-class, 4 in active service and 1 more to be commissioned); Type 092 submarine (NATO designation Xia-class, 1 in active service); and Type 096 submarine (NATO designation Tang-class, under development).

China's first SSBN, the Xia 092 class was commissioned by 1983. This gives an idea of how advanced they are in SSBN design.

The Type 094 Jin-class is believed to have Russian influence. It will carry 12 JL-2 SLBMs with 3 to 4 MIRVs (perhaps 90 kilotonne each) to some 8,000 km range. An article in the Naval Submarine League magazine *The Submarine Review*, stated that with the successful implementation of the JL-2 onboard the Type-094, China now possesses a weapon capable of reaching any target in the world.

AIRCRAFT CARRIER

Since 1985, China has acquired four retired aircraft carriers for study: the Australian HMAS Melbourne and the ex-Soviet carriers Minsk, Kiev and Varyag. Since September 2012, the

PLA Navy is operating an aircraft carrier called Liaoning. This is originally a Soviet aircraft carrier called Riga launched in 1988, and later named Varyag by Russia in 1990. Ukraine sold the unfinished hull to China, where it was completed and commissioned as Liaoning. This is a 58,600-67,500 tonne Kuznetsov-class aircraft carrier. It is believed to carry some 24 Shenyang J-15 aircrafts (based on the Su-33) and some 12 helicopters. Currently, it is being as a training ship, intended to allow the Navy to practice with carrier usage and has not been assigned to any operational fleet.

On December 31, 2015 it was reported by several news sources that China was building a second aircraft carrier using entirely indigenous design. Earlier reports had indicated that they would be making two Type 089 carriers of 60,000 tonnes or so and based on the Varyag.

NAVAL AIR ARM

The PLANAF has roughly 700 aircrafts of various types under the navy's command. This is a considerably large naval aviation force considering the lack of aircraft carriers. It operates aircraft similar to the air force, including fighters, bombers, strike aircraft, tankers, reconnaissance, electronic warfare, maritime patrol, seaplane, transport, training and helicopter types.

PROBLEMS IN THE WAY OF CHINA'S ASPIRATIONS OF A TRUE 'BLUE WATER NAVY'

The augmentation of the Chinese naval fleet with guided missile destroyers and destroyer escorts and with an increasing number of new attack submarines provides the Chinese with a blue water operational potential and the capability of seeking and attacking enemy strategic naval at increasing distances from the Chinese mainland. But this is not the same as being a true 'Blue Water Navy'. The main problem areas are:

- Not having aircraft carriers presents one area of weakness in the PLA Navy and it comes in the way of their aspirations of possessing a true 'Blue Water Navy'. And once they make a carrier it must serve as an airbase for carrier-based aircrafts to project power, as the US, British or French navies do. The carrier is the primary weapon and the escort of destroyers and cruisers is intended to protect and support it. On the other hand, the Soviets had envisaged the Admiral Kuznetsov as a heavy aircraft carrying cruiser, intended to support and defend strategic missile-carrying submarines, surface ships, and maritime missile-carrying aircraft of the Russian fleet.
- Then unlike US submarines, Chinese submarine officers have very limited experience in offensive submarine operations far from the Chinese coast. Each US attack submarine sails on an extended patrol once or twice each year and six to 16 submarines are constantly forward-deployed lurking off foreign coasts—no doubt including China's. US SSBNs have conducted over 3,600 deterrent patrols over the past 55 years. The Cold War was a great training academy. That's a definite handicap with China. This overall lack of operational experience is a cause of concern. Given China's intentions and capabilities in the Taiwan Strait, any cross-strait naval assault with surface ships and subsequent supplies would be impossible to protect or sustain without significant submarine forces well-versed in sustained operations far from home. Unless they acquire this critical operational experience, they will have to limit the Chinese submarine force's mission to coastal defence and sea denial near China and Taiwan—they would not be really able to use it for force projection.

THE PAKISTANI NAVY

Pakistan has a small navy. But keep it in mind that they have a much smaller coastline to defend too. They have also more or less declared that if Karachi is blockaded again as in 1971, they could go nuclear. They do not have an aircraft carrier—that's a major shortcoming.

DIESEL-ELECTRIC SUBMARINES

They have three Khalid-class (2,083 tonnes) diesel-electric hunter-killer submarines. They are improved version of the Agosta 90B class with greater battery life, diving depth and lower noise signature. One was built entirely in France; the second was assembled in Pakistan; and the third was made in Pakistan. There are two Hashmat-class (1,788 tonnes—Agosta 70 class) hunter-killer submarines also plus 3 midget submarines for troop delivery, mine laying, etc commando type operations.

They are supposed to be in the process of acquiring 8 Yuan-class subs from China (four each to be built in Pakistan and China) but it is expected to materialize during 2022-2028.

FRIGATES

They have four Zulfiquar-class frigates (3,144 tonnes) and five Tariq-class destroyers (3,250 tonnes). There is one guided missile frigate called PNS Alamgir (4,200 tonnes) acquired recently in 2010. There are a few mine hunters and three missile boats also.

NAVAL AIR ARM

The Pakistan Navy's air arm is based on 7 Lockheed P-3C Orion for naval surveillance/anti-submarine warfare aircraft/

airborne early warning/airborne and bombing missions; 8 Aérospatiale SA-319B Alouette III for SAR transport/anti-ship role; and 6 Westland Sea King Mk.45 for anti-submarine/anti-surface warfare role. They also have some 32 old Mirage V planes in anti-ship role. They are supposed to be replaced by JF-17 Thunder (Block II).

CHAPTER 4

The Real Face of Wars: Separating Facts from Fiction

WHAT THE INFANTRY REALLY DOES OR CAN DO?

HYPE VERSUS TRUTH

Most people derive their notions of war from films. But what really happens out there is entirely different and certainly not as glamorous or heroic as the films depict. It is sheer drudgery—no wonder, the US army slang for an infantryman is 'grunt'. Yes, we are all aware of the tremendous courage which the Poor Bloody Infantry (PBI) is, at times, required to display. After all, it is only the infantry which could still be obliged to fight on a man-to-man basis. Artillery men shoot from as much as 30 km away and there is nothing heroic about a shell falling on the poor guy's head out of nowhere. About the role of tanks, I have written separately. The infantry is the only macho and honourable way of fighting. But, it is a myth that a war isn't over until your infantry, the ultimate arbiter of victory, walks into the other fellow's cities and takes up residence. You can very well win a war with bombers. The US won the first war with Iraq by carpet bombing alone. Much hype was built around the resistance which the Iraqi army would offer and how great and committed fighters the Republican Guards were. Poor guys never got a chance to fight at all. The nation buckled before they got anywhere within shooting range.

Quite against popular misconceptions, infantry warfare is

not all about fixing bayonets and charging with lusty battle cries—leave that to the third-rate films. Try that and you will be mowed down. Soldiers all over the world abandoned this stupidity after the disastrous experience of the First World War. One who still persists with it would qualify to be called incorrigible. Infantry warfare is not about commando-style attacks either as you saw in the Bollywood film 'Lakshya'. **Extremely few operations by Special Forces take place and, history stands witness, they are good only for becoming the stuff of legends; the course of wars is still decided by the blood and sweat of the 'grunts'.**

PRIMARY TASKS

The fact is that the primary tasks of the infantry both in peace and war, in decreasing order of time devoted to them, are defending a position or just manning it hoping that it could perhaps be attacked (as we do all along the border and the LOC); patrolling in their respective area of responsibility, and rarely attacking.

ARTILLERY SUPPORT VITAL

If at all they go into attack, it is almost necessarily preceded by and covered by artillery fire; the infantry basically walks in, takes a few prisoners, and keep on going. There is no modern infantry attack without the artillery. Artillery is the king of battle. The attacking infantry runs into serious trouble wherever the terrain or some other problem does not permit delivery of effective fire of artillery on the enemy positions to pound them into submission—it may so happen that the artillery fire only helps to keep their heads down—the defenders get up and fire as soon as you go anywhere near them. This is what had happened in the Battle of Mount Tumbledown in the Falklands War and to some extent on most heights in Kargil.

DEFENDERS' ADVANTAGES

The defender has, in fact, a number of advantages. First, he is under cover, customarily dug in. He is difficult to see. The attacker is nervously aware of this invisibility whereas he must get up and expose yourself to enemy fire—if the enemy too has been delivering some effective artillery fire of his own, the outcome of the attack becomes quite uncertain, eventually getting decided by some chance or situational factor or someone losing nerve first.

Even if armour has also been attacking along with the infantry, experienced soldiers know that it is easy enough to crawl off somewhere and hide, or just keep one's head down as the enemy's armoured vehicles rumble past. Fighting to the death exists more as a fiction than as an infantryman's goal in battle. Survivors of the artillery bombardment try to quickly get out of the bottom of their holes or dugouts and set up anti-tank and other heavy weapons.

INFANTRY ATTACKS AND HOW THEY DEVELOP?

Ground forces attacks generally follow a pattern. Assuming that the defender is not caught by complete surprise, the first day is generally the day of the heaviest fighting. The attacker wants a quick decision and the defenders are fresh. The defenders want to prolong the fight, as this allows time for reinforcements. If the first day's push does not succeed, the attrition now favours the defenders on the second day. If you are still not able to overrun them on the third day, it means that you have encountered fortifications and/or obstacles. Now, trying to reduce enemy fortifications is more expensive and risky than going after normal defensive positions. If fortifications have been prepared with some foresight, they must have been prepared in considerable depth. Multiple lines of fortifications over a depth of several kilometres are not unusual. Hereafter you have to slug out and results become more unpredictable.

EFFECT OF OTHER FACTORS

Then you have to consider other factors also, such as, whether you have ground attack aircraft or not (attacks proceed better if you have air superiority, superior reconnaissance, inferior enemy air recon, and relative freedom from air strikes); what is the nature of the enemy's air defences; and whether the terrain lends itself to the use of armour or not. Armour's mobility is reduced by rough terrain (mountains, hills, riverbanks) as well as by soft ground (swamps, sand dunes) and numerous obstructions (forests, built-up areas). The range of direct firing line-of-sight weapons is cut by obstructions, particularly by forests, underbrush, hills, and buildings. The range of observation is also cut by obstructions. Above all, these allow the defenders to conceal themselves more easily and prepare ambushes.

PARADOX OF INFANTRY WARFARE

The paradox of infantry warfare is that even as they spend maximum time in defending, defence rarely produces victory. If you stop the enemy attack once, there will likely be another one. If you do manage to really clobber the attacker, you are often rewarded with an order to counter-attack when you will face the same problems which the enemy had faced hitherto. But you do not really have to defeat the enemy summarily or in a comprehensive manner. If the leaders planning and leading the attack are skilful enough, they can destroy the key positions, allowing troops to bypass many of the remaining ones. This way, the assault can be carried out with minimal losses to the attacker. Reckless bravery does not help, as it just gets more attackers killed.

MILITARY OPERATIONS IN URBAN TERRAIN

Infantries still prefer warfare in open country. MOUT (Military Operations in Urban Terrain) or FIBUA (Fighting In Built Up Areas) is the infantry's nightmare. The Second World War was a first-time learning experience for everybody—hence everybody suffered heavily. As they developed the science of fighting in urban areas, the developments in the weaponry available to the defenders kept pace with them. In fact, unless the artillery and the air force can deliver some very accurate and heavy fire, the defenders do have an advantage in urban warfare. The Russians learnt it very painfully in the Battle of Grozny.

All their lives, the Indians have been preparing for tank warfare in the 'classic tank country', on the pattern of the battles in 1965 and 1971. But if we are going to be ambitious against Pakistan (you know the quintessential boasting of the army officers of having a 'chhota peg' in the Lahore Gymkhana Club—how childish!), we may have to fight with armour in urbanized terrain and for that we have neither any doctrine nor preparation. The Russian armour ran into a sea of troubles against the Chechen rebels in the urbanized terrain of Grozny the moment they encountered some unconventional methods of fighting. The extensive experience of the fighting in the towns of the Second World War proved to be of no use. The Israelis are acutely conscious of the possibility of fighting in the urbanized terrain of Lebanon and have accordingly introduced several modifications in variants of the Merkava tank for that purpose. They include an internally operated 60 mm Soltam mortar for situations where landing indirect fire may be necessary. The Merkava 3 Baz features one Browning .50 calibre machinegun that can be fired from inside; extra protection against grenades and netting that protects optics and ventilators; and a rear camera for better navigation in narrow streets. Some of the Merkava tanks were fitted with ambulance capabilities also. The Merkava ARV called Nammer, is an armoured recovery vehicle based on a Merkava chassis. It is capable of rescuing stuck tanks and carries a back-up power plant for the tank. We have done nothing special of this sort.

MYTH OF THE ARMOURED PERSONNEL CARRIER (APC)

Another myth is the APC (Armoured Personnel Carrier) or the IFV (Infantry Fighting Vehicle) as an important tool and the very symbol of mechanized infantry warfare. But the fact is that the IFVs have not seen sufficient action in modern warfare to enable one to develop theories on the basis of that. The experience with Russian IFVs (BMPs) in Middle Eastern wars was not encouraging for their users. The experience of American IFVs in the Gulf War was not conclusive because the IFVs did not get a sustained workout. Israel has, in fact, gone out of its way to produce a new tank but saw no compelling reason to develop an IFV. The simple reason is that the APC or the IFV basically provides security from enemy small arms fire; it still remains highly vulnerable to anti-tank weapons which the other side might have. Hence, it remains to be seen whether the APC/IFV would remain basically a source of additional firepower through its 20-30 mm cannon, .50 machinegun or automatic grenade launcher, or would like to engage enemy IFVs which are similarly armed and are also immune to small arms fire.

THE IMPORTANCE OF ARTILLERY IN MODERN WAR

POUNDING THE ENEMY INTO SUBMISSION

When you consider all the wings of the armed forces together, the war-making capacity, the will, the fighting spirit of a nation is broken by the air force first and the other wings essentially complete the job of polishing off. But on the ground, if someone were to ask me what is the most important, the most decisive arm of the land forces in the modern era, my unequivocal answer would be the artillery. Ask any soldier what bothers him most on a battlefield and his reply would be the artillery. Please note that here by artillery I mean both tube-launched shells and rockets launched from multi-barrel rocket launchers. You can't fight artillery, it is always out of sight; it is unpredictable and brings death and mutilation with it. The Indians could scrape through the Kargil conflict only on the strength of superior artillery. According to the authoritative globalsecurity.org, the Indian artillery fired over 2,50,000 shells, bombs and rockets during the Kargil conflict. Approximately 5,000 artillery shells, mortar bombs and rockets were fired daily from 300 guns, mortars and MBRLs.

These days the infantry merely polishes off what has been prepared by the artillery. As far as the land forces are concerned, an enemy is pounded into submission essentially by the firepower of the artillery and not by the heroics of an infantryman. The rule of thumb is that you first beat the shit out of the enemy using your artillery and then move in with the infantry to finish the last vestiges of resistance.

VARIOUS TYPES OF ARTILLERY FIRE AND THEIR EFFECTS

During a major operation, as many as 500 shells per gun per day may be fired. That could be over four hours of steady firing, but it's rarely all at once. Usually bursts of a few shells, or a few dozen, are fired interrupted by displacement to new positions, maintenance, and, if the front is close by or the enemy has broken through, defence against ground attack. You remain in one place for more than a few minutes and you are in trouble. The crews must always be alert to the danger of air attack, and the dreaded counter-battery fire.

Modern indirect fire is delivered in two forms: barrage and concentration. A barrage is literally a wall of fire—shells exploding in a line—that is employed to screen troops from enemy observation or to prevent enemy movement. Historically, a great deal of romance is associated with artillery barrages. A rolling barrage moves forward at a pre-planned speed in front of an advance. If this is done properly, the advancing troops will reach the defending positions right behind the exploding shells, leaving the enemy little opportunity to fire back. A concentration is high-density fire for the purpose of destroying a specific target. Barrages and concentrations are fired at three levels of intensity:

- **Harassment or Suppression:** Up to 10% damage, enough to keep the troops' heads down but not suitable for non-human targets.
- **Neutralization:** About 25-30% damage, causing a 'temporary' inability of the unit or the target entity (office, factory, whatever) to perform. This is the most popular type of firing mission. 'Temporary' means ranging from a few hours to a day.
- **Destruction:** 50-60% damage, resulting in disintegration of the unit/target or long-term ineffectiveness. Requires a large quantity of ammunition.

Interdiction is similar to, but a heavier form of, harassment fire. It is employed on critical supply roads or routes behind enemy lines for the purpose of stopping or slowing down movement of men and material. You will be hearing a lot of it in the context of the next war between India, Pakistan and China because a lot depends on keeping the supplies moving through.

COUNTER-BATTERY FIRE

The term counter-battery fire refers to the concept of detecting the source of artillery (shells or rockets) landing on friendly forces and then firing back at them with artillery, suppressing or destroying them in order to protect the friendly forces and reduce enemy artillery strength. By definition, it must aim at enemy artillery rather than infantry or fortifications. Originally, counter-battery fire relied on ground or air-based artillery observers noticing the source of the artillery fire (due to muzzle flashes, smoke, spotting the artillery pieces, etc) and estimating firing solutions to strike back at them. Artillery spotting, along with reconnaissance, was one of the roles for early aircraft in warfare. Modern counter-battery fire relies on counter-battery radars, which are able to calculate the source of incoming artillery shells very accurately and quickly. Radars coupled to computers can accurately track a projectile in flight back to its firing point. As you can see, how important counter-battery fire is. An army which does not have these, will be in trouble against an army which is stronger in artillery.

SHOOT-AND-SCOOT: THE TOWED VERSUS SELF-PROPELLED ARTILLERY DEBATE

The rise in counter-battery abilities has driven field artillery to adopt 'shoot-and-scoot' tactics emphasizing constant manoeuvre within a designated position area, usually from hide point to firing point and back again. It is difficult to do this with towed guns, as the time required to break down the guns and hook them up to the transport vehicles and then drive away is significant—by that time counter-battery fire may already be falling on the position. In this respect, rocket artillery like the US Multiple Launch Rocket System (MLRS) is superior as all the rockets can be fired in a short period and then the launching vehicles can be driven away almost immediately. Some self-propelled guns (such as the US M109 Paladin or Soviet 2S1 Gvozdika) also use this tactic but they can only fire a limited number of shots (due to their slower rate of fire) before moving on, and may require some time to retract jacks and such which afford them stability while firing, before they can move.

Although three or more times as expensive as towed artillery, self-propelled artillery has several important advantages:

- SP artillery can keep up with mechanized units and go places towed artillery cannot.
- Towed artillery takes about 30 minutes to prepare for firing; SP guns need about half that time.
- SP guns are also faster moving out of a firing position, taking a minute or two.
- Its armour makes it more resistant to enemy artillery, and more capable of delivering direct fire and surviving.

ROLE OF TANKS IN MODERN WARFARE: MYTHS AND REALITIES

TANKS' PLACE IN WARFARE: WHY AND HOW TANKS HAVE CAPTURED PUBLIC IMAGINATION?

Tanks have fascinated people ever since they were developed. For most people, the enduring image of a victorious army is that of their tank formations blowing enemy tanks to pieces in tank battles and then triumphantly marching into enemy territory to capture it. Talk of land battles and people talk of tanks only. The tank is to modern warfare what the knight in his plate armour was to medieval warfare. Impervious to small arms fire of the infantry, the tank creates the same problems for the infantry which the knights created for the infantry in the medieval age. As medieval war planners were obsessed with finding ways to contain the knights, modern war planners are obsessed with containing the tanks.

In the First World War, tanks were invented with the sole purpose of crossing obstacles (barbed wire entanglements and ditches/trenches) and attacking the infantry from their armour rendered them immune. When the enemy also fielded tanks, tank versus tank battles became necessary. Since tank guns packed a much heavier punch than any infantry weapon, tank armour had to be made still heavier and tanks guns even more powerful. This trend continues even now. The ability to ride roughshod over all sorts of terrain, of course, remains unchanged.

Throughout the Cold War, the nightmare which haunted the NATO commanders most was the spectre of the massive Armada of thousands of Soviet tanks steamrollering Western Europe in their inexorable advance. Tactical nuclear weapons were invented with the sole purpose of halting a relentless advance of the Soviet tank divisions.

Tanks are glamorous things, no doubt about it. Great tank battles have helped weave many myths about the prowess of tanks which have sunk deep into the collective subconscious. As a result, modern ground combat still revolves around tanks. Tanks account for about a third of a mechanized army's firepower and over 20% of its equipment cost. They are to ground warfare what battleships were to naval warfare once upon a time.

TANKS' ROLE IN OFFENCE

If you have to define the role of tank in modern warfare, it would be "to punch holes in enemy's defence formations and to provide fire support." Tanks' major role in a battlefield is to overwhelm the enemy positions and infantry-held lines by using sheer fire power, mobility and manoeuvres, along with mechanized infantry which provides assistance and later helps in securing the confronted targets. When the enemy armour opposes it, then they have to fight them in those orgasmic battles of which films are made.

In spite of all such beautiful things about tanks, the fact is that tanks and tankers' skills have, however, never been really tested in tank-to-tank battles since the Battle of Kursk salient in the Second World War. We waited for a conflict in Western Europe; it never came. We really wanted to see how the NATO tanks claimed to be technically superior than the Warsaw Pact tanks would fare against the vast Soviet Armada of allegedly somewhat less sophisticated tanks; but the opportunity never arose. We cannot draw meaningful conclusions from smaller conflicts like the 1965 India-Pakistan war or the Yom Kippur war. The use of the Abrams tank in Iraq during the Gulf War does not prove a thing; the Iraqis and their T-72s were no match for the Americans in any case. Tanks still prepare primarily for tank-to-tank battles and the Americans persist in carrying nothing but anti-tanks shells on their tanks. The very large power output of a tank engine (say 800 to 1,500 hp) ensures that it will always leave a distinct thermal signature. One of the reasons for the one-sided tank-to-tank fighting during the Gulf Wars was that tanks like M1 Abrams had almost four times the night time infrared scanning range of T-72s used by the Iraqi army.

Against good infantry in 'busy' (forested or urban) terrain, tanks cannot operate efficiently by themselves. In practice; most of the time the tanks creep forward under the eyes and ears of the infantry. When the tank is 'buttoned up' with all hatches closed, the crew can see only through slits, gun sights and periscopes. This makes tanks very vulnerable to infantry, especially in close terrain or built-up areas. Firing down from multi-storey buildings allows rather easy and 'cheap' shots at the soft upper turret armour of the tanks. If tanks cannot be accompanied by infantry, which usually slows them down, its only other recourse is for the commander of every tank to keep his head out of the hatch. The Israelis use this technique. You may win battles, but you lose a lot of tank commanders. A well-sited defender (or still better a group of defenders) has a clear advantage over a tank. Correct siting of anti-tank weapons and proper use of the three dimensional space is critical.

Unlike what they show in films, they cannot operate in massed formations in which they are highly vulnerable both to anti-tank weapons from the ground/artillery and the ground-attack aircrafts. A massed fornation is tanks operating closer than 100 metres from one another. Normally, multiple platoons of 4 tanks each would coordinate with mechanized infantry and utilize their mobility and firepower to penetrate weak-points in enemy lines.

To avoid the unpleasant prospect of being surprised without the eyes and ears of the infantry, tanks usually spend most of their time hiding or looking for a place to hide. But still, no one would like to be found without the concentrated combat power of tanks which makes them, of all the combat arms, capable of forcing a decision quickly and decisively. That is the dilemma of the tanks.

TANKS IN DEFENCE

While tanks have the above-mentioned limitations in attack, they are superb in defence, especially against other armoured vehicles. Tanks have firepower, mobility, and protection. The classic 'mobile defence' relies on good planning and reconnaissance. The planning involves picking out several positions for each tank unit to fall back to as they shoot up the advancing enemy. The reconnaissance ensures that you don't lose track of the larger enemy force. If that happens, your tanks are liable to being ambushed themselves.

When used defensively, tanks are often sunk into trenches or placed behind earth berms for increased protection. The tanks can fire off a few shots from their defensive position, then retreat (reversing) to another prepared position further back and drive behind the berms or into the trenches there. These positions can be constructed by the tank crews, but preparations are better and quicker if carried out by combat engineers with bulldozers. When defensive, they would wait in prepared positions, or use any natural terrain elements (such as small hills) for cover. The favoured position is on the reverse slope of a hill. This is called 'defilade'. A tank sitting just behind a hill crest ('hull down') exposes only the top of its turret, with the gun and sensors, to the enemy—providing the smallest possible target while allowing it to engage almost anything on the other side of the hill. The tank depresses its gun and, while facing the direction of enemy advance, backs down that slope until all the enemy can see is the gun and top of the turret. Even this much need not be shown until the enemy is in range, as it only takes a few seconds for the tank to move up the slope and into firing position. It is equally easy to back down and move off to the next firing position when the enemy gets too close. That's where the abilities to depress the main gun below the horizontal level and the traction to keep standing on a high slope become important. One little-recognized aspect of gun design is the gun depression in degrees; the greater the depression, the better. Western tanks can depress their main guns farther that Russian tanks—this means Russian tanks must expose more turret when in defilade.

An attacker would have to be some 10 times more numerous and able to manoeuvre in order to brush aside a tank-based defence. Ironical, isn't it?

ANTI-TANK OPERATIONS

In the modern era, tanks have become highly vulnerable to anti-tank fire of static defences and even more so to anti-tank guided missiles which come at a very minute fraction of their cost. As the US Marines put it: "Hunting tanks is fun and easy"—ever more so when the tanks charge ahead of their own infantry.

ATGMs and RPGs

They remind us of the armoured knights and the crossbow men. The knights, those flowers of chivalry who used to spend entire lifetimes training and developing skills of combat, could be killed quietly from a distance by crossbow men who might not know anything about combat! Very unfair! But life is like that! You can attack tanks in two ways—M-Kill (mobility kill) or C-Kill (catastrophic kill). Usually, even a M-Kill suffices. The Taliban (in Afghanistan) developed the technique of forming armoured-vehicle hunter/killer teams that worked together with as many as 15 RPGs to destroy armoured vehicles, aiming for a mobility kill by firing at the tracks to stop the tank from moving, then attempting to destroy the main armour while the tank was disabled.

One must understand that ATGMs have not rendered tanks obsolete nor are they free from problems in use. To better appreciate the problems of using ATGMs, consider the following situation. Armoured vehicles are first seen approaching 800 metres away. They are moving at 30 kilometres an hour (that is, eight metres a second). Your ATGM crews can get off a maximum of three or four missiles before surviving vehicles are on top of them. The missile crews may not survive that long, as their first shot can easily reveal their position. The tanks' machinegun fire will often spoil the missile operators' aim. The tanks also can throw a smoke screen in front of themselves, or call artillery or mortar fire on the exposed missile operators. With these deficiencies, why have ATGMs still proliferated? Simple, they are cheap. You can afford a miss without going bankrupt. Then the missiles are light enough for the infantry to carry and operate easily.

Anti-Tank Mines

The most feared anti-tank weapon in practice is not guns or missiles, but the 'dishonourable' anti-tank mines. It is utterly unglamorous to use them. But they have become a whole new field of technology and very deadly specimens are now available. Some mines result in only a Mobility-Kill (M-Kill) whereas some result in a Catastrophic-Kill (C-Kill). A M-Kill still leaves the tank armament and its crews able to carry on fighting. The most devastating anti-tank cluster bomb is the one that carries track-buster mines. A fighter-bomber can carry over a dozen cluster bombs, enabling it to spread track-busters to cover an area over 100 metres along with each bomb. A tonne of track-busters (1,200 mines) can cover an area 1,000 by 100 metres. Each tank entering such a minefield would have a 70% chance of losing a track. The only reliable countermeasure to track-busters is to equip the lead tanks with plows, which will literally plow any track-busters out of the way. This slows the advance considerably and makes the advancing tank unit more vulnerable to other anti-tank weapons.

Now we have 'thinking mines' or 'smart mines' too which can read characteristic magnetic or seismic signatures of the vehicles. There are off-route mines too which fire a shaped charge into the side of an AFV. The family of scatterable mines (SCATMINEs) which can be delivered by 155 mm shells, a ground dispenser or by air, provide a rapid and flexible means of delaying, harassing, paralysing, canalizing, or wearing down the enemy forces in both offensive and defensive operations. The WAM (Wide Area Munition) uses a passive infrared sensor to detect the target and fires an Explosively Formed Penetrator (EFP) at a vulnerable area from a stand-off distance to provide a mobility-kill.

Gunships and Ground Attack Aircrafts

Helicopter gunships and certain specially developed fixed-wing ground attack aircrafts (for example, the great American A-10

Thunderbolt) use ATGMs and automatic cannon like the GAU-8/A Avenger Gatling gun firing 30 mm rounds at a frightening 3,900 rounds per minute! Helicopters' relatively slow speed exposes them to the risk of ambush, while the faster fixed-wing craft can use speed as a form of protection.

THE REALITY OF AIR WARFARE

REAL ROLES OF THE AIR FORCE AND HOW IMPORTANT ARE DOG FIGHTS?

Contrary to popular perceptions, air war is not all about dogfights in the air. What is the reason of this obsession with dogfights or the Top Gun Complex ('my slave can whip your slave', or 'my dog can lick your dog' syndrome)? Simple! The reason is that the glamour quotient of dogfights and fighter pilots is very high. Glamour attracts people. Fighter pilots are extremely well-trained smart guys. They are young, very fit and quite often good-looking too—even if they are not, they look damn smart in their G-suits. Then the planes they fly are the fastest, smartest and most complicated of all the flying machines. Flying them automatically speaks of the tough training they have had. They are turning, twisting, rolling and doing what not to get to the tail of the other guy so that you may shoot him down. How exciting! Air combat in popular perception has therefore become synonymous with dogfights.

But, for the purpose of a real war, air forces have got two distinct roles. The tactical role is to support the ground forces. The strategic role is to penetrate an adversary's air defence system (which may include its fighters) and deliver a high explosive payload. Where? Once strategic air power meant unrestricted bombing of targets, now it may not be so. Certain key industries and infrastructure may be spared so that once the conflict is over, reconciliation is easier and the recovery could begin quickly. In between the two comes the glamorous part; the air-to-air combat. Air forces must consciously eschew the desire of getting obsessed with fast jets' aerobatics and the kinetic application of force. Air-to-air combat is the means and not the end of air war.

AERIAL COMBAT DEMYSTIFIED

Various Types of Combat Aircrafts

The capabilities of modern aircrafts show such a pronounced degree of overlap that a clear-cut distinction is not always possible. Still, it helps sometimes to think in terms of classifications. A fighter aircraft is a military aircraft designed primarily for attacking other aircraft. Fighters are comparatively small, fast, and highly manoeuvrable, and have been fitted with increasingly sophisticated tracking and weapons systems to intercept and attack other aircraft. You need fighters to achieve and maintain air superiority. A ground attack aircraft is one specializing in attacking ground targets like armour, light armoured vehicles and infantry. A strike fighter is a fighter aircraft used to attack surface targets of high value, including ships. The definitive strike fighter is the US Navy's F/A-18 Hornet. An interceptor aircraft (or simply interceptor) is a type of fighter aircraft designed specifically to intercept and destroy enemy aircraft, particularly bombers.

Various Types of Combat Missions

Interception missions are intended to intercept incoming enemy aircraft. Strike Missions are called 'air-to-mud' missions, that is, against ground targets.

Aerial Combat

Dogfighting relies on offensive and defensive Basic Fighter Manoeuvring (BFM) in order to gain an advantage over an aerial opponent. They are tactical movements performed by fighter aircraft during Air Combat Manoeuvring (ACM). Dogfight is the art of manoeuvring a combat aircraft in order to attain a position from which an attack can be made on another aircraft. A faster, heavier aircraft, for example, may not be able to evade a more manoeuvrable aircraft in a turning battle, but can often choose to break off the fight and escape by diving or using its thrust to provide a speed advantage. A lighter, more manoeuvrable aircraft, on the other hand, cannot usually choose to escape, but must use its smaller turning radius at higher speeds to evade the attacker's guns, and to try and circle around behind the attacker.

All manoeuvres in dogfight have only one purpose: to shoot down an aircraft, you must get to his rear. Why? This gives you two advantages. The first is that you can fire a simple heat-seeking missile that will lock on to its extremely hot exhaust. The second is that it is still difficult to fire something behind your back and thus the plane being targeted has an obvious disadvantage. In an effort to get the better of it, the Russians went on to develop tail-mounted radar and rear-firing missiles—clever, isn't it? With modern Beyond Visual Range Air-to-Air Missiles (BVRAAM) and Advanced Medium-Range Air-to-Air Missile (AMRAAM) guided missiles greatly extending the general engagement range of jet fighters, many people feel that dogfighting may be headed toward extinction. However, till such time that suitable technology becomes available on all the planes, you will have to bear with it.

You will also get to hear terms like climbs; turns; barrel rolls; displacement rolls; turn performance; pursuit curves; high and low Yo-Yos, and repositioning manoeuvres such as displacement rolls; combat spread; defensive split;

Immelmann, Split-S; Scissors; unloaded extension; Pugachev's Cobra; Cobra turn; 'Kulbitinscy' or 'Kulbit'; and Herbst Manoeuvre or J-Turn etc. From those who are throwing jargon at you. They are matters of not-so-necessary details but if you want to learn a great deal more about them, please see my treatise *Indian Defence: Crisis and Challenges*. As far as the aircraft itself is concerned, the technical aspects that matter include thrust-to-weight ratio, wing loading, and the 'corner speed' (the maximum/minimum speed at which the aircraft can attain the best turning performance). But do remember one thing. Air shows have little relevance with real combat. Real life is different. Some aircrafts may perform astoundingly at air shows. It does not mean that will necessarily win aerial combats, not to speak of winning aerial wars.

IS NUMERICAL SUPERIORITY THE DECISIVE FACTOR?

It is agreed that we have an undisputed overall numerical superiority vis-a-vis Pakistan. But real life is not so simple. The fact is that India cannot deploy or use all of its frontline fighters on the Pak border. They will have to keep a strong component on the Chinese border also lest China take advantage of the situation, either by just posturing or taking some offensive action to grab territory. Moreover, the number of aircrafts that can be profitably deployed depends on the number of airfields within say, a 1,000 km of the border. Numerical superiority in respect of fourth-generation fighters—the Su-30s, MiG-29s and Mirage-2000s of the IAF against the F-16s and JF-17s of the PAF; eventually enjoying a 2.6:1 superiority—means that they can, if nothing else, sustain more combat losses without feeling the pinch. But, if India envisages a very short war, the question of attrition becoming decisive would not even arise.

THE EFFECT OF AIRCRAFT DESIGN/PERFORMANCE PARAMETERS AND PILOT TRAINING

Contrary to popular notions, the outcome of a dogfight is not a simple function of the training of the pilots and the design/ performance parameters of the aircrafts. It is a far more complex affair. More than half a century after the Korean War, the Americans still love to analyse the famous air battles between the MiG-15s and the F-86 Sabre jets through extremely sophisticated simulated animations; they do the same thing for the air battles of the Vietnam War also between the Vietnamese MiG-17s and MiG-21s on one hand and the American F-4 Phantoms, A-1 Skyraiders and A-4 Skyhawks on the other. Why? They do it because they were and still are perplexed by the outcomes of the battles that had taken place. Had they been convinced of the superiority of their pilots and aircrafts, there was no need to carry out that analysis.

Since there has never been any real combat test of modern high-performance and extremely costly aircrafts, kids, journalists and equally ignorant self-styled experts wax eloquent about how the pilots of this country beat the pilots of that country in such-and-such exercise—as if exercises make the outcome of a war a foregone conclusion! Well, if it were to be so, then the matter is decided. Why should we have air forces at all if we know that such-and-such is going to win or lose? There is little point gloating over the results of the exercises. Who got invited to Top Gun, who beat whom in Red Flag, Maple Flag, etc is all childish stuff. In fact, it has also been alleged that because some people wanted the F-22 Raptor to be pushed and hence other planes were made to deliberately underperform or that they did not bring their best equipment or pilots.

Even if you lend some credence to the results of an exercise, do remember that design/performance parameters of an aircraft on paper are not everything it is going to deliver. In 2015 it was reported that a 40 year old F-16 beat the technologically most advanced F-35 Joint Strike Fighter. A mock air battle was held over the Pacific Ocean between the cutting-edge F-35, meant to be the most sophisticated jet ever, and an F-16, which was designed in the 1970s. But according to the test pilot, the F-35 is still too slow to hit an enemy plane or dodge gunfire. So far, the F-35 has cost the US military more than $350 billion. The dogfight, which was staged in January near Edwards Air Force Base, California, was designed to test the F-35's ability in close-range combat at 10,000 to 30,000 feet.

But, according to the F-35 pilot's report, which has only recently been made public, the jet performed so appallingly that he deemed it completely inappropriate for fighting other aircraft within visual range. He reported that the F-35, designed by Lockheed Martin, was at a 'distinct energy disadvantage for every engagement' despite the F-16 being weighed down by two drop tanks for extra fuel. The F-35 pilot reported a number of aerodynamic problems, including 'insufficient pitch rate' for the jet's nose while climbing—all resulting in the plane being too cumbersome to dodge enemy fire. He said that a half-million-dollar custom-made helmet that gives pilots a 360° view outside the plane meant he was unable to comfortably move his head inside the cramped cockpit.

It is not to say that the great technological systems of the F-35 are not really great. They are great alright but I only wish to impress it upon you that the result of a combat does not depend on technology alone. Technology is fascinating but real combat is more than just a clash of technologies.

The cardinal rule of air-to-air combat is to hit the other fellow while he isn't looking. Obtain the favourable position (usually high and behind the enemy) and get in the first shot. The average plane-to-plane combat is over is less than 90 seconds. Anyone can land the lucky punch in this time—in jargon we call them situational factors. Tactics gains an advantage only when ALL other things are equal.

MODERN NAVAL WARFARE: REAL-LIFE COMPLEXITIES

NAVIES MUST BE CLEAR ABOUT THEIR OBJECTIVES

The basic purpose of navies in all ages is to protect their merchant shipping, or preventing the enemy from using theirs. A nation which is placed differently, must devise its own concepts of naval warfare that are especially suited to it in terms of the weapon systems that it has got. The point being made is that no one should blindly ape the Americans. The Americans have many carrier groups with unimaginably tremendous and accurate firepower contained in them—their strategy is projecting their might in any corner of the world. This obviously does not suit India, for example, with just one carrier.

The US mission is to maintain sea access. The Russians developed their own concepts of denying sea access to the oceanic powers. Send enough submarines against the West before it can mobilize its forces, and you can deny it use of the oceans. They developed the large number of cruise missiles for this purpose only. The Russian Navy had a lot of small, heavily armed ships so that it could hit as many of targets (ballistic missile submarines, aircraft carriers, nuclear attack submarines, and enemy shipping) as possible in the shortest time.

A small Pakistani Navy means that they would not bother to engage India in a one-to-one contest or try to blockade some port—we are way too strong for anything like that. Basically their strategy would be to go for opportunistic kills by their submarines. For us, a 1971 type attack on Karachi does not appear to be as easy now with much better surveillance assets available in this age.

ATTACK AND DEFENCE WITH MISSILES AND MINES

Missiles and mines can be expected to play a major role in the next war—gone are the heroic days of the booming guns of the battleships. The accuracy of the missiles would depend mainly on the navy's reconnaissance aircrafts. The recon aircraft only have to track the task forces' radar emissions. To counter this, the defenders could turn off all radars quickly; only one or more radar aircraft in the air could keep their radars on.

In defence, non-carrier task forces must use ship-based helicopters to give additional detection capability, as well as whatever land-based and satellite reconnaissance resources are available to all naval vessels. Electronic countermeasures play a very significant role in defence, as it is possible to hide yourself by deceiving the enemy's sensors. For an incoming missile, you could also jam the three forms of terminal homing that missiles use to hit their target. All of this seeking and jamming has to go on during the last five or ten seconds of a missile's flight. With so much to be done in so little time, speed, accuracy, miniaturization, reliability and luck (situational factor) become the arbiters of success. You can also activate all the Phalanx guns (close-in weapon system or point-defence system), or use chaff and flares to deceive heat-seeking or active radar guidance. To counter that, an intelligent attacker could use a combination of air and land-based cruise missiles, plus some launched from small ships, delivering something resembling a coordinated attack.

Mines are the weapon of choice for the little guy. If you are about to get clobbered by a larger navy, you build and use a lot of mines. You don't have much choice. Russia, no matter how large its fleet got, always maintained the world's largest stock of naval mines.

SUBMARINE AND ANTI-SUBMARINE WARFARE

This is yet another unglamorous way to fight. Submarines are deadly customers if they get off the first shot. Even a diesel-electric submarine can take out a nuclear ship if it hits first. That makes anti-submarine warfare very important. You can take a shot at a submarine only when you detect its presence in the first place and then locate it precisely. The same argument applies to the subs also.

The standard detection equipment these days is the sonar. Sonar equipment is similar to radar in that it broadcasts a signal, in this case sound, and listens for that signal as it bounces off distant objects. The underwater world is dark, murky, and full of distracting sounds and that's why you need excellent electronics and signal-processing software to filter the noise. You also require a powerful computer and a library of sounds from a very large number of sources enables you to classify sounds quickly and accurately most of the time. This must be updated frequently. Good libraries can identify individual ships by their 'signature' noise. There are so many factors complicating the functioning of sonars such as varying temperatures (giving rise to thermal layers) and salinity, etc that it actually becomes a battle of technologies.

There are several types of sonar available: towed arrays (used both by ships and subs—the best can detect up to 100 km away); sonobuoys (dropped from aircrafts—good up to 10-20 km); dunking sonar (dunked by hovering helicopter—good up to 8 km); and hull-mounted sonar (used both by ships and subs—good up to 5-10 km). US submarine war games have shown that up to 40% of potential targets were not even detected, and 20% of those that were could not be successfully tracked and attacked. Experience with Russian-made subs indicates that their record was (and still is) even worse. Once again, you see, how uncertain real battles are and how small situational factors dominate.

Chapter 5

What Decides Victory or Defeat in Conventional Warfare?

INTRINSIC IS NOT IMPORTANT, EXTRINSIC IS

THE ROLE PLAYED BY IMPONDERABLE AND UNPREDICTABLE FACTORS

With a million imponderables and unpredictable factors, the only thing certain about war is that nothing is certain. The outcome of any battle or engagement depends, among other things, on intelligence about the enemy; your own preparation and strengths versus the preparation and strengths of the enemy; climate and terrain/topography, and how you have incorporated them in the battle plan; the element of deliberate surprise on either side; in what manner does the battle plan invite counteractions by the enemy; the manner in which the opponents choose to respond (it is his assessment—he may like to retreat; he may like to slug it out; he may like to just harass you; he might lure you into a trap; and the degree of risk which you incorporated in your battle plan (there is always a need of optimization as neither great risks nor too few risks pay.) At a given moment, anything may swing to anyone's advantage or disadvantage. Situational factors thus play the most important role—they constitute the classic 'fog of war'.

HOW FAR NUMBERS AND HIGHER TECHNOLOGY ARE IMPORTANT?

Numbers matter, but only to a limited extent. The defenders' advantage is well-known in military science and hence the attackers do require larger numbers. If they cannot muster that, they are in trouble.

Quality of the weapon systems and the equipment that you carry matters but only if there is a generational gap between your stuff and your enemy's stuff. Slight differences do not make any difference. The rate of automatic fire is important for a point-defence system like the Phalanx gun firing on an incoming missile. Every ounce of lead or explosive that is thrown, matters—you never know which one of them could hit the missile. It is, however, not at all important for an automatic rifle firing on a human target. It does make any difference whether you are pouring out 30 rounds in 3 seconds (at the rate of 600 rounds per minute) or 2.6 seconds (at the rate of 700 rounds per minute)—the human targets in front of you will not be able to tell the difference—you cannot say that the target can take evasive action if the rate of fire is 600 rounds per minute and cannot take such evasive action if the rate of fire is higher; giving him 0.4 seconds less time—human reflexes are, in any case, far slower.

The concept of 'constant tactical factor' must always be kept in mind—technology, per se, is not the final word. Many new advances have tended to cancel each other out. Many so-called military revolutions, simply raise the ante for all participants so that warfare continues at a higher intensity and cost, without either side gaining any permanent advantage. (Interested readers may refer to my treatise *Strategic Thought and the Art of War*). Technology increases strains also. In general, the greater the degree of technological sophistication of weapons and their platforms, the greater the amount of logistic, electrical, and mechanical repair effort required to support them. The tactical or operational impact of technical revolutions is more often overestimated in retrospect than underestimated at the time of their first fielding.

As Martin van Creveld has argued persuasively: "Using technology to acquire greater range, greater firepower, greater mobility, greater protection, greater whatever, is very important and may be crucial. Ultimately it is less critical and less important than achieving a close 'fit' between one's own technology and that which is fielded by the enemy. The best tactics are based on bypassing the enemy's strengths while exploiting the weaknesses in between. Similarly, the best military technology is not that which is 'superior' in some absolute sense. Rather it is that which 'masks' or neutralizes the other side's strengths, even as it exploits his weakness."

Acquiring modern weapon systems is fine—one cannot fight modern wars with .303 rifles and Sherman tanks—but before one acquires weapon systems, one must know and should be able to explain how they fit into his war-fighting strategy and the national grand strategy. One cannot be allowed to make the nation pay through its nose for something and yet not be sure as to how exactly he proposes to use them. They cannot be allowed to purchase anything and everything simply because the nation can somehow fork out the money. For any country, procurements without policy are a waste of resources as mindless acquisitions do not solve fundamental problems. There is no running away from strategy. It cannot be concealed under the cover of operational secrecy. Elsewhere in the world, people have been publishing research papers about war-fighting strategy. The broad concepts cannot be kept secret. They cannot be allowed to cover up their intellectual bankruptcy under the pretext of secrecy.

In all countries of the world (except the USA, Russia, China, England, France, Germany, Japan and Israel which produce their own weapon systems), the defence forces and their apologists in the media and the so-called think tanks try to create an impression that the nation must purchase every single thing that the defence forces ask for and if it is not done the security of the nation would be in serious jeopardy. The fact is that in general, and this applies to all nations, an army which claims that it can fight only if it is given the best of the best is cheating its nation. Scouring the world arms market constantly for ever new weapon systems is often a sign of either lack of intellectual capacity in the commanders to devise proper war-fighting strategies (the feeling of insecurity which results from incompetence compels them to seek new weapons systems in a compensatory gesture) or simple corruption in purchases.

HOW FAR SOLDIERS' PERSONAL QUALITIES AND FANCY TRAINING ARE IMPORTANT?

We must learn to be intellectually honest and spare ourselves juvenile rhetoric like "it will be the grit, determination and valour of our leadership and men that will finally make the crucial difference between defeat and victory". This sort of fallacy has been in existence since centuries and has repeatedly been proven wrong. In the beginning, First World War strategy was dominated by the offensive thinking that had been in vogue since 1870—the so-called 'Spirit of the Offensive' where Generals, sounding almost mystic, maintained that the soldiers' personal attributes, such as his discipline, training, bravery, and determination—all backed by the iron will of the officers—would make him relentlessly pushing on the offensive. This led to nothing but a bloody slaughter. Curiously, this mystical belief in the personal qualities including bravery, fanatical devotion to duty, disregard for his life, and 'attitude' in general persists even now amongst many—particularly in Third World and Asian countries.

Wars are complex affairs and, as shown above, their outcome depends on a mind-boggling array of mutually-influencing as well as independent factors. It is pathetic that even now people make a reference to such utterly simplistic and juvenile notions as bravery. Not only that it shows how simplistic a view that they hold and how limited is their capacity to grapple with complexity. Military history of the world shows that intellectually challenged generals who were incapable of formulating a sound strategy or even battle plan sought to compensate for it by demanding such qualities from their soldiers. (Interested readers may refer to my treatise *Historic Battles of India* for elucidation and scores of examples.) Fact is, while good strategy may compensate for poor tactics; tactics, however good, can never compensate for poor strategy. Wars cannot be won on the strength of the personal qualities of the soldiers; wars are won by a complex interplay of generalship, strategy and resources.

Do not be misled by military parades. They are impressive, but for kids or those who have the intellectual level of kids. Frederick the Great's post-1743 fall manoeuvres (Herbstübung) in Prussia were very cleverly designed to earn the awe and admiration of foreign observers who had little military mettle in them. Military hardware alone or the smart turn-out of the soldiers has never been instrumental in deciding a modern war.

Training is important; however, fancy training, quite like fancy weapons, is not. Most people fail to realize that fancy training is often used to showcase the organization for vested interests. This is particularly true of the training given to the Special Forces in various armies even as they constitute but a small fraction of the total strength of the armed forces of that nation. Since they are the best, the strongest, the fittest, the smartest, have the best and the most exotic weapons and gadgets, and receive the most difficult training, they are also the most presentable face of the armed forces of a nation through which they can befool the people and further their organizational interests.

TV programmes made on the Special Forces are fine for amusement but the fact is that the actual combat value of the training given to these Special Forces, after they were deployed in real life situations like Iraq and Afghanistan, was found to be highly doubtful. Let us get it straight, the American or the British commandos do not have a very impressive track record in either place. A rag tag band of the Taliban militia ensured that the ISAF, its formidable firepower and weaponry notwithstanding, could not defeat them decisively in so many years—rather they were forced to hold secret parleys with them. What weapons they had; what training infrastructure they had? By the time of writing this book, President Ashraf Ghani of Afghanistan was forced to sign a 'peace deal' with the warlord Gulbuddin Hekmatyar in September 2016—a man who had earned the soubriquet of the 'Butcher of Kabul' and who was declared a 'global terrorist' by the US in 2003 and whose Hizb-e-Islami was placed on the UN list of foreign terrorist organizations. Thus, a war in which the state-of-the-art technology was used against a militia and which, according to the US CRS (Congressional Research Service) cost a whopping $685.6 billion, could not achieve its basic objective of defeating the Taliban decisively. What a shame!

Given the fact that a band of ill-fed, ill-equipped, ill-trained, ill-educated and almost primitive people have given a tough fight to the very best soldiers in the whole world, one must admit that real combat is infinitely different from simulated combat in training fields. Performance of an army in real combat depends on many factors other than your individual worth as a soldier. Hence, next time if some army guys start blabbering about their training and how their men can whip the other nation's men, smile condescendingly.

COMBAT EXPERIENCE IS VITAL

On the other hand, experience counts and counts greatly. It is only combat experience that provides you with a realistic attitude towards warfare and confronts you with real-life problems—no amount of simulated exercise can make up for the real McCoy. Real life throws up problems which cannot even be anticipated in an exercise. The Taliban had acquired valuable experience of fighting in that terrain from the Mujahideen war against the Soviets; the coalition troops, in spite of their better physical conditioning and weaponry, did not have that hands-on combat experience for that place. In comparison to other nations of the world, the Americans have acquired tremendous combat experience since the Second World War. The Korean War; the Vietnam War, the two Gulf Wars, the war in Afghanistan and military interventions in Grenada, Beirut, Libya, Panama, Somalia, Haiti, and Yugoslavia have all given them experience which nobody in the world has. The Russians' lack of combat experience was very much evident even in their small intervention in Ukraine, not to speak of the fumbling in Chechnya—the Chinese had fumbled in Vietnam. In the Indian subcontinent, none of the contestants have any combat experience.

THE ECONOMIC AND INDUSTRIAL BASIS OF MILITARY POWER

Warfare is expensive. There's no such thing as a cheap war. Depending on how wealthy a nation is, and how many weapons and munitions it can buy, the cost of killing each enemy soldier killed can vary from several thousand to several million dollars. Be prepared to dish out a huge amount of money before you start shooting. Poor nations must avoid going to war just for the sake of some macho ego. To speak of money is a rather simplistic way of putting things. When we say money we mean all the resources necessary for conducting a war. If you are going to run out of artillery shells midway the war, how are you going to fight—you should not only have money but also the industrial base to produce shells yourself or import it from reliable sources that won't ditch you in a crisis.

Economic power does not translate directly into military power but if you have to have military power, you must have the economic resources to create it and sustain it. The converse is not necessarily true. Further, money alone is not everything. A nation may have money or economic capacity from say, the services sector. That, by itself, is not enough to automatically make it into a military power also. For a nation to become a genuine military power, its economic capacity must have a strong industrial capacity or base. A nation cannot aspire to become a major military power unless it has a very strong industrial base and manufacturing sector of its own. Prevailing in lengthy wars of attrition depends not only upon the military forces a State could initially muster but also upon its ability to mobilize the underlying economic and industrial capacity of the State to produce combat power during war.

THE OUTCOME OF TANK BATTLES: WHAT REALLY MATTERS?

CAN YOU FACE OFF INDIAN, PAKISTANI AND CHINESE TANKS ON PAPER?

No way! it has been the favourite pastime of defence journalists, army officers and their friends in the academia to confound the lay man with a lot of jargon about tanks' design and performance parameters. I do not deny that performance parameters like power to weight ratio; speed; armour thickness and effectiveness; nature of power plant (the diesel versus gas turbine debate); mobility; type of the main gun (the smooth bore versus rifled gun debate); efficacy of fire control system; and target acquisition, aiming and gun stabilization systems do not matter. But they are not everything. Unless there is a generational gap between two tanks fighting each other, there is no combat experience to prove that a small difference in performance parameters would be decisive. There was indeed a generational gap between the Abrams and the T-72.

How tanks are designed, depends to a considerable extent on the war-fighting philosophy and priorities of the nation. The basic design of a tank can be described as a compromise of the three main issues: armour, firepower (weapon) and mobility. A defensive tank (for example, the British Chieftain and the Challenger) favours firepower and armour over mobility. During Operation Desert Storm a Challenger 2 tanks shot an Iraqi tank at 5 km! Israeli tanks contain even mortars which can be operated from within the tank, enhancing the anti-personnel capabilities and allowing it to engage targets which are behind obstacles—all because they are required to fight under those circumstances. The Americans have been emphasizing fire control; fire on the move capability, which can be linked to stabilization of the gun; rate of fire; integrated sights; acquisition ranges, and weapon range etc. The French and the Russian tanks went for autoloaders for the tank guns from the beginning; the Americans did not. Soviet design has never bothered about crew comfort.

Then there is also the factor of mechanical reliability—something for which the Sherman tank was famous in the Second World War even as the German Panzers were technically decidedly superior, but not as reliable. Russian tanks are said to break down, on average, every 250 kilometres. Western vehicles last about 300 kilometres. You must know that a division of 300 tanks moving 100 kilometres (three hours' marching) will average 100 or more breakdowns. Modern tanks require extensive maintenance, proficient operators, and skilled mechanics, as well as daily resupply of large quantities of bulky petroleum products such as fuel, oil, and grease. For your information, eight man-hours a day is not unusual if you use the vehicle a lot and want to maintain it in excellent condition. The amount of equipment being added to tanks is increasing, especially electronics. Tanks therefore cannot operate successfully without adequate recovery and repair units.

Depending on the tanks' condition, the crews' maintenance training, and the efficiency of the tank-maintenance units, a division will lose 2 to over 20% of its vehicles per hour of movement. Most of these crippled vehicles will get going again and catch up, but the effect will be disorganized units, run-down vehicles and crews, and generally less effective combat divisions. The glamour is wearing off, isn't it?

In the light of this much knowledge, we are now ready to face off the Indian, Pakistani and Chinese tanks. According to sources in the public domain like Wikipedia, the Indian Army has about 1,250 T-90 tanks, 248 Arjun tanks and 2,414 T-72 tanks. The Pakistani army has 300+ Al Khalid, 600 Al Zarrar, 320 T-80UD, 300 Type 85-IIAP, and 400 Type 69IIMP tanks. China has 610 Type 99, 2,500 Type 96, 500 Type 88, 200 Type 69/79, and 2,360 Type 59 tanks.

If you look up the Internet forums, every Indian and Pakistani kid and all those adults with the intellectual capacity of kids are anxious to know what would happen if our respective tanks (such as Arjun versus Al Khalid) do clash at all? Well, I empathize with their anxiety but the fact is that nothing very exciting is likely to happen. No one side is likely to steamroller the other. By any standard, it is not going to be a cakewalk for any side. Remember one thing about real life battles. They are short. Hence it all depends on who gets that lucky shot first. There are many other vital things that precede the shot from the main gun. You have the war planning; mobilization; deployment; the numbers; whether you have had that element of surprise or not; air support; and so on. Finally the tanks roll out and manoeuvre. And even then they do not get to shoot too many rounds before they themselves are shot out or develop a snag. Eventually it is some very small situational factor, some mistake on somebody's part; somebody's bad luck or some such unpredictable, uncontrollable factor occurring in a fraction of a second that decides who will get that lucky shot. Your training, your maintenance, your machine's capabilities have all a role to play, but certainly a small one. They will not guarantee that you and you only will get that lucky shot.

I will explain the concept further. There was a History Channel programme called 'Deadliest Warrior' (2009-2011) in which detailed information on historical and/or modern warriors and their weapons was used to determine which of them was the 'deadliest' in a clash. Long back, a similar effort was made to make Muhammad Ali fight Rocky Marciano. The show was characterized by its use of the data compiled in creating a dramatization of the warriors' battle to the death. Now because any warrior could get that lucky shot, their programme ran possible engagements between the two warriors a thousand times just to eliminate the chance factor. This is precisely what does not take place in real life. You do not get a thousand chances in real life. That's why situational factors decide the issue.

Artilleries of India, Pakistan and China

There is great confusion regarding the numbers of artillery pieces in respect of India and Pakistan—estimates vary widely. However, certain broad trends can be made out. The Indians have been complaining of the lack of sufficient number of 155 mm howitzers since long—they have about 200 of the Bofors. They also have some 900 M-46 130 mm howitzers. But they have the 105 mm Gun in very large numbers—some 2,400. Our self-propelled artillery consists basically of the 110 2S1 Gvodzika 122 mm and 80 FV 433 Abbot SPG (UK) 105 mm howitzer.

In comparison, by all accounts, Pakistan seems to have paid considerable attention to self-propelled artillery: 60 M110 in 203 mm, 150 M109A2, and 115 M109A5 in 155 mm. In towed artillery also, they have, in 155 mm, 72 MKEK Panter, 148

M198, 144 M114, and 30 M59 howitzers; in 203 mm they have 28 M115. In sub-155 mm calibres, they have some 1,656 pieces.

In rockets, India has 150 batteries of the BM-21, 80 of the Pinaka, and 62 of the Smerch MBRL. Pakistan has 52 batteries of Type 83, 40 of KRL 122, and 42 of the A-100E.

China is a different ball game altogether. China has probably the largest, combat ready, artillery force on the planet. This force includes some 6,246 towed artillery pieces of 79 calibres, 1,710 self-propelled guns of various calibres, as well as 1,770 multiple rocket launcher systems. China has developed some interesting new systems, including GPS guided WS-2 406 mm rockets, carried in self-propelled rocket launchers. The WS-2 is similar to the US 610 mm, 1.8 tonne ATACMS (Army Tactical Missile System) rocket but costs one-tenth of that. Such heavy emphasis on artillery is obviously a relic of the Second World War Soviet war philosophy. Once again, the crucial question is how do you fit your weapon systems into your battle plans.

BETTER LOGISTICS WINS: THE EXTREME IMPORTANCE OF LOGISTICS

GOOD ARMIES MEANT GOOD LOGISTICS

Most people do not understand, not to speak of appreciate, the extreme significance of logistics in war. Students of military science and history who only read accounts of battles and casualties or territory captured, do not understand this. Most people derive their notions from films and novels where they show only the glamorous part of fighting. Unfortunately, logistics is not the sort of thing that gets the attention of most of the commanders and in peacetime. But it is the donkey work which makes fighting possible. Keeping the troops furnished with arms, ammunition, food, medicines, fuel etc is a huge effort. It was difficult even in the past centuries. When Napoleon spoke of armies marching on their stomachs, he was only being poetic and being the astute general that he was, he meant everything that the soldiers needed.

I will illustrate the effort required in logistics with a concrete example from history. Take the standard 12-pounder Napoleon gun which was the mainstay of almost all the 19th century battles. Do you think that all it needed was a couple of gunners to fire the guns which you see in films? No! Batteries required extensive support systems. A battery of six guns in the field required 152 men and 149 horses! The battery carried a total of 1,344 rounds with it. Nearly the same number of rounds was carried in the reserve park too. Why so many horses? Well, the gun carriage including its wheels weighed 1,128 lbs; the concerned limber weighed 725 lbs; the caisson weighed 792 lbs; and the limber of the caisson weighed 695 lbs. You needed horse power to haul all that stuff. And I have not even mentioned the horse feed! A good horse weighing 900 lbs (they ranged from 600-1,200 lbs) needed about 14 lbs of hay and grain per day. That meant hauling over 2,000 lbs of horse feed alone every day. Thus effective use of guns in the battlefield demanded not only good gunners but also an efficient administration that could ensure reliable logistic arrangements. If, in spite of all these problems, some armies could effectively deploy and use the guns in battlefields repeatedly, they must be given due credit. Now you can understand the pride which the armies took in their artillery and valued the generals who could win wars with them!

Remember, valour is no substitute for logistics. You cannot shoot from an empty machinegun and the days of heroic bayonet charges are passé. You may, if Lady Luck is exceptionally kind, kill a man or two with bayonets. After that your own epitaph will have to be written. Leave that to third-rate films.

COMPLEXITIES OF MODERN DAY LOGISTICS

How Much?

Just to give you an idea of what sort of things are required to equip modern American soldiers, I will tell of how NATO forces classify their supplies: Class 1: Food; Class 2/7/9: Individual equipment/medical/spares; Class 3: Fuel; Class 4: Barrier and construction material; Class 5: Ammunition. Fuel includes fuel for generators also. Food includes canned and other long-shelf-life combat rations, as well as fresh provisions for units in stable situations. Spares include all the spare parts to keep equipment going and keep the troops in good health. This means, it also includes medical supplies, normal replacements for clothing and equipment, and so on. A modern infantry soldier also needs about 15-30 lbs (average 22.5 lbs) of food, water, change of clothing, and ammunition of his personal weapon every day. The requirements of squad machinegun which could fire up to 5,000 rounds in a day, and mortars etc are in addition to that.

Mechanized armies need nearly ten times more material per day per soldier, the most important of them being fuel. Further, since weapons mounted on vehicles consume much more ammunition than a rifle or machinegun carried by a man, that too adds greatly to the total weight. In typical pursuit operations, 75-80% of the weight of supplies moved is fuel; ammunition takes up some 17-21% of the weight transported.

The requirement of supplies varies in different types of operations, as discussed above. However, on an average, an American infantry division requires 1,309 tonnes of ammunition; 461 tonnes of fuel; 79 tonnes of food; and 65 tonnes of spares—1,914 tonnes in all per day! When it is conducting an offensive operation, the total requirement would shoot to about 3,816 tonnes per day including some 2,500 tonnes of ammunition and 1,210 tonnes of fuel.

You can get an idea of the weight of the ammunition from the following. In the US Army, for example, each 155 mm gun is expected to fire an average of 205 rounds a day. This means that each heavy 'armoured' division with 54 155 mm guns needs 11,070 rounds a day, or 554 tonnes of 155 mm ammo a day! And they do not fire it for fun.

Artillery cannot do wonders. Typically and as a rule of thumb, for neutralization of soft targets you need to land at least one 155 mm shell in a square of 32 m side (that is, 1,000 sq m) and one shell in a square of 10 m side (that is, 100 sq km) if you are firing on armoured units. Suppose you have to neutralize a battery of towed artillery (that is, inflict about 30% damage) which is there in the open. This will require you to fire as many as 150 rounds of 105 mm gun, or 60 rounds of 155 mm gun, or 90 rounds of 120 mm mortar, or 120 rockets of 122 mm, or 60 rockets of 220 mm. Artillery deals with heavy stuff. One shell of 155 mm weighs 43.2 kg; the packing is extra; the 105 mm shell weighs 19.08 kg, and the 120 mm mortar bomb is 16 kg. A single 122 mm rocket weighs 66.6 kg; a 220 mm rocket weighs 280.4 kg. If they are in what is known as 'dispersed defence', your requirement increases greatly.

When the division is in offensive operations, the requirement would go up to 2,300 tonnes per day. In defensive operations, they would need up to 3,000 tonnes a day! All the heavy vehicles of the mechanized units are fuel guzzlers and require an enormous amount of fuel every day. Mechanized combat divisions, with all their high-tech weapons, unless constantly replenished with their copious supply of fuel, munitions, and spares, turn into fists of iron having feet of clay. If you are doing a lot of moving around in pursuit operations, you consume a lot of fuel; in defence, you consume a lot of ammo. A Western-type division carries over 3,000-5,000 tonnes of artillery munitions with it, a Russian or Third World division about half of that. You see, you are likely to run out of ammo pretty quick.

And How?

Now how do the fighting units get all that stuff? In India, the full rake of a goods train consisting of 40 BCN wagons can haul about 2,200 tonnes. For military supplies, depending on the shape and size of the loads, you may have to provide flatbeds etc and the total carrying capacity might get greatly reduced—in the US it is just 400 tonnes per freight train. Moving by roads is much costlier. In the Indian subcontinent, nobody has built or bought specialized cross-country military transports like the 10-tonne, cross-country HEMTTs (Heavy Expanded Mobility Tactical Trucks) trucks of the US. Then there is a more fundamental problem. There may not be a rail head near your battlefield. This means that considerable road hauling would also be required before the stuff lands with the units fighting. That provides for two objects of vulnerability to the enemy aircrafts. If they disrupt any one of them, you are in trouble.

The half million coalition troops massed for the war in 1991 piled up over 7 million tonnes of supplies to support their war efforts. This could be done because they were not facing any serious threat from the Iraqi air force, artillery/rockets or sabotage—movement by road from the supply bases was practically risk-free. Above all, they had the advantage of ports being there. Fighting in Afghanistan became a terribly costly affair because practically everything had to be airlifted and you could not spend them lavishly. Anyone who was not a believer in the importance of logistics before Afghanistan turned a believer after that. An enemy who can get into your rear and destroy the supplies kept even in bases rather far from the combat area also, will have, for all practical purposes ensured that you start croaking quickly.

Maintaining Reserves

Peacetime logistics efforts are primarily concerned with maintaining war-reserve stocks and the regular flow of spare parts, fuel, and food. War-reserve stocks are stockpiles of supply that, it is hoped, will get units through the first 30 or more days of combat. The war-reserve stocks include everything conceivable needed including ammunition, fuel, food, spares, and supplies of every description. A three-to-five-day supply of all such items is carried by each division at all times. Theoretically, reserves of up to 1-3 months can be kept in areas close to the combat area so as to make movement easier. But that makes them highly vulnerable to air attacks, land missile attacks and sabotage. This was done during the Gulf War.

Complexities of Repairs and Maintenance

Now keeping reserves is not as easy as it seems. Modern weapon systems, vehicles, aircrafts and every single bit of military equipment are complex. Field repair would demand a lot of electronics and precision components besides highly skilled technicians. Spare parts are as essential as fuel and ammunition to keep a modern armed force functioning. Hence, the standard practice is to make military gear modular. Entire assemblies are taken out and replaced, even if only a single component of the assembly is defective. It makes for easier storage too. But the problems do not end there. Each component in an aircraft comes under different types of stress, depending on what the aircraft does. Different types of missions wear out different components at different rates. One does not know exactly how the aircraft will be used in wartime. Hence all you can do is to make educated guesses as to how many of what spares to stock. Aircraft usage depends a lot on what the enemy is going to do to you, and you do not know this. In the end, not only you could end with the wrong mix of spares, there may also be too few of them.

Take my word, in combat requiring extensive use of weapon systems, complex weapons systems would quickly, rather painfully quickly, run out of spares. Now you will understand why we speak of reliable weapon systems. High technology is not necessarily the best solution.

Implications for India in a Future War

If you intend to fight seriously, your choice of battlefield gets automatically narrowed down by the considerations of logistics mentioned above. You cannot fight just about anywhere you happen to point on the map. You have to plan the logistics for that point first. In any country, that's where generals must put their foot down if any unreasonable demand is placed on them. For planning purposes, norms must be established so that operations can be planned without exceeding available supplies.

Now you would also understand why it is so important for the enemy to damage railroads and roads. Imagine the situation in difficult terrain like Ladakh and Arunachal Pradesh. There could be but few roads, tunnels or bridges for supply. If the enemy aircrafts or shelling damages them and keeps it threatened, your supplies would be cut off. To replace these items is also costly in time. While portions of the transportation network are being rebuilt, additional expense is incurred in detouring around blown bridges or tunnels. And please, do not listen to anybody who tells you exciting stories of camouflaging supplies. The enemy aircrafts will hunt you down. If the aircrafts do not, their missiles could. If they have accurate intelligence on your supply dumps or the movement of your supplies through satellites, HUMINT or whatever, you are in trouble.

If you want to determine who is going to win a future war, examine the supply situation first and take note of the vulnerabilities of the supply lines of each side. Particularly in the context of China you will find that their supply network is not only decidedly better but more extensive too, providing for easier detouring—when you have but a very limited number of supply lines, detouring becomes very difficult.

Logistics suffers from a fundamental and intrinsic problem. You never know how a particular front will develop. There may be intense fighting in some unexpected place, thereby placing great demands on logistics and which might not have been catered to in the original plans.

FACTORS ON WHICH THE OUTCOME OF AN AIR WAR DEPENDS

There is no way of finding out exactly now two roughly equivalent air forces would fare in an air war. Hence stop speculating about it. Still, there are some very important and often unappreciated factors besides the training of pilots and aircraft design/performance parameters on which the outcome of a war would depend. They are discussed below.

SURGE AND SUSTAINED SORTIES RATE

You may recall that the Americans flew as many as 1,00,000 sorties in six weeks with 2,000 aircrafts in the Gulf War. In a typical campaign, you would have two days of surge (your maximum capacity) and many more days of sustained sorties (your enduring capacity for several days or weeks). An American F-16 squadron, which used its 20 aircraft, 40 pilots and very energetic and well-trained ground crews to fly 160 sorties in 12 hours. Most Western aircraft can fly three or more sorties per day for two or three days, and one or two per day indefinitely as long as the spare parts and ground crews hold out. India, Pakistan and China keep such things secret. Hence I do not know what they are capable of.

Durability and Maintainability of the Aircrafts

High-performance aircraft literally burn up many of their components, mainly in the engines. The reason is simple. The components of the engines of the high-performance aircrafts have to cope with extremely high pressures, temperatures and speeds. This puts tremendous strain on the components and as a result of the metal fatigue they need to be replaced every few hundred or few thousand hours, depending on the aircraft and the amount of stressful manoeuvring it has done. An aircraft engine is not like the engine of a diesel locomotive. Their high performance comes from operating on the edge.

Hence, between sorties, an aircraft must be checked out visually and electronically to see if all key components are operational or approaching failure. Fuel and munitions are loaded. The pilot must be briefed on the mission, which can take from a few minutes to over an hour. After a sortie, the same cycle must be repeated before another takeoff. The sortie rate (both surge and sustained) and the readiness rate are, in turn, related to the durability and maintainability of the aircrafts that a nation has. This is a very critical issue. You are aware of what has been happening to the MiG-21s in India. If you cut corners in maintenance, it increases the risk of losing the aircraft and/or sending it up with some capabilities crippled. Hundreds of man-hours and 10-20 tonnes of supplies are needed to launch one sortie. The F-16, for example, requires 1,010 tonnes of supplies of all kinds to the airbase per 100 sorties. How many sorties would be flown depends on the type of war you are fighting.

Western air forces have long used high sortie rates as a key component of their air power. This is one reason why Western warplanes are so expensive. They are built to fly a lot, especially in combat. This means they are easier to maintain, despite their heavy use of electronics. The Americans take great pride in this and are consistently improving upon it. For example, F-15/16 class aircraft must spend 30 minutes on the ground between combat sorties; the F-22 Raptor cuts that in half. The speed with which malfunctioning aircraft can be repaired is also very critical in war. Currently only about 25% of malfunctions can be fixed in under four hours. The F-22 claims to increase this to 75%.

Before any nation of the world purchases a plane, it should know all such things pertaining to its maintenance and upkeep besides its combat record. There is no way of finding out such things except from combat record and user opinion. Manufacturers are notorious for making unusually tall claims. Remember, buying planes is not like buying lingerie off the shelf or from amazon.com. Even for purchasing lingerie there is a system of a trial room and most women would get formal user reviews or informal user opinion from friends—going by looks alone or brand names can prove a costly mistake!

YOUR DETECTION, ACQUISITION, AND TRACKING CAPABILITY

Detection

Electronic warfare, that is, ECM (electronic countermeasures) and low flying are the favourite ploys of attacking enemy aircrafts for avoiding detection. You can try countering them by AWACS (Airborne Warning and Control System). Everyone has problems getting enough AWACS to cover everything. Further, the US AWACS can only stay on station for six hours, unless it gets an in-flight refuelling. Twelve hours in the air is the usual maximum because of the need for ground maintenance on the aircraft and the complex radars and computers.

Acquisition

Once an aircraft has been detected, it must be 'acquired'. That is, you must confirm that it is an enemy aircraft and determine exactly where it is and where it is going. You want to know when the aircraft will be within range of your weapons. For a tactical air-defence system with a maximum weapon range of 20,000 metres, every second counts. All of this occurs is an atmosphere of uncertainty. Why? The reason is that even as a typical ground radar can spot aircrafts up to 550-kilometres out and 30 kilometres high, the probability of making a positive detection at this range is only 50%. At 370 kilometres the probability is still only 90%. A daring pilot can take advantage of this uncertainty to fly most of his mission at high altitude before descending to the more dangerous and nerve-wracking flying at treetop level for the final approach to target.

Tracking

You have to maintain your 'track' of the enemy aircraft long enough for your guns or missiles to do their job. Tracking generally commences outside the range of the weapons it serves. Missiles without independent guidance systems (that is, most of them) depend on continually successful tracking.

Air-Defence Weapons

The key to successful air defence is therefore layers of defence at multiple depths and altitudes. For poorer nations, they range from anti-aircraft guns to portable SAMs, medium-range SAMs, and long-range SAMs—that is, all on the ground. Western nations view air superiority is seen as the primary air-defence technique.

HOW WELL THEY SUPPORT THE DIRTY AND DANGEROUS FIGHTING ON GROUND

There is a popular allegation against air forces of the world that they would rather be fighting the war of their own in their stylish way and on their own, without getting mixed up with the grubby work of the infantry. **But if you have to win an air war, you must**

force the air force to do all that they want to avoid. Hats off to the Americans; they did it most admirably in the Vietnam War—close air support was often just a radio call away. You are ambushed and have been taking casualties—call for the air force, and they would be right there in a few minutes dropping napalm on the Viet Cong. But unfortunately, things have changed in the USAF also. It was witnessed in Afghanistan. They used to circle high above the target area (like Kunduz) and wait for the Special Forces troops on the ground to spot targets and identify them with their lasers. But then the American ground forces went on to argue, "If the air force won't give us support, we'll get it any way we can." Precisely for this reason, the US Marine Corps has its own air force and receives superb ground support from it, and this experience is not lost on the US Army.

There are published views of top-ranking army officers on how the Indian Air Force had behaved when the going got tough in Kargil. They include the papers 'Kargil Controversy: Mismanagement of Higher Defence' by Lt Gen Harwant Singh, former Deputy Chief of Army Staff; and 'Kargil Controversy: Army Trashes IAF Perspective' by Lt Gen Mohan Bhandari, both in the *Indian Defence Review*. You can read more about them in my treatise *Indian Defence: Crisis and Challenges*. All such tendencies must be ruthlessly curbed in future wars.

RECONNAISSANCE MISSIONS

Reconnaissance is one of the primary missions of air power and they must be made to do it. If you allow an argument that you can't waste very costly planes on such mundane tasks, you will suffer. The ground-forces commanders need the following from the air force recon missions:

- **Tactical Reconnaissance:** For the troops in a combat division, or the area immediately around a naval task force.

- **Operational Reconnaissance:** For army and theatre commanders. Tactical reconnaissance may extend from right in front of your combat troops to about 20 or even 100 kilometres behind the enemy lines.

Besides these, the national command would expect strategic reconnaissance from the air assets—jobs of the type the SR-71 Blackbird did or what the satellites do now. The E-8 JSTARS (Joint Surveillance and Target Attack Radar System), first used during the 1991 Gulf War, ushered in a new era of air reconnaissance. This is an airborne command and control aircraft. Unlike the AWACS (Airborne Warning and Control System), which handles only air operations, the JSTARS' primary job is tracking ground activity and was designed to better integrate air and ground operations by quickly locating targets for our aircraft and coordinating those attacks with friendly ground operations.

WILL OUR NUMERICAL SUPERIORITY BE THE DECISIVE FACTOR?

Contrary to popular perceptions, it is not really so. Numerical superiority would play a decisive role only if the war is long enough to cause attrition to have an appreciable effect. In the Cold Start type limited objective war, the numerical superiority would not get to play a decisive role for the simple reason that the number of sorties itself would be limited due to various unalterable factors discussed above—such as your repair and maintenance facilities; the very design features of your aircrafts; the use of surface-to-surface missiles by the enemy, and so on. That automatically limits the number of possible engagements. How many enemy aircrafts you can shoot down in them?

In a limited objective war, ground support to the army would be critical. If India can do that, Pakistan will have much to worry about. Presently I do not expect much from the fixed-wing aircrafts in this—attack helicopters would perhaps render more service.

The numerical edge of the IAF does not really mesh with the strategic objectives which India might have in a somewhat drawn-out conventional war. Having beaten the Pakistanis over their skies might serve as an ego trip for India but it is doubtful whether it will have a material effect on the outcome of the war per se. Remember, the Indians are in no position to execute the 'shock and awe' of the Americans. India is not in a position to carpet bomb Pakistan the way the Americans pounded Baghdad. More important than attrition is your ability to cope with attrition and continuously adjust your strategy accordingly. Many air forces get terribly perturbed at an attrition rate of 2 per cent (that is, 20 per 1,000 sorties). In the end, the fundamental problem with a war of attrition is that the enemy would not be prepared to fight that and would rather prefer to terminate it quickly by using TNWs (Tactical Nuclear Weapons).

CHAPTER 6

A Conventional War with Pakistan

THE PERILS OF CONDUCTING 'WARS ON PAPER'

It has long been a favourite pastime of the army officers and their friends in the media and academia to imagine all sorts of scenarios—how Pakistan would launch the 'Army Reserve North' (ARN) through the Shakargarh bulge; how they would try to interdict the NH1A; how they would threaten the Madhopur head works; how they would like to exploit the spatial bias in north from Marala Headworks through Shakargarh Bulge; and so on. The 'Army Reserve South' (ARS), it is argued that, is likely to be employed in semi-desert/desert terrain south of Sulaimanke head works on the Sutlej. It could be deployed either west or east of the Indus. If located to the west, it gives them more options for employment but makes the force vulnerable to interdiction while crossing the Indus; locating to the east of the Indus reduces the options for employment—our guys know the business of the Pak army better than their own Generals, you see! It is also argued that having one infantry division and an independent armoured brigade short in comparison to the ARN, the ARS is thought to lack offensive capability and is supposed to be more suitable for a riposte or counter offensive tasks.

In other words, they would have you believe that the Pakistanis do not have many options; that they can fight only in certain fixed manners; and that they can be given a resounding beating in all those scenarios. Everything, every possible move and countermove has been worked out on paper. While this sort of speculation could be tolerated for a moment for academic interest, one must pause to think that the Pakistanis would not be such fools as to be so predictable.

Given their poor understanding of military science and military history, the problem with such people is that they are absolutely incapable of thinking beyond numbers and ORBATs (Orders of Battle). Friends, Indians, countrymen, if you ponder to think, there is a clear Freudian angle to such an obsession with size. Knowledgeable readers would understand immediately. Warfare is not an organ-measuring contest of schoolboys—period! And, by God, if these people have worked out the result of every move and its possible countermove; if everything in strategic planning is so obvious and predictable, we could invite the Pakistanis for a seminar (or be their guest, or go to some neutral exotic locale) and slug it out on a map or in a specially designed video game—what is the need of actual bloodshed? If the 'tale of the tape' were to decide the outcome of boxing matches, what is the need of having boxing matches in the first place?

Gentlemen, real life is not a C-grade Chinese kung fu movie where, in some elaborate but highly unnatural choreography, every move, every punch, every kick of both the fighters is met by a block or countermove straight from the textbook. Somebody should ask as to why should then a fight end in one fighter's defeat or victory at all? The fight should theoretically go on indefinitely. Their answer is that the victor comes up with something strange at the very end and the defeated guy asks in wonder, "Hey, what style was that? Is your school's kung fu better than my school's?"

WHAT COULD MAKE PAKISTAN GO TO WAR?

PAKISTAN'S QUEST OF CASUS BELLI

We have already discussed the flashpoints from India's perspective earlier. Pakistan too can take initiative in launching attacks as they have done in the previous wars. We should not think that they cannot do that again. Somehow or the other, ever since people have started talking of Cold Start in India, people have formed a notion in their minds that only India will take the initiative. There is no good reason to believe that Pakistan cannot attack first.

According to an independent research site pakistanbodycount.org maintained by Dr Zeeshan-ul-Hassan Usmani, a Fulbright scholar, deaths from suicide bombings up to October 2016 were 6,492 with 16,508 injured. According to the Pakistani newspaper *Express Tribune*, terrorist attacks staged in Pakistan have killed over 35,000 people, 5,000 of which are law enforcement personnel, and caused material damage to the Pakistani economy totalling $67 billion by the IMF and the World Bank. The irony is that, in spite of their well-known overt and covert support to terrorism in Jammu and Kashmir since 28 years, Pakistan has been falsely accusing India of instigating insurgency in Balochistan and covertly supporting other acts of terrorism in the country. The Pakistani military and civilian leadership have repeatedly alleged that the Indian intelligence agency RAW has been funding and training Tehreek-i-Taliban Pakistan (TTP) members using a network of Indian consulates in Afghanistan along Pakistani border. According to the Pakistani allegations, when the TTP emerged, Afghan and Indian intelligence were quick to seize the opportunity to infiltrate and utilize some of its elements, particularly Baitullah Mehsud's kin, against Pakistan and its armed forces. Hence, at least for the sake of argument, albeit falsely, in case there is any major terrorist attack in their country, they can blame it on India and find a casus belli.

They can also take recourse to what is popularly known as 'Water Wars'. You may recall that following the notorious Uri attack, through the famous "Blood and water cannot flow together" speech of the Prime Minister Narendra Modi, India gave indication of stepping up exploitation of India's share of water in the Indus Water Treaty. It was enough to really rattle Pakistan. So severe was the rattling that Sartaj Aziz, advisor to Pakistani Prime Minister Nawaz Sharif, said that they would approach the United Nations and the International Court of Justice if India unilaterally suspended the Treaty. "Pakistan will not accept Indian aggression in any form, and any Indian step for disrupting water flow as [an] upper riparian state will pertain to considerable risk of war and hostilities," Aziz said. Pakistan does not possess water storage facilities and is hence dependent on the river flow for irrigation. Hence it is very easy to raise the bogey of drought and famine in Pakistan caused by India cutting off the water. It would naturally be a highly emotive issue and would get instant support of millions of ill-informed farmers in Pakistan.

The Indus Water Treaty of 1960 gives Pakistan control over the three western rivers (the Indus, the Chenab and the Jhelum) and India control over the three eastern rivers (the Beas, the Ravi and the Sutlej). The Treaty resulted in a partitioning of the rivers, rather than a water sharing system. It also states that while India is allowed to use 20% of the western rivers for irrigation and power generation, it cannot build projects, such as dams, along the rivers. The three western rivers are estimated to carry 123 million acre feet (MAF) of water while the three eastern rivers carry 233 MAF of water. Within the bounds of the Treaty, India will draw up plans to exploit its share fully—20% of the waters of the west flowing rivers. For example, India could use waters of the three rivers to irrigate 9,12,000 acres which can be increased by 4,20,000 acres. At present India irrigates only 8,00,000 acres. The Indus Water Treaty also permits India store up to 3.6 MAF of water; however it has not done so—it could do that now.

India could also look at exploiting the hydroelectric power potential of the three eastern rivers, estimated to be 18,600 MW, of which only 11,406 MW was either being used or are part of plans for usage. New Delhi would also review a 1987 decision to stop the construction of the Tulbul barrage on the Jhelum. The Tulbul project is a 'navigation lock-cum-control structure' at the mouth of the Wullar Lake. It envisages regulated water release from the natural storage in the lake to maintain a minimum draught of 4.5 feet in the river up to Baramulla, during the lean winter months. This is to ensure year-round navigation from Anantnag to Srinagar and Baramulla, a distance of over 20 km.

THE PERCEPTION OF PAK ARMY OFFICERS

Then, given the preeminent position which the army enjoys in Pakistan, the perception of Pak army officers is vital. What they think of India, will have an important bearing on the nation's policies. Now how do we determine that? One important tool is the Pakistan army's *Green Book* which contains essays by serving officers and is published every two years by the Pakistan Army's General Headquarters. This allows us, as Christine Fair described it, to listen to the Pakistani army talking to itself—the former Army chief, Gen (retd) Ashfaq Parvez Kayani had described it as "a platform where the intellectual context of national security could be crystallised."

They have expressed their views on many issues. Analysing Pakistan's failure in Balochistan, they alleged that "India jumped into Balochistan affair to teach Pakistan a lesson in response to its involvement in Kashmir." It was from this that Indian journalists started speaking of the 'hidden hand' of the Pakistani Generals that guided India-Pakistan engagement. Then they are paranoid about deepening India-United States strategic relationship. Maj Gen Shaukat Iqbal spoke of an Indo-

US nexus and said that the two nations hoped Pakistan was tamed and sufficiently weakened to act in the form of a colonised State which should serve US interest and oblige to the dictates of India. He said that the United States wished to use the war on terrorism as an instrument to get the Pakistan army bogged down, weakening its war stamina, and creating a wedge between religious forces and the army. Maj Gen Asghar Nawaz called the US "as much a liability as a friend." It can also be seen that 1971 still haunts them. They say that India would not hesitate in attempting to dismember Pakistan yet again if it reckoned that the military adventure would pay off. They also seem to be acutely conscious of the issue of Pakistan's self-respect as a nation. One essay says: "Pakistan is not willing to live as a surrogate of India as it can compel India to pay a heavy price if it uses its military instrument to browbeat Pakistan. It is determined to chart its own course and strengthen its Islamic connection with rest of the Muslim countries."

THE PROBLEM OF MESHING DESIRE WITH STRATEGY

Thus finding casus belli is not difficult for Pakistan. A more difficult thing is to fix the objectives of the offensive. What exactly they would want to achieve with the offensive? Remember, this is not 1971. Therein lies the nightmare of the Pakistani General.

As far as India is concerned, an objective of Cold Start or something similar to it could be to quickly grab some territory which could be used as a bargaining chip in negotiations. Theoretically, even Pakistan could think along similar lines. But the question is can Pakistan bring such overwhelming firepower to bear upon India as to push its forces back and capture some territory. I have doubts about it. They will have to invent a Pakistani version of the Blitzkrieg for that. I wonder if they can find a Heinz Guderian amongst them.

INDIA'S SO-CALLED 'COLD START' STRATEGY

THE SUNDARJI DOCTRINE

Under the so-called Sundarji doctrine, pursued by India between 1981 and 2004, the international border was protected by seven defensive 'Holding Corps'. In a war, after the Holding Corps halted a Pakistani attack, the Strike Corps would counterattack from their bases in central India (I Corps in Mathura, II Corps in Ambala, and XXI Corps in Bhopal) and penetrate deep into Pakistani territory to destroy the Pakistan army's own two Strike Corps through 'deep sledgehammer blows' in a high-intensity battle of attrition.

THE LEARNING EXPERIENCE OF OPERATION PARAKRAM

Operation Parakram ended the myth of the Sundarji doctrine. To the horror of the Indian Army top brass, from the time the mobilization order was given, the armoured columns of the Strike Corps took nearly three weeks to make their way to the international border area. In this intervening period, the Pakistan army was able to counter-mobilize on the border, and more importantly, the US got involved. Under US pressure, President Musharraf was made to deliver his 'about turn' speech on January 12, 2002. In view of his denunciation of terrorism in the name of Kashmir and the pledge of a renewed crackdown on militant groups in Pakistan, by the time the Strike Corps reached the border region, India's political justification for military action had been significantly reduced.

It was argued that a war-fighting strategy that called for massive armoured thrusts to dismember Pakistan was too crude and inflexible a tool to respond to terrorist attacks and other indirect challenges. Furthermore, mobilizing the entire military was not an appropriate policy to pursue limited aims.

CONCEPTUALIZATION OF A NEW DOCTRINE

In April 2004, it was reported that the Indian Army has developed a new limited war doctrine that would supposedly allow it to mobilize quickly and undertake retaliatory attacks in response to whatever the Indians could deem to be unacceptable at the hands of the Pakistanis. There is no official confirmation regarding this whether the doctrine exists or not. I am therefore commenting only on those aspects of the 'presumed' theory which have already appeared in public domain in the works of numerous scholars.

The concept of 'Cold Start' envisages troops moving from peacetime quarters directly into battle—and hence the word 'cold' in the doctrine. That saves on the time in 'assembly'. The goal of this 'limited war' or 'limited objective' doctrine is to establish the capacity to launch a retaliatory conventional strike against Pakistan that would inflict significant harm on the Pakistan army before the international community could intercede, and at the same time, pursue aims narrow enough to deny Pakistan a justification to escalate the clash to the nuclear level.

This was not something out of the blue which has supposedly taken Pakistan by complete surprise and has paralysed them. It was reportedly developed with the help of external strategists like Stephen Cohen, and borrowed also from Israeli tactics, notably from the 1967 Arab-Israeli War besides NATO's famous "come as you are" war doctrine. As such, the basic concept was in the public domain since long.

CONCEPT OF INTEGRATED BATTLE GROUPS

This doctrine requires reorganizing the Indian Army's offensive power away from the three large Strike Corps into eight smaller division-sized 'Integrated Battle Groups' (IBGs) that combine mechanized infantry, artillery, and armour in a manner reminiscent of the Soviet Union's operational manoeuvre groups. The eight battle groups would be prepared to launch multiple strikes into Pakistan along different axes of advance. It is envisioned that the operations of the IBGs would be integrated with close air support from the Indian Air Force and naval aviation assets to provide highly mobile fire support. In simpler words, the doctrine sought to "mass firepower rather than forces". At the same time, the Holding Corps (re-designated 'Pivot Corps'), which would be bolstered by additional armour and artillery, would concurrently man defensive positions and undertake limited offensive operations as necessary. All elements would engage in continuous operations, day and night, until their military objectives were achieved.

A major emphasis of Cold Start is on the speed of both deployment and operations. The argument is that forward-deployed division-sized units can be alerted faster and mobilized more quickly than larger formations. If the battle groups and the pivot corps start closer to the international border, their logistics requirements are significantly reduced, enhancing their manoeuvrability and their ability to surprise.

In execution, it is argued that moving forces simultaneously into unpredicted locations at high speeds and making decisions faster than their opponents can, the IBGs would seek to defeat Pakistani forces in the field by disrupting their cohesion. It is also argued that the use of multiple units increases the challenge for Pakistani intelligence's limited reconnaissance assets to monitor the status of all the IBGs, improving the chance of achieving surprise. One more amusing argument is that if Pakistan were to use nuclear weapons against Indian forces, divisions would present a significantly smaller target than would corps.

Although the operational details of Cold Start, if at all it exists, remain classified, it appears that the goal would be to have three to five IBGs entering Pakistani territory within 72 to 96 hours from the time the order to mobilize is issued. The objective would be to make shallow territorial gains say, 50-80 km deep, that could be used in post-conflict negotiations to extract concessions from Islamabad.

The probable objective areas for Cold Start have been conjectured by different people to be:

- Ravi-Chenab corridor from two directions—an IBG along Jammu-Sialkot-Daska axis and another across the Ravi to link up with the first IBG;
- in the south against Reti-Rahim Yar Khan-Kashmore complex;
- along the Jaisalmer-Rahimyar Khan axis; or
- along the Barmer-Mirpurkhas axis.

CRITIQUE OF THE COLD START DOCTRINE

PROBLEMS IN EXECUTION OF COLD START

Difficult Demands of C4I

In terms of military theory, as we mentioned above, the Cold Start is basically an attempt to copy NATO's "come as you are" war doctrine. The NATO doctrine demanded an integration of three levels—the 'Combat Command'; the 'Battle Groups'; and the 'Combat Teams'. The doctrine was supposed to optimize resource management for the battle commanders by funnelling information of a continuously-evolving complex community of people, devices, information and services onto a single platform. Executing such extremely fluid and complex manoeuvres would be impossible without a highly sophisticated C4I (Command and Control, Communications, Computers and Intelligence) network or Net-centric system. Even the Americans are still trying to debug and streamline a functional Net-centric system. In India's case, this is far away from becoming a reality.

Resource Intensive and Expensive

Such a doctrine is prohibitively expensive strategy. It demands huge stockpiles of spares, fuel and ammunition near the staging bases, heavy-duty air lift capacity, highly sophisticated C4I network, resource hungry training, and the highest levels of mission-readiness all year around. There are serious doubts whether the Indian Army possess the resources necessary to execute Cold Start? The integrated battle groups will require organic self-propelled artillery to have the mobility and firepower necessary to accomplish their mission. Then there are doubts about the helicopter airlift capability to move men and material. Close air support is also a doubtful field.

Numerical Advantage Not Decisive

Let us not forget that India is obliged to man two borders. That would provide a roughly 1:1 balance of forces in the immediate theatre at the start of any crisis. Since the Pakistani army's deployment on the Afghan border is variable, it may account for a little difference to the ratio. Now we can apply some conventional wisdom. The conventional wisdom (see, for example, John Mearsheimer) is that the attackers must have a numerical superiority of 3:1 in offensive strength at the tactical level as a requirement for successful breakthrough operations. This has been a topic of great dispute and I must emphasize that it cannot be a hard and fast rule. Still, the basic point to be noted is that the attacker must enjoy a significant numerical superiority to have a decisive edge. How much it should be exactly is, of course, a matter of debate and it is difficult to quantify it. But India does not seem to possess a decisive numerical superiority.

Coming to the issue of numerical advantage in tanks, a large numbers of tanks on both sides are vintage second-generation platforms. If we confine our discussion to just the modern high-performance tanks (third generation T-80UDs and Al-Khalids of Pakistan and India's T-90 and Arjun tanks of India), India has a numerical advantage of 1.3:1. But this should be viewed in the backdrop of the fact that Pakistani armoured units are primarily stationed in the vicinity of the international border, while India's are primarily based in central India—thus the ability to mobilize and deploy rapidly goes to Pakistan's advantage.

On the other hand, we have seen that Pakistan is in a comfortable position regarding self-propelled artillery. However, the professional issue is that the advantage of self-propelled artillery lies more in offence and not in defence. Thus Pakistan might not derive a great advantage from them in defence; however, India would feel the pinch of their shortage in self-propelled artillery in offence.

India's Shortage of Ammunition

There are also issues of shortages of ammunition also. A serving officer like me cannot comment on it but journalists have written at length on it. For example, Rajat Pandit and Sharma and Datt write that as of August 2014, the army lacked ammunition to undertake more than 20 days of 'intense fighting' with less than seven days of reserves of key stocks of artillery ammunition, anti-tank missiles and a 'critical shortage' of ammunition for its main battle tanks that would run out after ten days, hardly enough time for additional forces to make a difference.

In this connection, I must add that according to some unofficial accounts and media reports the Indian reserves of the shells of 155 mm Bofors howitzer had run dangerously low during the Kargil conflict and they had to hurriedly import some 50,000 Israeli/South African/Russian manufactured shells during the conflict—they had fired about 2,50,000 shells during the conflict. Had the war been not confined to a frontage of just about 150 km, or if it had dragged for some more time; India could have very well run short of other types of ammunition also, such as for the 130 mm medium guns too.

The Issue of Support of Other Services

As an army concept for warfare on land with major emphasis on ground offensive, Cold Start places the other two services in a subordinate and supportive role. This is especially applicable to the air force. Cold Start employs airpower according to the army's own vision of joint warfare, where elements of all three services are under the control of a unified (presumably army) commander. India is known for inter-service rivalries. No one can deny it. This doctrine also runs counter to the Indian Air Force's own concept of joint operations, which involves the services fighting wars separately but according to a coordinated plan. The air force has traditionally been gearing itself for air superiority, deep attack and strategic reach—not close air support. Thus eventually, the load will fall on attack helicopters.

Poor Alignment with India's Broader Strategic Goals

While Cold Start represents a significant advance in India's conventional capabilities, it is a concept that is poorly aligned with India's broader strategic goals. It is, in fact, an example of creative military problem-solving on paper. Cold Start presumes that you would be conducting offensive operations in such a manner so as to prevent Pakistan from crossing the nuclear threshold. But that's what the Indian Army believes. Is there any reason to believe that the Pakistanis would accept it?

Cold Start rests on the presumption that Pakistan would play by India's rules. We cannot expect them to 'cooperate' with us and comply with our wishes. Why should they? Who in the world is going to believe that? The concept of limited war in the 'Cold Start' strategy is dangerous strategic thinking.

Unrealistic Presumptions about Pakistan's Response

Cold Start presumes that the Pakistani military will fold instantly and the Indian forces will be able to destroy the Pakistani forces without inflicting damage to the Pakistani civilian population. There is no reason to believe in this assumption. The Pakistani army is not going to behave like a coy bride waiting for the bridegroom in the shape of the Indian Army to arrive to her room on her wedding night and do whatever he wished with her.

Cold Start envisions 'limited' thrusts into Pakistan to a depth of 50-80 km. But the historical fact is that in no past war between India and Pakistan has there been a penetration of the territory of the other side beyond 15-20 km. This means that there is greater uncertainty associated with the likely Pakistani response. There is no way of knowing where they would draw the line of going nuclear.

Nuclear Escalation

Wars have a way of taking on a life of their own. What prevents the Pakistanis from going nuclear? As Pakistan's former army chief Gen Ashfaq Parvez Kayani had emphatically pointed out, proponents of the use of conventional force in "a nuclear overhang" were charting a course of dangerous adventurism whose consequences could be both unintended and uncontrollable. Whoever thinks that a limited war with decisive results is possible completely ignores the perception of the other party. Pakistan has to decide how they would react.

How can the Indians take decisions on behalf of the Pakistanis? Clausewitz had cautioned that war is a reciprocal engagement: "In war, the will is directed at an animate object that reacts." It is true even now.

They also overlook the fact that in a crisis the nuclear threshold will be indeterminate and will depend more on psychological factors, the prevailing public mood, the pressure of the media, and the perceived desperation—how they are evaluating the situation and its effect on the leaders' personal as well as national interests. In fact the popular perception in Pakistan is that why has the nation made nuclear weapons after spending billions upon billions if the government does not have the guts to use them—have they been made just to keep them as showpieces? As Shireen Mazari claims in a lighter vein, Pakistan's nuclear escalation ladder has only 'one rung'.

Imponderables Ignored

In military parlance there is a concept referred to as 'balance', which relates to the time-distance between forces; a force is said to be in a state of balance if it is capable of sustaining itself to achieve the assigned mission in a time period within which reserve forces can arrive, permitting the initial force to go further, whether in defence or attack. In attempting a Cold Start there is an inherent risk to the maintenance of balance between the forces that have joined battle and those leaving barracks to reinforce them. There are too many imponderables, and the operation has to be impeccably planned to work.

Pakistan's Geographical Advantages

The advantages of Pakistan lie in shorter lines of communications, as well as prepared fighting positions that leverage natural and man-made obstacles to protect defensive forces.

American and Pakistani Assessments of the Cold Start

It would be of considerable academic interest to know as to what the then US Ambassador to India had to say on the Cold Start. As revealed in the Wikileaks, Tim Roemer had concluded. I present some excerpts.

The Indian Army's 'Cold Start Doctrine' is a mixture of myth and reality. It has never been and may never be put to use on a battlefield because of substantial and serious resource constraints, but it is a developed operational attack plan announced in 2004 and intended to be taken off the shelf and implemented within a 72-hour period during a crisis.... Although the plan reportedly has a significant air support component, it is unclear to us how much joint versus parallel planning has taken place. We have not heard of a major operational role for the Indian Navy or parallel sea-launched attacks.

Cold Start is not a plan for a comprehensive invasion and occupation of Pakistan. Instead, it calls for a rapid, time- and distance-limited penetration into Pakistani territory with the goal of quickly punishing Pakistan, possibly in response to a Pakistan-linked terrorist attack in India, without threatening the survival of the Pakistani State or provoking a nuclear response.

Indian leaders no doubt realize that, although Cold Start is designed to punish Pakistan in a limited manner without triggering a nuclear response, they cannot be sure whether Pakistani leaders will in fact refrain from such a response.

The existence of the plan reassures the Indian public and may provide some limited deterrent effect on Pakistan. Taken together, these factors underline that the value of the doctrine to the GoI may lie more in the plan's existence than in any real world application.

Even if the plan is never actually implemented—and there is considerable question as to GoI intent to ever implement it—news of Cold Start's existence has already paid dividends to Indian policymakers by providing reassurance to the Indian public that the GoI has the means to punish Pakistan for attacks on Indian soil without triggering potential mutually-assured nuclear destruction. From the Indian perspective, the unimplemented plan has the added virtue of accentuating Pakistani discomfiture and angst, which in theory may have some deterrent value.

The GoI refrained from implementing Cold Start even after an attack as audacious and bloody as the Mumbai attack, which calls into serious question the GoI's willingness to actually adopt the Cold Start option. Second, the Pakistanis have known about Cold Start since 2004, but this knowledge does not seem to have prompted them to prevent terror attacks against India to extent such attacks could be controlled. This fact calls into question Cold Start's ability to deter Pakistani mischief inside India. Even more so, it calls into question the degree of sincerity of fear over Cold Start as expressed by Pakistani military leaders to USG officials.

Cold Start is not India's only or preferred option after a terrorist attack. Depending on the nature, location, lethality, public response, and timing of a terrorist attack, India might not respond at all or could pursue one of several other possible options.

In Pakistan, Lt Gen Khalid Masood Khan (retd) believes that the Cold Start doctrine is only a deterrent which can never be implemented. It is designed to keep the Pakistani Generals preoccupied and busy. Commander Muhammad Azam Khan (retd) of the Pakistan Navy describes it as flirting with Armageddon.

PAKISTAN'S LIKELY STRATEGY FOR A FUTURE CONVENTIONAL WAR

EXPECTED THEATRES AND NATURE OF OPERATIONS

Any Indo-Pak ground conflict can take place only in one or more of the four major theatres, each varying in geography and, to a lesser extent climatically. All of them lend themselves to different types of operations. The theatres of operations are:

- Along the Line of Control—Northern Kashmir region
- Southern Jammu and Kashmir and Punjab sectors
- North and Central Rajasthan
- South Rajasthan and Gujarat

An Indian offensive through Kashmir, if at all made, is likely to be a First World War style affair, that is, artillery bombardment followed by infantry assaults as the terrain is not suitable for mounted manoeuvre. From a professional perspective, the military objectives of such a venture could include the capture of Skardu to cut off the main glacier zone in Baltistan. Moreover, a strong offensive aimed at capturing Muzaffarabad from the North and the South of the Jhelum, and the neutralization of the Haji Pir (Bedori) Bulge would also be important objectives.

In the Southern Jammu and Kashmir and Punjab sectors, stretching down into North and Central Rajasthan, there are a series of formidable obstacle defences for hundreds of kilometres, called ditch-cum-bunds (DCB) and irrigation canals on both sides. These defences or fortified defensive fighting positions, combined with the existing natural ground features once again make large-scale mechanized operations rather difficult even as military bridging has been developed into a speciality in itself.

In the Northern/Central Rajasthan theatre and further below in south Rajasthan and Gujarat, considerable scope exists for the large scale use of mechanized formations in the desert and semi-desert sectors—the stuff of films.

PAKISTAN'S FUNDAMENTAL APPROACH TO A CONVENTIONAL WAR

Given the fact that any future war has to be fought in one or more of these theatres only, there is little scope for giving free reins to your imagination and innovativeness. The wars can be fought only in a limited number of ways—the combinations of attack and defence are necessarily limited. Hence no bolt out of the blue can be expected. The chances of someone coming up with such a brilliant piece of strategy that the other guy is left flummoxed are extremely rare.

When looking at these theatres of operations, it must be borne in mind that Punjab and Kashmir are politically very sensitive areas for the political establishments in both countries. It is, therefore, hardly likely that any major loss of territory in either of these two areas would be acceptable. In fact, the real vulnerability of Pakistan lies, not so much in a lack of 'strategic depth', but in the fact that so many of its major population centres and politically and military sensitive targets lying very close to the border with India.

One of the original nightmarish scenarios for the Pakistanis was a powerful armoured thrust in the southern Rajasthan sector, striking at Pakistan's vital north-south road and rail communication links where they narrow to a waist hardly 70 kilometres across, south-west of Rahim Yar Khan. This could cut off Punjab and the North-West Frontier, where most of Pakistan's air and ground force military assets are based, from the port at Karachi, the Navy, and resupply of oil and strategic goods from abroad—effectively bisecting Pakistan at its weakest point in the Sindh Province.

OFFENSIVE-DEFENCE, RIPOSTE AND DISPROPORTIONATE RESPONSE

Then the question arises as to where do they fight and how? Remaining on the strategic and tactical defensive was ruled out due to lack of strategic depth. It was realized that a 'stand and fight' doctrine would probably result in deep penetration by Indian forces, without Pakistani forces being able to manoeuvre effectively.

The doctrine of 'Offensive Defence', evolved by General Mirza Aslam Beg [supposedly tested in 1989 in exercise Zarb-e-Momin (Strike or Blow of the Believer)], is characterized by retaining adequate reserves at successive force levels, surprise, and aggressive leadership. This strategy would call for the Pakistan army to detect the initial enemy thrust at the earliest, take effective countermeasures to limit penetration, and simultaneously attack the adversary to capture or threaten a strategic objective.

The 'Riposte' is believed to have evolved from operationalization of the strategies which were developed and supposedly tested during the Azm-e-Nau (New Resolve) I, II, and III exercises conducted for four years (2009-2013). In fact, the Pakistani Inter-Services Public Relations (ISPR) clearly said after the conclusion of the exercise that the 'new concept of war fighting' was aimed at pre-empting India's 'Cold Start Doctrine'. It calls for Pakistani 'Strike Corps' to take the initiative in a war with India, pushing deep into Indian territory while other corps hold back the initial Indian advance. In the 'Riposte' strategy, their two Strike Corps [I Corps (Mangla) and II Corps (Multan)] would conduct a limited advance along narrow fronts to occupy Indian Territory near the border The Riposte was remarkably simple in concept in that Pakistan would accept some loss of territory in Indian penetrations, but would conduct a limited but powerful advance along narrow fronts with the aim of occupying territory near the border to a depth of 40-50 km. Pakistan believes that this would give it a bargaining chip to be used in the aftermath of a ceasefire brought about by international pressure after up to four weeks of fighting. They claim that under the new concept, the Pakistan army could mobilise in far less time as compared to India. It is not clear whether it is a bluff or they have developed something special.

Pakistan must know that if India is able to gain superiority in the air, it can inflict serious damage on any army that is advancing towards it. It is obvious that such a situation must be prevented at any cost. This means that they must watch out for pre-emptive air strikes by India to ensure maximum destruction of their airbases and aircrafts very early in the war, which will be immediately followed by swift shock attacks. In other words, the Pakistanis must be extremely wary of India doing to them what they had attempted on India in 1971.

Pakistan's War College has scrupulously and diligently run all the permutations and possible combinations for an India-Pakistan conflict. As far as remaining non-nuclear is concerned, they would like to:

- occupy their wartime locations earlier than the Indian Army confers on it the ability to pre-empt Cold Start;
- create more armour-dominated brigade-sized reserves from the existing resources if possible, and a more flexible military system and structure;
- an aggressive counterattack into Indian territory that bypasses the advancing IBGs—the classic 'offensive-defence';
- activate fifth-columnist action or terrorist sleeper cells in India for effecting some spectacular terrorist strikes in the country to disorientate the leadership and produce intense consternation amongst the people and the media; and

- simultaneously provoke rioting/civil unrest in places like Kashmir that immediately attract international attention and project the civil unrest and terrorist strikes as a continuum representing popular opposition to India within India.

What if Riposte does not work? On the basis of certain documents obtained by them, *The Hindu* paper revealed in December 2013 that Pakistan's official Army Doctrine calls on the country to invoke 'disproportionate responses' in future wars with India. The Doctrine argues that "a disparity at the conventional plane continues to grow disproportionately, which too disturbs the strategic equilibrium of the region." It does not state what the red lines compelling nuclear weapons use might be, but says future strategic "force development centres around developing and maintaining credible minimum deterrence, based on a land, sea and air triad, including an assured second-strike capability to an Indian nuclear first-strike."

Disproportionate response means that Pakistan was prepared to use its bigger nukes also. It must, however, be noted is that this doctrine was developed before they had made the Nasr battlefield missile and the TNWs (Tactical Nuclear Weapons) operational. The TNWs have changed the scene materially since then. Since the TNWs do not necessarily present an inevitable threat of an Indian response by nuclear warheads much bigger than the TNWs themselves, this means that now Pakistan would be more inclined to use nuclear weapons in the form of TNWs.

CHAPTER 7

Factors which would Necessarily Make the War Tortuous

DILEMMAS OF A 'LIMITED OBJECTIVE' WAR

INABILITY TO SURPRISE THE ENEMY, QUICK MOBILIZATION NOTWITHSTANDING

A 'limited objective' war rests upon the presumption of a quick mobilization and penetration. A quick penetration is likely to succeed only if it surprises the enemy. But the question is, is quick mobilization enough to effect complete surprise so as to catch the enemy unawares? No. Anyone can run through the history of wars. Even in the ancient age, there was always a political build-up to the actual outbreak of hostilities. Except for local potentates who could summon their two hundred horsemen on a bugle call and dash to the nearest village of the enemy, everybody else needed some time and resources to mobilize his forces—above all; they needed a reason to go to war.

At least in the context of India and Pakistan, it is difficult to contemplate a situation where India, on fine night, suddenly mobilizes its armour in absolute secrecy and then launches a fierce attack on Pakistan. It does not happen in real life. There has to be some build-up of tensions preceding that. We are not a country which will deliver a knockout punch, a bolt out of the blue just like that, for no good reason. As we have discussed earlier, there have to be some political reasons for going to war or, may be, one of the numerous precipitating factors such as an obnoxious terrorist strike. Now, if anything of that sort has happened between India and Pakistan, that would, unless they are completely dumb, alert them to the possibility of an Indian response. They have been hearing since years that India would not take it anymore. The nature of response may be a matter of debate or conjecture but, following the occurrence of one of the precipitating factors, the Pakistanis must get alerted to the fact that India might react militarily. That is enough time for them to mobilize their own defences and offensive elements. If we can mobilize quickly, so can they—after all, we have not discovered some such secret of rapid mobilization which was hidden in some ancient scroll.

In fact, even if the speed of mobilization were to become the decisive factor; given that all other factors are almost equal, Pakistan will have an advantage for the simple reason that it has to move its forces much shorter distances.

CAN WE DO A PEARL HARBOUR ON PAKISTAN?

Can India take Pakistan by complete surprise and do a sort of Pearl Harbour on Pakistan? The answer is a categorical no! Even the real Pearl Harbour was not as unexpected as it is generally made out to be. On the 70th anniversary of Pearl Harbour, the attack that had propelled America into the Second World War, a declassified memo shows that Japanese surprise attack was expected. As Jacqui Goddard reported in *The Telegraph*, President Franklin D Roosevelt was warned three days before the attack that the Japanese empire was eyeing up Hawaii with a view to 'open conflict'. Its contents are revealed by historian Craig Shirley in his new book *December 1941: 31 Days that Changed America and Saved the World*. Unfortunately, Washington dismissed red flags signalling that mass bloodshed was looming and war was imminent. US leadership was guilty of a 'failure of imagination' in its inability to translate warning signs into a specific prediction of the horror that lay ahead.

In warfare, the seemingly impossible also must not be dismissed as absolutely impossible—one must always expect the unexpected. In the context of Pearl Harbour, the American top brass was kind of in denial because they didn't think anybody would be as audacious to move an army thousands of miles across the Pacific, stop to refuel, then move on to Hawaii to make a strike like this. The French had never expected that Hitler would violate the neutrality of Belgium and bypass their formidable Maginot Line to attack France. The Germans had never expected that even after the fierce fighting and terrible losses incurred in the Battles of Moscow (October 1941 to January 1942) and Stalingrad (August 1942 to February 1943), Stalin would, against the advice of his generals, launch a general counteroffensive that was to lead to the decisive Battle of Kursk Salient (July-August 1943). In Stalingrad, the Axis forces (Germans, Romanians, Hungarians and Italians) had suffered nearly 8,75,000 casualties, besides some 900 aircrafts, 500 tanks, and 6,000 artillery pieces. The Soviet casualties were nearly 1.13 million, 4,341 tanks, 15,728 artillery pieces, and 2,769 aircrafts! In the wake of such frightening losses, the Soviet generals thought that a large counteroffensive could not be logistically supported. But Stalin insisted, "We must grind the Germans down with all speed, so that they cannot attack in the spring." With this, the conduct of the war changed from Defence in Depth to Deep Operations, the war of manoeuvre which many senior Red Army officers had been preparing for before the Great Purge. Thenceforth, the Wehrmacht was only to retreat all the way to Berlin.

Given the sort of acrimony that exists between the two nations, Pakistan would be guilty of extreme naiveté, if they do not gird their loins at the slightest hint of trouble brewing.

COMPLICATIONS INHERENT IN THE CONCEPT OF A SHORT AND SHARP CAMPAIGN

Now, our inability to spring a surprise means that the enemy must be expected to be prepared and put up a serious resistance. We need not debate the nature of resistance as the enemy preparations are not known to us. However, as I have shown earlier, tanks are indeed highly vulnerable to prepared defences. Resistance means that the offensive would lose speed, its very forte. If we are not able to achieve a quick breakthrough, the main objective of the 'limited objective' campaign is as good as lost.

It is commonly believed that since we are bigger and heavier in the 'numbers game', our advantage is loud and clear. However, India's military advantage over Pakistan in a short and sharp or 'limited objective' campaign of the Cold Start type is much less substantial than is commonly believed. An analysis by Christopher Clary has arrived at the same conclusion. The principal difficulty with limited objective campaign strategy is that it prevents India from taking advantage of its main advantage: its larger ground forces. Simply put, if India chooses to employ only a portion of its army, Pakistan would choose to employ a larger portion of its own forces to stop the attack and perhaps open up other fronts on terrain favourable to Pakistan.

I do not think that Pakistani Generals are so unrealistic as to think of defeating India outright in whatever way. A realistic objective would be to configure their forces in such a way as to deny India 'victory on the cheap'. That throws the ball in the court of India. India will have to take a call on whether it wants a 'costly victory' for politically not-so-significant gains or would it like to escalate the war further for politically more substantial gains. But the problem with such escalation is that it brings the war closer to the nuclear threshold or red lines of Pakistan.

Pakistan's military dilemma is that it cannot defeat India; India's military dilemma is that it cannot 'punish' Pakistan adequately without bringing the war dangerously close to a nuclear one.

Not only that, 'limited objective' wars are riskier in the sense that failure of the limited campaign will bring the combatants under strong pressures to escalate and attempt to achieve more decisive political results.

THE EFFECT OF CHINESE CIVILIAN CASUALTIES

An Indian attack could result in Chinese civilian casualties amongst Chinese workers working for the China-Pakistan Economic Corridor (CPEC) connecting Xinjiang in China with Gwadar in Pakistan. Chinese workers are to be found in Pakistan-occupied Kashmir, opposite the Jammu international border and along the entire border with India. Casualties amongst them may provide enough reason for China to at least mobilize its forces and carry out more aggressive patrolling if not actually start fighting.

The Depsang plains incident in 2013 is repeatedly cited as an example of how Chinese columns will cross into Arunachal Pradesh, without fear of being 'tailed or followed', pitch tents, and occupy Indian land without firing a shot. It is said that the PLA had practised occupation of the Indian Air Force's Advance Landing Ground during its Strike series of exercise in 2010. If we push them, it will be war. If we do not, we lose face.

FIFTH-COLUMNIST ACTION BY TERRORISTS AND ESPECIALLY TRAINED SABOTEURS

One thing which probably no planning has factored in is protection of vital lines of communication of the army (such as bridges, roads, railroads, etc) from sabotage due to fifth-columnist action. I have been writing on this since long that steel bridges in particular are rather easy to destroy by explosives—concrete bridges in comparison are somewhat difficult. The elementary techniques to destroy bridges are very much available in public domain and terrorists do not need any special ISI course for that—for example, the US Army Manual Explosives and Demolition, FM 3-34.214 (FM 5-250) [US Army Manual Explosives and Demolition, FM 3-34.214 (FM 5-250), July 2007, https://info.publicintelligence.net/USArmy-Explosives.pdf] deals with the subject at adequate length. Then there are numerous other sources also in public domain. And for all you know, the Pakistanis could especially train saboteurs. If the terrorists or saboteurs know their business, the army's supply lines can be easily cut to the utter detriment of any campaign. There is nothing easier than sabotage and we cannot afford to deploy the army or the paramilitary forces at the myriad targets that need to be protected. Besides communication links, other favourite targets of the saboteurs include electricity sub-stations, high-voltage lines, and mobile communication towers, etc. They may not have a direct effect on the operations of the armed forces but they have great effect on the general public and thus serve to spread panic.

AIR WAR'S LIKELY SHAPE IN THE CONTEXT OF A 'LIMITED OBJECTIVE' WAR

AIR SUPREMACY VERSUS STRATEGIC BOMBING

The air balance between India and Pakistan is believed to heavily favour the larger and technologically more sophisticated IAF. But there is a catch. The question is what exactly we propose to do? Indian Air Force would eventually be able to establish air supremacy over the skies of Pakistan; the battle would still be hard fought and would take time. What are its implications? It means that the longer the fight for air supremacy, the longer it will be before the IAF can focus on supporting ground forces in the event of substantial ground clashes. In any case, achieving air supremacy is not an end in itself. Where do we go from there? War is not about beating fighters only.

Can the IAF undertake strategic bombing (destroying the enemy's morale or its economic ability to produce and transport war material to the theatres of military operations) or damage Pakistan's critical industrial infrastructure significantly? I do not think so. I do not envisage carpet bombing or bombing on strategic industrial targets for the simple reason that the IAF does not have such assets which can deliver heavy explosive loads sufficient enough to damage them substantially. The sort of loads which can be carried by our assets can take on military targets only.

The outcome would also depend on what Pakistan does for its air force in the time before the next war. After all, the next war is not going to take place the next day and the Pakistanis would be expected to do something for their air force in the mean time. Given that they are starting with a handicap, they are likely to pay more attention to modern fighter aircraft with beyond-visual-range capability as well as new airborne early warning and control aircraft.

CLOSE AIR SUPPORT OR AIR SUPERIORITY?

That India cannot spring an absolute surprise on Pakistan has an important bearing on the role of the IAF in the war. It means that a sudden pre-emptive airstrike that would destroy a large portion of the Pakistani Air Force (PAF) assets on the ground is not possible—a repeat of the Israeli action against Egypt in the 1967 Six-Day War cannot be envisaged. That leaves the following three options before the IAF:

1. Focus on providing Close Air Support (CAS) to the armour.

2. Concentrate its assets on achieving air superiority before initiating ground operations.
3. Contend with the PAF while simultaneously providing close air support (CAS) to ground forces.

We will analyse them one-by-one.

Providing Close Air Support (CAS)

For a limited objective war, the Indian armoured thrusts will necessarily have to be supported by the IAF. Otherwise, there are standard methods of taking on an armoured thrust and it can be ground to a halt. Throughout the Vietnam War, the American ground forces were eternally grateful for CAS and artillery support. Wherever the infantry was beleaguered, they could count upon the aircrafts and the artillery to come to their rescue. We have not had a culture of this type, the air force clearly preferring the glamorous tasks; first air-to-air combat and then strategic bombing. It is not merely a question of inter-service coordination on which the self-styled experts love to write; it is more of a matter of the role which the air force has assigned to itself in its own perception and what it thinks of itself. The Kargil war is a good example of this and; take my word; it is not an easy problem to overcome. According to media reports (such as, Josy Jospeh's), the Army was keen on wresting control of all future attack helicopters from the Air Force—this could point towards a realization that for CAS, the army will have to fend for itself.

The question is to what extent the IAF can provide effective close air support.

In the first place, this requires detailed integration of each air mission with fire and movement of these forces. Detailed integration is important because of proximity, fires or movement of friendly forces. Close air support requires excellent coordination with ground forces. In advanced modern militaries, this coordination is typically handled by specialists such as Joint Fires Observers (JFOs), Joint Terminal Attack Controllers (JTACs), and Forward Air Controllers (FACs). This should not be taken for granted—the IAF and the Indian Army will have to make conscious efforts to develop this mindset and synergy.

Secondly, the CAS assets including helicopter gunships must do their job using rockets, missiles, small bombs, and strafing runs. Unlike the USAF, the IAF has never had dedicated assets for this role or assets that were specially modified for this role. The Americans built the famous A-10 Thunderbolt; the Soviets produced the Su-25 Grach. The F/A-18E/F Super Hornet, as the name itself indicates, comes in CAS configuration also and performed this role both in Operation Iraqi Freedom and in Afghanistan. Even the venerable high-altitude B-1B Lancer provided close air support in Afghanistan using precision-guided munitions. As a US army officer fondly recalls, there are few better sights than some A10's streaking over, hitting some ground targets with that big 30 mm GAU-8 Avenger Rotary Cannon (Gatling gun, then banking hard ... little dots leaving them and heading down ... the aircraft still leaving hard and roaring ... and then the ground just exploding from all the cluster bombs. Wow!

Thirdly, India was heavily dependent on the Jaguars and the MiG-27s for this role—their gradual phasing out has affected the IAF's ground attack capability.

Fourthly, CAS systems themselves are not immune to enemy counterattacks or countermeasures. The very ability of an air force to target defenders in well-prepared fighting positions, even with precision guided munitions (PGMs) is limited. Lambeth (1999) supports this contention and says that the role of the IAF in Kargil is a pointer to it.

Achieving Air Superiority

This is where their heart and the material lie and, there are reasons to believe, they can do it. It will be difficult to make a conjecture about the effectiveness of Pakistan's air defence systems and its effect on the IAF offensive. There are two reasons. First, every country keeps it classified. Second, no such system has been combat tested. As I have been mentioning, mere technical specifications do not tell the whole story.

Doing Both Simultaneously

A difficult task, particularly in view of the fact that the ground attack will lose any semblance of surprise.

Surface-to-Surface Missiles could Upset the Equation and Change the Scene Materially

Aircrafts can shine against other aircrafts, that is, as long as they are fighting a symmetric war. They become irrelevant when the enemy goes asymmetric and starts using his surface-to-surface ballistic or cruise missiles against you. Aircrafts cannot do anything against them. A very important thing which generally self-styled experts lose sight of is that if the Pakistan Air Force determines that it cannot successfully use its airpower in reprisal raids on Indian soil, Pakistan may use its conventionally armed cruise and ballistic missiles. Despite whatever claim any nation of the world might make about ABM (Anti-Ballistic Missile), the fact is that air and missile defences would not be able to stop incoming missile attacks. (For details of the shortcomings of Ballistic Missile Defence systems, interested readers may refer to my treatise *Indian Defence: Crisis and Challenges*.) Missile attacks, albeit conventional, on Indian targets could prompt India too to launch its conventionally armed missiles and thus take the war in a different direction altogether where the expensive toys of the air force would be rendered irrelevant. Ballistic missiles costing just $1.4 million each could render a modern fighter costing $220 million irrelevant for the simple reason that you could fire several of them with zero loss and nearly 100% assured hits. In the end the Top Gun fighters of both sides would be just sitting and watching the show of missile duels.

SURGICAL TRANS-BORDER AIR STRIKES: MYTHS AND REALITIES

INTRINSIC LIMITATIONS OF SURGICAL STRIKES

Surgical strikes by the IAF on terrorist targets across the border in Pakistan or POK are also a favourite subject of speculation by the journalists and TV anchors. Most of them would have you believe that it is just a matter of our taking the decision—after that, the supersonic jets would screech across the border, hit the terrorist targets, destroy them and be safely back home before the Pakistanis realized what hit them. Really? Is that so simple? Once again, real life holds much more complexity than what the journalists and self-styled experts can comprehend. The so-called precision air strikes are not India's best option now or for the foreseeable future.

The question is can we pull it off successfully? Professionally, the following issues must be considered before pronouncing a judgment:

1. The very fact that the media of and other people of this country have been talking of surgical strikes since long, means that Pakistan does expect it. There are several things they could do in this regard, particularly after sponsoring some obnoxious terrorist attack in India. First and foremost, they would alert their own air force and the air defence systems. This means resistance to our aircrafts. If we get shot down without being able to do much, we lose face before the world.

2. Second, they could plant misleading 'intelligence' about the possible location of the terrorist targets. If we hit the wrong target, we risk international opprobrium.
3. Third, they would indeed take steps to camouflage possible targets so as to mislead the aircraft on to other innocuous targets.
4. Fourth, if possible, they could arrange to completely vacate the targets of the terrorist elements. The terrorist camps are, in any case, makeshift affairs and can be vacated, camouflaged or even dismantled on short notice.
5. Fifth, the very accuracy of the precision-guided munitions that we have, does not guarantee that they will always hit the correct target. As I have written elsewhere also, the drone strikes of the US are successful because they come with very accurate HUMINT (human intelligence). In contrast, our HUMINT has been of such quality that in the past 28 years, we have never been able to publicly produce a single photograph or video of any terrorist camp/assets in Pakistan or POK of enough evidentiary value (in the sense that it proves the land to be that in Pakistan and with evidence of date/time) for the world to see and shame Pakistan.
6. Sixth, terrorism and terrorists, by their very nature, do not present such fixed targets that, once reduced, would permanently cripple their capacity to revive. Terrorists are not short of volunteers to their ranks and the support system which they need is fundamentally minimalistic. Like the mythical Hydra, you cut off one head, another would sprout.

All this means that even if IAF aircrafts do succeed in penetrating the Pakistani air space and hitting targets, they could hit either targets of no value or worse, hit something innocuous. In the latter eventuality, Pakistan could cry before the world of collateral damage and civilian casualties at the hands of India. This means that even if we acquire the Predator and Reaper drones, the outcome would still be questionable. And, by any chance, if the targets happen to be large, the explosive payload of the drone would fall short of the requirement.

Possibility of Backlash

USA and Israel have come to be regarded as the models of forceful trans-border military action to strike terrorists and related infrastructure. Their success has been tempting many people to clamour for India to emulate them. What they do not understand is that there is a fundamental difference between the situation of USA and Israel on one hand (with respect to Afghanistan/Iraq or Yemen, Gaza and Lebanon) and India (with respect to Pakistan) on the other hand. Afghanistan/Iraq or Yemen, Gaza and Lebanon are not nuclear armed; Pakistan is.

Even if India strikes targets strictly inside the POK, it would still have to contend with the possibility of a strong backlash from Pakistan as the Pakistani government would be under severe domestic pressure—from both the military, radical Islamist groups, and a nationalistic public—to mount a response to an Indian attack. History stands witness; nations do not submit a case first to their supreme courts for deciding on the legality of mounting a response before it is done. Hence a presumption that attacks in the POK will not permit Pakistan to retaliate is ill-founded. Attacks by the USA on terrorist targets on Pakistani or Afghani soil using their drones or manned aircrafts are not the same thing as that by India. Pakistan has its compulsions with the USA; it does not have the same with India. And the fact remains that American drone strikes have indeed generated considerable resentment in Pakistan. This is because people regard it as unfair in the sense that technically one of the most advanced weapons platform is pitted against people with rifles and living in primitive huts. And hence there is a modicum of sympathy for the Taliban. The public does not regard it as a fair fight and also gets incensed over the collateral damage (as reported by, for example, Farhat Taj, the Dawn, and Declan Walsh and Ismail Khan).

It therefore stands to logic that highly limited surgical strikes in POK, even if they do not escalate into a war, would eventually be reduced to an essentially symbolic act, intended more to appease the aroused public sentiments in the country than to achieve any militarily significant result or inflict substantial harm on the terrorists. The TV channels may go ballistic over the strikes, papers would have screaming headlines, and there may be fiery speeches—yet, it is eminently questionable whether that would help 'solve' the problem of terrorism from across the border. If they escalate into war then the issue of damaging terrorist targets would obviously get relegated to a secondary position and more important issues will come to the forefront.

As for terrorist targets inside Pakistan, precision bombardment of targets in Pakistan can be done only after air superiority is achieved. But unfortunately, the targets that are of lowest risk for a limited objectives strike are also those of least value.

THE NAVAL WAR

India's substantial quantitative and qualitative naval superiority is unlikely to be an important factor in a short, limited war because it is difficult to conceive of a strategy in which the naval might of India could be committed to good effect in that short a period. The question is not so much of the ability of the Indian Navy but of the effect it can produce in the given time frame. There do not seem to be many options in which Indian Navy could beat its Pakistani counterpart so decisively and quickly that it might alter the strategic situation on land. The ocean is big, much bigger than the land and Pakistani naval targets would not be waiting.

Establishing even a partial blockade is difficult, takes time, and it takes even more time for that blockade to cause such shortages on land that are noticeable. On the other hand, over the last decade, Pakistan has increased its ability to sustain a blockade. In addition to the main commercial port of Karachi, Pakistan has opened up new ports further west in Ormara and Gwadar and built road infrastructure to distribute goods from those ports to Pakistan's heartland. The new overland routes to China are likely to further protect Pakistan from strangulation from the sea. To close off these ports to neutral shipping could prove particularly difficult since Gwadar and the edge of Pakistani waters are very close to the Gulf of Oman, host to the international shipping lanes for vessels exiting the Persian Gulf. A loose blockade far from shore would minimize risks to the Indian Navy from Pakistan's land-based countermeasures but would also increase the risks of creating some political incident with neutral vessels.

CHAPTER 8

Nuclear Concerns and Strategies of India and Pakistan

INDIA'S NUCLEAR DOCTRINE

India published its 'Draft Report of the National Security Advisory Board on Indian Nuclear Doctrine' (we may call it the 'Draft Nuclear Doctrine') in August 1999. The doctrine has yet to be authorized as an official Government document. The reasons of the delay in authorization of this draft or why a different policy is not being adopted are not known in public domain. I cannot comment on matters of Government policy.

The Doctrine states that the purpose of India's nuclear weapons is the "deterrence of the use or the threat of use of nuclear weapons" by other states, and declares that India "will not initiate any nuclear attacks". These are interpreted by various people as 'credible minimum nuclear deterrence' and 'no first-use' of nuclear weapons. 'Credible minimum nuclear deterrence' is seen as a policy based on 'retaliation only', in which great emphasis is placed on survivability of nuclear forces, although no reference is made to concrete levels of force size. Since the doctrine does not specify exactly what level of force constitutes a 'credible minimum nuclear deterrence', this ambiguity has resulted in various interpretations and arguments.

INDIA'S NUCLEAR CONCERNS WITH PAKISTAN

Pakistan presents a unique case because tensions between the two countries are prone to a very quick build-up and also because so many people in both the countries regard the other country as a 'natural enemy'—as such crisis stability between the two countries is a matter of doubt. Pakistan operates from the position of a cornered opponent—they cannot hope to match India's resources in conventional weapons; they lack strategic depth; and they are dangerously emboldened by their nukes. Add all this to the emotive (meaning irrational) manner in which many of their leaders have been addressing the political issues with India and you will find that the chances of a rash act with respect to nukes are enhanced.

India might be perfectly logical and might be acting in a highly calibrated manner—what matters is how the Pakistanis perceive it. It is precisely for this reason that options like 'hot pursuit' of terrorists across the LOC, or even surgical air strikes on terrorist camps across the LOC are likely to be misread by many in the Pakistani establishment as Indian attempts to liberate the POK or some bigger design on Pakistan, and might result in lowering of the nuclear threshold.

There have been a series of confidence-building measures like the Agreement on Prevention of Air Space Violations; the Agreement on Advance Notice of Military Exercises, Manoeuvres and Troop Movements; the extension of the hotline between the two countries; and the exchange of instruments of ratification for an agreement regarding not attacking nuclear facilities. All of them had been in place long before Kargil and could do little to prevent or defuse Kargil.

From an Indian perspective, the Pakistani nukes have ensured that the strategic equations in the subcontinent can never be solved now. Since Pakistan's strategic problems are fundamental, it means that they will, for all times to come, flaunt their nukes for every small thing—we have to learn to live with it.

WHY PAKISTAN RUSHED TO BECOME A NUCLEAR POWER?

Why did the Pakistanis rush with their nuclear tests in 1998? The whole world knew that they had the capability for quite some time. But they rushed to conduct the tests within 17 days of the Indian tests. Why? On paper and for the consumption of the world, they might have said that it was for 'restoring the regional strategic balance'. But, from a purely Pakistani perspective, there were other factors too and which were not so 'diplomatic' in character:

- To use the opportunity and excuse of the Indian tests without having to attract the harsher censure that Pakistan would inevitably have attracted from the world community had it conducted the tests unilaterally at some other time. By conducting the tests in response to those of India, Pakistan sought to dilute global criticism and reaction, which would be divided over both the countries and, to some extent, rightly put the blame on India for initiating the nuclear arms race in South Asia.
- To 'prove' Pakistan's nuclear capability in the eyes of India—to confirm what was hitherto the matter of conjecture.
- Denying India the political, diplomatic and prestige advantages that would have accrued to it had it become the only nuclear power in South Asia.
- To prevent a situation from arising in which India, after misreading or underestimating Pakistan's 'unproven' nuclear capability, could have embarked upon any misadventure against Pakistan.
- Acquiring political, diplomatic and prestige advantages for itself, particularly in the Islamic world.

SIZE OF PAKISTAN'S NUCLEAR ARSENAL

According to Paul Kerr and Mary Beth Nikitin, writing for the US Congressional Research Service in August 2016, Pakistan has about 110-130 nuclear weapons, although it could have more. Dr Samar Mubarakmand, a scientist closely involved with the country's nuclear weapons programme, stated in a 2016 interview that only China, France, Russia, and the United States have more nuclear weapons than Pakistan. We do not know how many of them are tactical but according to an article in the Japanese paper *The Mainichi*, Dr Mubarakmand has stated that Pakistan has 15 different types of warheads according to their yield and size. By all accounts, their nuclear arsenal is comparable to India's, if not bigger. On August 27, 2015, it was reported by the Carnegie Endowment for International Peace and the Stimson Centre in a study 'A Normal Nuclear Pakistan', Pakistan could have 350 nuclear warheads sometime in the next decade, becoming the world's number 3 nuclear power by outpacing rival India and several other nations in bomb-making. The study says, "The growth path of Pakistan's nuclear arsenal, enabled by existing infrastructure, goes well beyond the assurances of credible minimal deterrence provided by Pakistani officials and analysts after testing nuclear devices."

PAKISTAN'S NUCLEAR COMMAND STRUCTURE

Gen Musharraf established Pakistan's overall nuclear command and control system in 1999, creating the Strategic Plans Division (SPD) in the Joint Staffs Headquarters to manage nuclear-related matters. In February 2002, Pakistan established the National Command Authority (NCA) to formulate policy and exercise employment and development control over all strategic nuclear forces and organizations. Musharraf, in December 2007, formally articulated the NCA's composition and functions: the President as Chairman, the Prime Minister as Vice-Chairman, the Foreign Minister, the Defence Minister, the Finance Minister, the Interior Minister, the Chairman, Joint Chiefs of Staff Committee, the Chief of Army Staff (COAS), the Chief of Naval Staff, and the Chief of Air Staff. When Musharraf left office in April 2008, Asif Ali Zardari became the nominal head of the NCA, though actual control over Pakistan's nuclear weapons remained with the military. In November 2009, however, President Zardari handed over his NCA powers to Prime Minister Yousuf Raza Gilani.

The SPD now acts as the secretariat of the NCA besides its other multifarious duties. The SPD Director General is responsible for the operational security of Pakistan's nuclear arsenal. The DG is drawn from the army but there are officers in the SPD from all the services. The SPD has about 10,000 troops for the security of the nuclear sites, replete with electronic systems. The employees are subject to security checks by the ISI called Personnel Reliability Programme (PRP) and Human Reliability Programme (HRP).

The three services do have their respective strategic forces command but the operational control theoretically remains with the NCA. The army commands the surface-to-surface delivery systems and the air force commands the aircrafts that could be used as delivery vehicles and also protects several of the nuclear facilities through air defence (those sites are designated as no-fly zones).

PAKISTAN'S NUCLEAR DOCTRINE

LET NO ONE BE FOOLED BY A PRETENCE

In realpolitik and in the wars of the real world, as history stands witness, many nations are apt to ditch their pre-war policies, announcements or promises. That's how life is. The neutrality of Belgium was violated in both the World Wars by Germany. The neutrality of Netherlands and Luxembourg was also violated. As William L Shirer writes in *The Rise and Fall of Adolf Hitler*, his Generals reminded him that those small countries were neutral. Hitler's response was: "Declarations of neutrality can be ignored.... Considerations of right and wrong do not enter the matter. The aim must be to deal the enemy a smashing, decisive blow right at the start." It was a strategic masterstroke to bypass the formidable Maginot Line of France on which they had placed so much trust. The Maginot Line was impervious to most forms of attack, including aerial bombings and tank fire, and had underground railways as a backup; it also had state-of-the-art living conditions for garrisoned troops. Had Germany attacked it directly, they would have run into some extremely choppy waters. The plan to bypass it by violating the neutrality of Belgium was so brilliant that France capitulated in just 45 days.

The same principles apply even now. Many self-styled experts have deluded themselves into believing that if a State has a certain doctrine, it is bound to obey it, come hell or high water. Alexei Arbatov, Vladimir Dvorkin and Sergey Oznobishchev point out in 'Contemporary Nuclear Doctrines' that a State's military doctrine including its nuclear doctrine, including its nuclear aspect, serves to send a message to other countries, both potential adversaries and allies, and contains a warning to the former and a set of guarantees to the latter, while explaining under what circumstances and in what manner the State will resort to military action.

A nation would not be tried in a court of law and convicted if it violated its own nuclear doctrine. Can it be? A doctrine, being a theoretical concept in military strategy, is simply an announcement of the posture likely to be adopted by a nation.

The so-called doctrine has not an iota of legal significance and the nation is not at all legally bound by it. There is no legal requirement by any international convention that a posture thus indicated must be very detailed or must be rigid. I do not think that Pakistan will bother so much about any doctrine it might have professed, if at all. They are not going to be hanged for going back on their public pronouncements. From their perspective, when one is neck-deep in shit, he thinks of options, not of doctrines.

China is the only great power that declares a commitment on no first use of nuclear weapons. Really? It is generally believed that a nuclear power that has committed itself to nuclear no first use must be drawing on the concept of and means for a retaliatory (second) strike. However, according to the estimates generally accepted by most scholars, the Chinese strategic nuclear forces, as well as missile early warning systems and combat control and communications infrastructure, are too vulnerable and could not guarantee a retaliatory strike after a potentially disarming nuclear attack by the United States or Russia. From this, it has been argued that the official doctrine of the People's Republic of China primarily as an instrument of politics and propaganda (similar to the 1982 Soviet commitment on no first use of nuclear weapons), which does not reflect the actual operational planning of strategic nuclear forces that are in reality geared to pre-emptive strike.

I therefore agree with Michael Krepon who says that the circumstances under which Pakistani leadership would resort to the first use of nuclear weapons have been deliberately kept imprecise and somewhat vague. It does make eminent sense from the point of view of realpolitik. The reason, in Pakistani perception, is quite simple—clarifying red lines might embolden Indian military actions just beneath them.

A Critical Analysis of the So-Called Nuclear Red Lines of Pakistan

Still, that does not prevent people from talking of red lines. In the case of Pakistan, an announcement to that effect was made by Gen Khalid Kidwai, former head of the Strategic Policy Division. His characterizations of red lines were released in an odd fashion, embedded in a trip report that included a summary of a conversation with two Italian non-governmental researchers. Now, given the sort of responsible person that Gen Kidwai has been, there is no reason to believe that it was done casually—he did it on purpose. Krepon, basing on his email correspondence with Paulo Cotta-Ramusino on May 19, 2012, says that before publication, the Italian co-authors sent their report for review to Foreign Minister Abdul Sattar, who did not object to their characterization of Gen Kidwai's remarks. Pakistani officials subsequently distanced themselves from this report, noting that it was not an official statement, nor a precise summary. But this should be viewed in the backdrop of the fact that Gen Kidwai is a very important person in the Pakistani nuclear establishment. He is a man who was made to continue as the head of the most sensitive SPD (Strategic Plans Division, which functions as the National Command Authority's secretariat and administers NCA policies over all of Pakistan's nuclear and missile programmes) even after his retirement and subsequent extension and this continuation in the post survived even the banishment of Gen Musharraf, the man who had placed him there.

As reported by the Italian researchers, Gen Kidwai offered the following explanatory remarks: Pakistani nuclear weapons are aimed solely at India. In case deterrence fails, they will be used if:

(a) India attacks Pakistan and conquers a large part of its territory (space threshold).

(b) India destroys a large part either of its land or air forces (military threshold).
(c) India proceeds to the economic strangling of Pakistan (economic strangling).
(d) India pushes Pakistan into political destabilization or creates a large scale internal subversion in Pakistan (domestic destabilization).

It is easy to see that Gen Kidwai was trying hard to envisage situations which could theoretically provide some sort of 'moral justification' for the use of the nuclear weapons. The red lines enumerated in the Italian report range from specific to general, and from likely to improbable. In fact, many of the situations are difficult to envisage in the era of the sort of conventional high-tech weaponry (including missiles of all sorts) which the nations possess now.

We can understand the 'space threshold' and the 'military threshold'. They are indeed emotive issues for the people of the nation even if in professional terms, the situation is not that bad or is still recoverable. The Soviet forces, after all, even as they retreated right up to Moscow in the Second World War, fought the Germans to a standstill and then pushed them back all the way to Berlin. Public perception of how the nation has been faring in a war may be fundamentally different from a proper military perception and might even prevail upon the leaders.

But take for example, the impression which the Italians got about the so-called economic strangling that it would include a naval blockade or the stopping of the waters of the Indus river. I have discussed the subject of naval blockade at length elsewhere in the book. It is both difficult and difficult to achieve in the time frame in which we expect to fight a war. Then what to speak of a total economic blockade? Since Gen Kidwai is not expected to be so ignorant as to not know the near impossibility of imposing an economic blockade, it would stand to reason that he was only trying to find some 'emotive reasons'. As for domestic political destabilization and internal disturbances, they can blame India alright but cannot possibly prove anything—the CIA has infamously been doing this in numerous countries since long and never got nailed. Thousands of books have been written on the subject.

The Pakistanis must know that covert intelligence operations, if done with any degree of finesse, remain actually covert. No intelligence agency is such a fool as to leave any trace of its 'provable' involvement anywhere. (For details of covert/clandestine operations, interested readers may refer to my treatise *Intelligence and Security Management*). In intelligence jargon, there is actually a colloquial phrase called 'sheep dipping'. The CIA made extensive use of it. The issue was simple. They might have to send in some Special Forces personnel, military officers or intelligence officers to some foreign country for some subversive activity there—ranging from bribing political leaders; engineering defections; influencing media and academia to create support for a given line of thought; blackmailing leaders by honey trap etc; sowing disaffection in the government service, police and armed forces; engineering communal or political riots etc; and committing acts of sabotage, etc—all aimed at manipulating or destabilizing the regime. But this was done with great finesse and it was ensured that even if some of the personnel thus sent got caught in flagrante delicto, their complicity could not be proved in a court of law. Towards this end, a simple precaution was taken. Before the personnel were sent in, they were, at least on record, made to resign from the service they happened to be in. In reality, the records went undercover. During the period of his covert assignment, all his service benefits were protected and he would get his medals once he came back successfully. However, if he ever got caught and prosecuted, the USA would officially disown him—here was a mercenary who had resigned from the service and whatever he was doing, he was doing on his own—the United States government was not responsible for it.

Incidentally who knows it better than the ISI? They were the conduit through which the CIA funnelled in $625 million worth of weapons and other material to the Mujahideen during their war with the Soviets in their Operation Cyclone. In spite of what you saw in Rambo III, the CIA or the US army never got a single man of theirs in the hands of the Soviets. Theirs was literally the 'invisible hand'. Brigadier Mohammad Yousaf of the ISI and Mark Adkin have written an interesting book called *Afghanistan: The Bear Trap: The Defeat of a Superpower* in which they have explained at length as to how the ISI procured the colossal cache of weapons for the Mujahideen which had not even a trace of the US funding. Even at this moment in 2016, it is well-known as to how the CIA is supplying weapons to the Syrian rebels!

CHAPTER 9

Indian Nightmare of the Pakistani Tactical Nuclear Weapons

WHAT ARE TACTICAL NUCLEAR WEAPONS (TNWS)?

Before we proceed with the discussion on tactical nukes, we must know what tactical nukes are? During the Cold War, nuclear strategists employed varied definitions of tactical nuclear weapons. These weapons were sometimes defined in relation to their intended use and zone of employment; their yield, range, or designated target; the type of delivery vehicle; or the level of command associated with the weapon in question. A particular weapon might be considered tactical by the United States and strategic by the Soviet Union, or vice versa, depending on its location, range, and intended target.

Some experts during the Cold War described tactical nuclear weapons as low-yield weapons that were not meant to cause widespread physical destruction. Instead, they were to be used discriminately against a variety of military targets on the battlefield, including enemy tanks and mechanized infantry, while generating as little collateral damage as possible. Range was clearly an important, although not necessarily a determinative factor, for categorizing tactical nuclear weapons. Thus tactical nuclear weapons are designed to engage objects in the tactical depth of enemy deployment (up to 300 km) to accomplish a tactical mission. We fully agree with this in principle. In the Indo-Pak concept, however, 300 km may be too large as Pakistan does not have enough depth.

The United States and Soviet Union deployed tactical nuclear weapons for use by their ground, air and naval forces. There were a staggering 53,000 of them; some 30,000 of the USSR and 23,000 of the USA. Some of these weapons, such as nuclear artillery, could be used at very short ranges of just a few kilometres. Yields varied, with some being in the sub-kilotonne range also. Types of tactical nuclear weapons included air-dropped free fall bombs and glide bombs; air-to-surface missiles and air-to-surface standoff missiles; cruise missiles; surface-to-air missiles; shorter-range surface-to-surface missiles; air-to-air missiles; artillery rounds; depth charges; torpedoes; and atomic demolition munitions.

PAK TACTICAL NUCLEAR WEAPONS AND THE NASR MISSILE

THE OFFICIAL CLAIM

On October 22, 2015, Pakistan publicly announced that TNWs (Tactical Nuclear Weapons) were essential for its national security, given India's threatening 'Cold Start' doctrine. Pakistan's Foreign Secretary Aizaz Chaudhary alleged in Washington that India had 'created a space for war', and that Pakistan's 'low-yield tactical weapons' would make it difficult for India to launch a war without inevitably breaching the nuclear threshold. "Our nuclear programme is one dimensional: stopping Indian aggression before it happens. It is not for starting war. It is for deterrence," said Chaudhary, in the first official comment on Pakistan's TNWs (Tactical Nuclear Weapons). It was the first time Pakistani officials acknowledged their intent to use low-yield, or so-called 'tactical', nuclear weapons in a potential future conflict with India. Ankit Panda adds in his report that India does not currently operate or plan to develop tactical nuclear weapons.

Zachary Keck discloses that in providing a worldwide threat assessment to the House Armed Services Committee in

February 2015, Marine Corps Lt Gen Vincent R Stewart, Director of the Defense Intelligence Agency, had discussed Pakistan's expanding nuclear delivery systems: "We anticipate that Pakistan will continue its development of new delivery systems, including cruise missiles and close-range 'battlefield' nuclear weapons to augment its existing ballistic missiles." According to the George C Marshall and Claremont Institute, the US intelligence community had expressed alarm about Pakistan's development of tactical nukes back in 2013.

The Nasr or Hatf-9 Missile

In April 2011, Pakistan first tested the Hatf-9 (Nasr) missile, which it called a 'Short Range Surface-to-Surface Multi-Tube Ballistic Missile'. In the official statement announcing the test, Pakistan's military said the Hatf-9 missile was nuclear-capable and had been developed to be used at 'shorter ranges'.

"Nasr, with a range of 60 km, carries nuclear warheads of appropriate yield with high accuracy, shoot and scoot attributes. This quick response system addresses the need to deter evolving threats," the statement said. It added that the "test was a very important milestone in consolidating Pakistan's strategic deterrence capability at all levels of the threat spectrum." Testing continued throughout 2012 and 2013, and Pakistan's Strategic Forces are believed to have inducted the missile into service following an October 2013 test. Pakistan has continued periodic testing since that time, most recently in September of last year.

Scientific Doubts

Jeffrey Lewis had expressed doubts whether Pakistan was capable of building nuclear warheads small enough to use on the Hatf-9. But that was in 2011. Aziz Chaudhary made his claim in October 2015. We do not know what transpired in four years. There is no reliable information about their having tested any such device. But they could have tested a very small device just to prove the design. It is also a fact that the Americans were able to make the world's smallest, the 23 kg W-54 warhead (27.3 cm dia × 40 cm length) for the Davy Crockett recoilless launcher in an era (1957-61) when computer simulation was not even available. Different versions of the warhead could produce yields of anywhere from 10 tonnes to 600 tonnes of TNT. Two Soviet researchers, Kaliski and Alt'shuler had published papers on a radically different design known as a bi-conical mini-nuke in the late 1960s. The fission cores of such bombs would have diameters of only 2.68 to 3.38 cm but still be capable of one or two kilotonne yields. And this is the 21st century! Usman Ansari, writing in the website defensenews.com, spoke of 0.5 to 5 kilotonne warheads. According to the website military-today.com, it is a 6 m long missile with a diameter of only 30 cm. This means that the warhead has to be at least like the W-54 if not better than it. I wonder if the Pakistanis actually did it.

Starting in 2012, Pakistan began firing the Hatf-9 in four missile salvos from what it called a 'state-of-the-art multi-tube launcher', which was also derived from Chinese systems. The Nasr missile itself is a derivative of the Chinese-made Weishi-2 (WS-2) short-range ballistic missile. The WS-2 is a 40 cm dia missile with a range of 200-350 km and delivering about 200 kg of high explosive. This was designed to enable the PLA to strike the west coast of Taiwan, including the capital Taipei and as a cheaper alternative to the expensive short range ballistic missiles in Chinese inventory. As a nuclear scientist, I am also not convinced of the claim but the issue is why would someone make a missile of this type if he were to throw only high explosive, and if he were not to make a large number of them like the Chinese? How would it fit into their war-fighting philosophy or the role assigned to this weapon? We do not know.

SCENARIOS OF THE USE OF TACTICAL NUCLEAR WEAPONS

HOW OUR SITUATION DIFFERS FROM THAT DURING THE COLD WAR?

Tactical nuclear weapons were championed during the Eisenhower administration as a cost-effective means of defending forward-deployed NATO forces and allied cities from being overrun easily, as well as to compensate for Washington's inability to match Soviet conventional force levels—the Americans were particularly afraid of the great Soviet tank Armada. It was apprehended that the numerically inferior NATO forces would find it difficult to check their relentless advance into Western Europe. That's how the Americans went on to develop even nuclear artillery so that even divisional commanders could have nuclear weapons to save themselves from being overrun. According to the US army's first field manual on tactical nuclear weapons, the FM 100-31, tactical nukes were to be used against enemy troop concentrations, command and control nodes, and logistical support facilities. At least on paper, though not expressed in such articulated words, Pakistan also intends to do the same. It would be incorrect to say (such as Saira Bano) that the concept is not valid in South Asia.

The Soviet Union had also amassed a huge stockpile of tactical nuclear weapons, notwithstanding the favourable conventional force imbalance it enjoyed in Europe. Soviet military planners viewed tactical nuclear weapons and conventional strike capabilities as integral parts of offensive operations. Theatre nuclear strikes were designed to destroy NATO's nuclear capabilities; defeat NATO ground combat forces; breach NATO defensive positions; and halt counterattacks. Striking first meant that tactical nuclear weapons needed to be distributed down to the brigade and battalion levels prior to the offensive. Nuclear strikes were intended to facilitate ground occupation of the European continent. Precisely how this would have occurred, in light of the devastation and radioactive contamination that would have been wreaked as a result of many nuclear detonations, is unclear—the Soviets were not known for bothering about such niceties.

Had the TNWs been absolutely worthless; had the very idea of ever inventing them been absurd; had they been the 'hair trigger' which would have unleashed an uncontrollable nuclear exchange, the USA would not have still retained about 760 and Russia 1,000-6,000 TNWs even now!

The Exact Destructive Potential of TNWs

The popular wisdom is that the Cold Start would entail launching multiple swift, shallow offensives into that country with overwhelming forces, led by tanks and air strikes. Pakistani planners, aware they would be overwhelmed, plan to deploy TNWs (Tactical Nuclear Weapons) along the border to threaten India with an early nuclear quick and clever reply to its armour.

Let us see what the TNWs can do? I will, on my authority as a nuclear scientist, give you an accurate idea of what small nuclear warheads can do. This is vital because lay men, journalists, and self-styled defence experts who are obviously not nuclear scientists harbour grossly, frighteningly wrong misconceptions about the effects of nuclear weapons. (For details, interested readers may refer to my treatise *Nuclear Weapons and International Security*.) We presume a standard air burst. For comparison, I will consider two warheads: one of 1 kilotonne and the other of 10 kilotonne. I will take assaulting tanks as the target as India's armour is the main concern of Pakistan and troops in the open are anyway highly vulnerable to other types of fire—why waste a nuke on them?

With a 1 kilotonne warhead, 50% of the personnel in the tanks in a circle of 900 m diameter (that is, an area of about 0.64 sq km) would be killed inside their tanks besides damage to the tank. Of course, one who gets out of the tank will be killed faster. The remaining tanks might not remain dependable as electronics and antenna etc would get damaged. With a 10 kilotonne warhead, this area would increase to a circle of 1,940 m diameter (that is, about 3 sq km). An area of 0.64 sq km is a square of 800 m sides; an area of 3 sq km is a square of about 1,730 m sides. Had it been anything less than a tank (say non-armoured vehicles), a 1 kilotonne warhead would have killed 50% of the occupants in a circle of 1,200 m diameter (approximately 1.13 sq km). A 10 kilotonne warhead would have killed 50% of the occupants in a circle of about 2,600 m diameter (approximately 5 sq km).

THE ACTUAL BATTLEFIELD EFFECT OF TNWS ON TANK FORMATIONS

A US Tank Platoon consists of just 4 tanks. A Tank Company has three platoons of four tanks each, with two additional tanks in the HQ platoon, for a total of 14 tanks. A Tank Battalion usually has four companies of tanks, each with 14 tanks. There are usually also two tanks in Headquarters Company, for a total of 58. In the USA, a Tank Brigade usually consists of anywhere from 3-5 Battalions, and will almost always have a mix of Battalions: some Infantry Battalions, some Tank Battalions—in the end about 118-126 tanks per Brigade.

Now, if the tanks were attacking in a mass formation, they should be about 100 m apart. Tanks could be deployed in various formations depending on the nature of the battlefield and the operation planned—column formation; staggered column formation; wedge formation; echelon formation; Vee formation; line formation; coil formation; and herringbone formation. We cannot waste time discussing all the possible combinations. For illustration, let us consider the wedge formation. The wedge permits excellent firepower to the front and good firepower to the flanks. It is employed when the platoon is provided with over-watch by another element and is moving in open or rolling terrain—sort of situation that I would envisage for the Indian attack. According to the concerned US Army Field Manual, a typical wedge formation of four tanks would have three tanks on one side of a triangle (400 m), and two tanks on the other two sides (300 m and 400 m each) with the lead tank at the apex. This triangle will have an area of 55,621 sq m (by Heron's or Hero's formula). Approximately 11.5 such triangles would come in the blast damage area of one TNW of 1 kilotonne warhead.

This means that a single 1 kilotonne warhead is likely to immediately disable about 23 tanks in open country and render the remaining tanks of the Company unreliable—not a very efficient method. A 10 kilotonne warhead would be able to damage about 136 tanks—that is, a little more than two tank Brigades. This is quite understandable because nuclear explosions are what we call 'point sources' of energy and not 'diffuse sources'. The effectiveness of the strikes can be increased if the target tanks are caught funnelling into bridge crossings etc.

The Real Purpose that would be Served by Using the TNWs

The calculation made above shows that a large number of TNWs will have to be used if the entire Indian armoured offensive is to be blunted. Pakistan would not like to do that as it might be regarded absolutely unacceptable by India. Then what they could have planned with the TNWs? Why they have spent so much money and research effort on them?

In the perception of Pakistan, the real objective of using the TNWs purpose would be to signal India to cease the offensive operations, and also to hasten international efforts to intervene and to put pressure on India to desist. In other words, the use of a single TNW would be a demonstration of the resolve of the Pakistanis to use nuclear weapons in the first place, and secondly, by stopping at one or two TNWs they would be further declaring that their intent is not to unleash a nuclear Armageddon but to put an end to hostilities.

TNWs will not be able to change the balance of war in a positive way—that is to say, they will not enable Pakistan to mount a counteroffensive and throw India back. After all, once an area is contaminated by radioactive debris, even the Pakistanis cannot enter that place. In the end, TNW would be a weapon to create great psychological impact, not some great military impact.

How the Indian Army or the Indian Government would react to the use of TNWs is a matter of Government policy and hence I would not comment on that. India might regard the use of even a sub-kilotonne nuke as Pakistan having crossed the Lakshman Rekha; it might not.

LET'S NOT HAVE A MORBID AND IRRATIONAL FEAR OF NUKES

There are many people in India who regard any use of nukes of whatever yield as crossing of the Lakshman Rekha and maintain that India must then go for massive retaliation [for example, Rajat Pandit had claimed (*TOI*, July 26, 2011) that the former Air Chief Marshal PV Naik had made a statement to that effect.] There are many people who say that India must retaliate massively only if Pakistan uses 10-40 kilotonne bombs on say, civilian targets. To my knowledge, since there is no Government policy on this subject to be found in public domain, I feel free to offer my personal views.

In the first place, the Pakistanis might be clever enough to use the TNW on their soil. Yes, winds might carry the fallout to our civilian areas (as argued, for example, by Jaganath Sankaran, and Reshmi Kazi), but generally they would still scream before the international community that they have not used the nuke on Indian soil.

> We must deny them a psychological advantage. By reacting too much to the Pakistani TNWs (Tactical Nuclear Weapons) we are exposing a raw nerve, if not the Achilles Heel of the nation. By making a reference to TNWs everywhere, we are indirectly admitting that we are as much rattled by the TNWs as the Pakistanis are rattled by the Cold Start. And God knows, the whole business of TNWs might be a pure bluff!

I have convincingly, scientifically shown that TNWs in the Indian context are not going to change the balance of the war. South Asia is not Western Europe of the Cold War era when the USA had made about 7,000 TNWs and the Soviets had made about 15,000-25,000—as nuclear mines, nuclear artillery, missile warheads, and so on. Their effect is more on the mind.

In fact, getting unduly perturbed by the Pak TNWs is a tacit admission of the fact that we regard nuclear weapons per se as some sort of taboo—the moment you touch them in any form, all hell would break loose. Or is there a specific taboo associated with small nuclear weapons? Let us be rational. If nations can make and keep strategic nuclear weapons, what is wrong with small ones? You cannot have double standards. Can anyone argue that keeping strategic nukes is moral but keeping TNWs (Tactical Nuclear Weapons) is immoral?

The CLAWS research team, for example, observes that the Pakistan army's lack of confidence in its conventional capability has led to some in the Pakistani establishment suggesting the use of low-yield tactical nuclear warheads if

Indian forces cross the international border. The question is, so what? Why in the world they should be obliged to fight on our terms? If I am a boxer or a karateka, why would I commit the mistake of wrestling with a man? Is there any good reason that the Pakistanis or for that matter anybody else in the world would fight on our terms. Why should they meet our armour with their armour, our artillery with their artillery in long-range artillery duels; and so on. Nobody in the world is fool enough to do that. War is not single combat or some modified version of single combat. By God, this is war, not a tournament!

Readers must understand that war is serious business between two nations in which a great part of their resources are employed. It has been so ever since the ancient era. Do not the Indians remember the Mahabharat War in which, according to the text itself, 18 Akshauhini armies had perished. An 'Akshauhini' is described in the Mahabharat (Adi Parva 2.15-23) as a battle formation consisting of 21,870 chariots; 21,870 elephants; 65,610 cavalry and 1,09,350 infantry. Allowing one man on a horse and two men each on the elephant and the chariot, a total of 2,62,440 × 18 = 47,23,920, that is, nearly 4.7 million soldiers had perished. Compare it with the casualties in some of the major wars in the world and you will find that the figure is not absurd. Yes, Bheem and Duryodhan did fight a duel but that was at the close of the war when Duryodhan was not left with any army to fight with and hence a single combat was proposed. There was no system that the war could be averted by the Pandavas fighting the Kauravas in single combat before the armies clashed.

The Samurais had a system of coming to the forefront before a battle, pronouncing their place of origin and challenge an equal opponent to fight, such as "I am Tadamori-No-Yoshi of Suruga province." Still, that was not a substitute for war—it just afforded an opportunity to the Samurai to show off. The armies clashed nevertheless—no duel between samurais ever averted a battle. The Pakistanis are not going to send their wrestlers to fight with our wrestlers in the battlefield and let that decide the issue. The Chinese are not going to ask their badminton players to have a match with our players.

If Pakistan is inferior to us in conventional ground force weaponry or in the air force and navy, nothing compels them to first match us item-by-item and then fight with us. They will fight with whatever they have and whatever they can use to give them an edge. That includes the use of the Mujahideen, fifth-columnists and saboteurs. This is what they did in 1947, 1965 and in 1999. Similarly, they would use whatever weapon systems that they reckon to be capable of giving them edge. We can 'punish' them for their misdeeds and crimes, but how in the world can we demand them to fight a *Dharmayuddha* (war based on certain ethical principles)!

The same argument applies to all that the so-called self-styled experts keep on talking about China's military modernization, capacity-building, infrastructure development in Tibet, and moves into the Indian Ocean. By God, they will—that's what realpolitik is all about. They will do all that they can to gain an edge. If they do not have a missile like BrahMos or an ABM system capable of countering BrahMos, they will try to compensate for it in other fields, such as cyber warfare, C4ISR, space, and IT.

CHAPTER 10

How and Why a Limited Nuclear War is Indeed Possible?

BALLISTIC MISSILES OF INDIA AND PAKISTAN

ISSUES OF WARHEADS AND ACCURACY

There has been considerable dispute and speculation about the actual operational status of both the Indian and Pakistani missiles and their numbers. We will not get into that controversy because that is an official secret. India has an edge in missiles over Pakistan for the simple reason that it has had a much older missile programme. The learning curve in this business is several years long.

You will be amused to note that Pakistan has a large variety of missiles of similar performance. Why? This is an indicator of how they have developed their missiles. They are not the result of a single dedicated programme like the Integrated Guided Missile Development Programme of India. That you have many different missiles of almost similar performance means that they have been developed from different sources—whatever they could lay their hands on, either from North Korea, China or indigenous research; they made a missile based on that and put that in the inventory. They were in a tearing hurry to achieve parity with India and hence took whatever that came to them. Do not bother about the claims of what is their 'latest' and what it can do. It is for the consumption of the gullible people in their own country and for the fools in the media and Internet forums.

Bother about what they have perfected and, more importantly, what they have in sufficient numbers.

There is no information in the public domain about the warheads carried on these missiles—whether eventually they will be the basic 10-20 kilotonne devices of the type used in the Second World War or any better; nobody has any idea. Generally, the media declares a missile 'nuclear-capable' simply because it can carry a warhead of about 500 kg or more—as if the payload were the only criteria of being a 'nuclear-capable'. Pity them.

Please also note that the claims about the accuracy of any missile in terms of the CEP (circular error probable) are simply claims—there is no way of an independent verification. But if you want to know the truth, you must go through the history of missile development in respect of the USA and the USSR and then you will understand how much research, experimentation and repeated tests are required for achieving a certain level of accuracy. The claims of the two countries must be weighed in the backdrop of how others had achieved that sort of accuracy.

PRITHVI MISSILE

Prithvi is one of our well-tested missile systems—its only problem is its low range of 150-350 km. It is a single stage liquid fuel system—red fuming nitric acid oxidizer with a 50/50 mix of Xylidiene and triethylamine fuel. It has dual motors. For field operations, Prithvi is transported on an all-terrain, eight wheel Kolos Tatra 4 × 4 truck. The missile is deployed off this vehicle and fired from a simple launcher. Dhanush is the naval variant of Prithvi.

AGNI FAMILY OF MISSILES

In this family of missiles, we have missiles from Agni-I to Agni-V. Agni-I is an MRBM (700-1,250 km range); Agni-II is IRBM

(2,000-3,000 km range); Agni-III is also IRBM (3,500-5,000 km range); Agni-IV is also IRBM (3,000-4,000 km range); and Agni-V is an ICBM under testing (5,000-8,000 km range). Agni-VI is under development.

The Agni family of missiles demonstrates India's coming of age in making large diameter solid fuel motors and making rockets of two or more stage. Agni IV is claimed to be equipped with indigenously developed ring laser gyro inertial navigation optionally augmented by GPS terminal guidance with possible radar scene correlation, and composite rocket motor. It can be fired from a road mobile launcher. Agni-V will have a canister launch making it operationally very flexible. All of them are capable of carrying warheads up to 1.5 tonnes.

Solid Fuel versus Liquid Fuel Motors

The advantage of a liquid fuel motor is that it is relatively easy to manoeuvre on-flight and they could be more accurate than the solid fuel rockets. The corrosive fuel, however, requires loading just prior to the launch of the missile. This imposes very obvious operational constraints in battlefield conditions. You will not be able to fire it on short notice. Solid propellant missiles are stable, easily storable, and easy to handle before launching. Unlike liquid systems, they do not need fuel loading before the launch, making it more efficient and less vulnerable to exposure.

PAKISTAN'S BALLISTIC MISSILES

Ghauri Missiles

The Ghauri missiles' propulsion system is a liquid rocket engine that uses a storable combination of inhibited red fuming nitric acid and kerosene—quite an old technology. Ghauri-I (or Hatf-V) and Ghauri-II are single-stage missiles.

Ghauri-I and Ghauri-II are believed to be based on the North Korean Nodong-1 missile which have a range of up to 1,500 km. The No Dong, in turn, is comparable to the Soviet R-17 missile. Iran's Shahab-III is also based on the Nodong-1. Ghauri-III was supposed to be a two-stage (both liquid) rocket based on the North Korean Taepo Dong missile. It is believed that the programme has been terminated.

SHAHEEN FAMILY OF MISSILES

The Shaheen series of solid-propellant missiles are believed to be based on Chinese technology. Shaheen-I is supposed to be based on the Chinese M-9 or DF-15 missile. It is believed that the so-called Hatf-IV and Shaheen-I are similar missiles; the Shaheen-I is a single-stage, railroad platform-based mobile variant of the Hatf-IV ballistic missile. According to NTI, it can reportedly deliver a 500 kg warhead over a range of 600 km; other reports suggest that with a smaller warhead, the missile could have a range of 800 km. Still other reports give it a range of 750 km with a payload of 1,000 kg.

Shaheen-II (or Hatf-VI) is believed to be based on the Chinese M18 missile. It is a two-stage solid system with a range of 2,000 km and a payload of a tonne. In March 2015, Pakistan conducted the first known test launch of the Shaheen-III ballistic missile. It was tested again in December 2015. Lt Gen (retd) Khalid Kidwai claimed that this has a range of 2,750 km.

NASR OR HATF-IX MISSILE

We have discussed it earlier. It was first tested in April 2011. Its most recent test, in September 2014, was done in salvo mode using a multi-tube launch vehicle (MLV). The road-mobile, solid-fuelled Nasr has a range of 60 km and is equipped with 'fire and forget' capabilities.

HATF FAMILY OF SHORT RANGE MISSILES

Hatf-I is a small 1,500 kg rocket, based on French sounding rocket technology—range about 100 km. Hatf-II is a two-stage solid system which can take 500 kg to 280 km. M-11, believed to have been acquired from China, is a single-stage solid propellant missile with a payload of 700 kg and range of 300 km. It thus appears to be comparable to the Prithvi. Perhaps 30 of them were acquired. Hatf-III or Ghaznavi is derived from the M-11. It is a two-stage solid system and would take 500 kg to 550 km or 800 kg to 290 km.

PAKISTANI CRUISE MISSILES

Pakistan shocked India and the world when it tested a cruise missile called Babur (or Hatf-VII) in 2005. Prasun K Sengupta had alleged in the New Delhi magazine *Force* that China's State-owned China National Precision Machinery Import and Export Corp (CPMIEC) had transferred this technology to Pakistan's State-owned National Development Complex (NDC). This 1.5-tonne, 22-foot long missile, launched from a MLV (multi-tube launch vehicle) is capable of carrying a 250-300 kg warhead to about 700 km. The air-launched version of the cruise missile is called Ra'ad (or Hatf-VIII). It is claimed to be able to carry 450 kg to about 350 km.

IF AT ALL THEY USE NUCLEAR WEAPONS: WHY, WHEN AND HOW?

PUBLIC PRESSURE DUE TO THE SPECTRE OF A CATASTROPHIC DEFEAT

In my opinion Pakistan's decision to use the nukes will be guided more by public opinion than by actual military situation. We have seen how farcical the so-called military red lines could be. It would be a matter of how the situation is perceived by the nation at large. The people could react to losses of territory; a large number of tanks; a large number of aircrafts; or any other thing in which people take pride or which is regarded as important. The psychological aspect of the impact of war on the people is all important. The Pakistani leadership cannot afford to ignore how the nation at large emotionally reacts to Indian military actions. The equation between India and Pakistan is not just military; it is more of an emotional affair. This is not 1971 and in this information age, it will not be possible for a country to conceal from its public as to how their military is faring in the war. Governments can befool their people but only to a limited extent. The very thought of the possibility of a repeat of 1971 is enough to make most Pakistanis irrational.

The tremendous influence of the public and the media can be seen from two relatively recent examples. In 1993, following the Battle of Mogadishu (the Black Hawk Down incident), the television images of the dead bodies of American soldiers, stripped of their clothes and being dragged through the streets by Somalis were too graphic for the American public to endure. It built so much public pressure that the US was forced to withdraw from Somalia. And this happened when the US had suffered just 19 casualties in killed, 73 wounded and one captured. Moreover, the US is a nation which is used to war and casualties. One can imagine the impact on a nation which has never been baptized by blood and fire in its history. Back in 1983 when the barracks of the Multinational Force in Lebanon were bombed in Beirut killing 305 men, it eventually led to the withdrawal of the International Peacekeeping Force from Lebanon.

Regarding the possibility of Pakistan using nuclear weapons, two things must be kept in mind. In the first place, the remarks which Gen Kidwai had made, were made before the Pakistanis had supposedly developed TNWs. He was speaking of larger nuclear warheads. The scene has changed materially since then and the red lines drawn by him become all the more irrelevant.

WHEN WOULD THEY USE NUCLEAR WEAPONS?

In their seminal newspaper op-ed, Agha Shahi (former Foreign Secretary and Foreign Minister), Zulfiqar Ali Khan (retired Air Marshal) and Abdul Sattar (former Foreign Secretary) had written that Pakistan was "not so unrealistic as to entertain" thoughts of the "use of nuclear weapons for war-fighting or seek to develop capability for pre-emptive attack." They quite understood that, "India is too large and too well-armed to be vulnerable to a disabling strike." However, they also reasoned that while Pakistan's victory in a nuclear war with India is unrealistic, denying India the pleasure of victory is indeed possible. The build-up of Pakistan's nuclear forces is based on this objective in mind.

Pakistan's combat strategy with nuclear weapons would depend on the situation in which they find themselves in a war and the psychological compulsions at that time. I presume that those who decide to use nukes are not crazy and bent upon their total annihilation. In other words, they should know that they must, in some way, leave the path to negotiation and eventual peace open. I also presume that Pakistan would understand it well that India would have kept its nuclear arsenal in such a safe and secret manner that taking out the Indian nukes would not be possible in some pre-emptive strikes. The same logic would, of course, apply to India also.

The use of nuclear weapons has to serve two purposes—to satisfy the public opinion and for some military objective. In my opinion, military objectives are not important because hurting India in its military vitals is difficult. As far as the Pakistani public is concerned, they will be satisfied with the mere fact that their country had the courage to use nukes—what damage they cause is irrelevant; propaganda can take care of that. For Pakistan, more important than the actual military advantage of nukes will be an open declaration of intent that nukes could indeed be used and that they were not kept as showpieces or for using on the occasion of Shab-e-barat, as some of their leaders have been speaking.

If they are facing a complete rout in the battlefields or a rebellion in the country against the regime, they might be tempted to use the bigger warheads alongside the TNWs, otherwise not.

THE COMPLEX PROCESS OF USING NUCLEAR WEAPONS

The Requirement of Extensive Planning

Nuclear weapons are serious things. You cannot go on simply dropping them just about anywhere on the map of the enemy. When, during the Cold War, a nuclear exchange loomed large between the USA and the USSR, both countries had applied a great deal of mind to how exactly use the weapons in the most effective manner. All sorts of theories were developed; never mind that many of them were of questionable merit. But they did apply mind to the problem furiously—which places to strike; with what type of waihead; the order of priority of striking various types of targets; dealing with various contingencies like a missile or bomber getting shot down; malfunctions; collateral damage; the whole lot. It was intellectually highly stimulating and fascinating to read all that discussion in the public domain. However, in the Indian subcontinent, at least in the public domain, we do not find such discussion.

Factoring in the Possibility of Pre-emptive Strikes

Pakistan will have to ensure that their ballistic missiles reach full combat readiness within a day or two of the strategic warning being received. However, they will have to pray that, by any chance, India does not launch a nuclear pre-emptive or decapitating first-strike out of the blue; or that India would not successfully pre-empt Pakistani nuclear assets by using conventional air-delivered weapons in a surprise attack.

The Problem with 10-40 kilotonne Warheads

In the business of making nuclear weapons, making physically large and heavy warheads of 10-40 kilotonnes is technologically much easier than making small warheads. Making 10-40 kilotonne devices is like passing a very difficult entrance examination—you make the bomb and you qualify for that elite club on the doors of which it is written 'entry only by force'. OK, so you get the much coveted label; but the question is what exactly are you going to do after that? What strategic objectives can you achieve with the nukes of that size? Nothing. In fact, the military utility of warheads of this size is so limited that the superpowers had quickly abandoned them and had progressed to warheads of 200-475 kilotonnes and 3-5 megatonnes. That's where the balloon of the euphoria generated by the making of the nukes gets punctured.

One nuke of 10-40 kilotonnes may take out a small town or may be some major industry. But India can afford to lose many more. Unless several such warheads are used simultaneously to take out the command centre, that is, Delhi, India can actually sustain the loss of smaller cities or parts of larger cities.

POSSIBLE INDIAN TARGETS AND THE REASONING FOR THAT

Delhi or Political and Military Command Centre?

Delhi or the political and military command centre is extremely tempting to the lay man, but might be considered the ultimate provocation and lead to disastrous consequences for Pakistan as India retaliates. Pakistan will have to keep in mind that unless they hit India with decisive force, they are likely to anger India more and it will prove costly for them. Hitting India with a single decisive nuclear punch does not seem to be possible for them as they do not have megatonne warheads. They will have to understand that the nuclear dynamics of India-China is materially different from that of India-Pakistan. China is capable of sustaining extensive nuclear damage and hence can take the risk of obliterating Delhi. Pakistan cannot take that risk because it is not in a position to sustain extensive nuclear damage.

Major Cities?

A nuclear strike on any urban centre will result in heavy casualties because of the high population density. Quite understandably, writings for the laymen harp on this aspect and go overboard in their imagination (see, for example, Abhishek Saksena). Because popular imagination has painted such a horrifying picture of nuclear attacks on cities that the human casualties will bring any government under tremendous pressure to escalate.

Critical Industries or Infrastructure?

In terms of war-fighting, damage to industrial capacity is more important than casualties. Moreover, by hitting industries, if the human casualties are relatively much less, the outrage produced in the public will also be less. That's where India has a distinct advantage over Pakistan. India has a huge size and the critical industries are widely dispersed. This means that India can indeed absorb nuclear attacks on its industries without the nation's industrial capacity getting crippled.

Military Targets

As we discussed in connection with the use of the TNWs, military targets will have a lesser probability of escalation associated with them.

Rationale

If Pakistan feels compelled to use nuclear weapons and yet leave the path of negotiation and eventual peace open of, its planners would have to ensure that they do not get annihilated in the retaliatory strike. This means that, in their perception, the use of nuclear weapons will have to be in the nature of 'one or two nuclear warning shots' against isolatable Indian military targets, just to demonstrate their resolve to use nukes while seeking to avoid such unacceptable damage to India which could lead to such retaliation that would threaten the very existence of Pakistan as a State. The bottom line is that it will have to demonstrate the resolve and the ability to cross the 'nuclear boundary' with great precision and yet not hurt India very seriously so that India does not regard it as Pakistan having crossed the nuclear Lakshman Rekha. Of course, the validity of this rationale depends on how India perceived it.

In view of the reasoning given above, I reckon, the logically possible targets could include:

- Attacking an Indian task force in the open sea would perhaps be a very 'safe' option that presents a purely military target with zero collateral damage and no problem of fallout in populated areas.
- Indian armour formations in the desert hit by TNWs (Tactical Nuclear Weapons). While the risk of fallout is there, they could still plead about using them on their own soil.

- A major defence industry like the Hindustan Aeronautics Limited, Bangalore where the Tejas is made, or the Heavy Vehicles Factory, Avadi where Arjun tank is made. But the problem with these targets is that they are close to major population centres and hence collateral damage could be high. India might not accept it. Alternatively, they may have to select a less-important factory which is not close to population centres.
- They could also select some important industry like a refinery (for example, the Jamnagar refinery of Reliance or the Vadinar refinery of Essar) or a major thermal power plant of the NTPC which are not strictly military targets but are important for the military potential of the country.
- They could also strike the fringe of a major city to demonstrate their resolve to use nukes and also hint that had they wanted, they could have hit the city itself. That would convey their intention of not hurting us badly enough. In their perception, that would also be an 'attractive' option.

The basic purpose of this exercise is to prepare us at least mentally for any such strike so that we are not left stupefied.

Possible Pakistani Targets for India

Incidentally, the very same arguments apply to India also should India decide to use nuclear weapons. Given our moralistic stance, we would all the more reason to keep our strikes confined to targets of military or industrial value only. The shrill calls of the people and the media notwithstanding, we will have to eschew the desire of bombing Pakistan back to the Stone Age. It would be almost mandatory for India to retaliate a nuke with a nuke but they may also avoid vital targets. The purpose is to let both nations survive as a functional society even after they are hit by a couple of nukes each.

CORRECT CONCEPT OF 'LIMITED WAR'

THE QUESTION OF TIME FRAME AND SPACE

The very term 'limited war' ought to be used very carefully. Many authors (such as Gen Deepak Kapoor (retd) in 'Limited Wars in the Indian Context', *India Strategic*, February 2012) have been committing the mistake of using the term 'limited war' inappropriately and incorrectly. Historically, the term has been used in the sense of a 'limited nuclear war'. (For details, interested readers may see my treatise *National Security and Global Strategic Issues*.) Otherwise, there has obviously been no war in entire human history that has been 'unlimited'.

From the impossibility of a war of attrition, it follows that the next war would be 'short' in time. How short is short, depends on your fancy. There is no universally accepted definition of shortness. It may range from few days to few weeks. With Pakistan, the geographical space available for war is also short; with China, the space is much larger and engagements could place under different commands altogether.

THE QUESTION OF INTENSITY

Another popular fallacy (for example, Deepak Kapoor, ibid) is that a short war would necessarily be a high-intensity war (that is, involving an intense exchange of firepower) and hence more lethal. There is no reason to believe so. Once again, it must be kept in mind that there is no universally accepted definition of intensity. In general terms and for all countries, the volume of firepower exchanged or tonnage of explosives unleashed per day depends on many other factors—above all, it depends on the 'real political intent' behind the war. There are occasions when wars are fought for the 'benefit' of the domestic audience or for playing to the domestic gallery. In such wars, the so-called intensity is necessarily low. For the domestic audience, the mere fact that a war is going on is more important. Their imagination can be fired by carefully selected or doctored videos or stories. They are happy with that. On the other hand, there are occasions when a vicious government secretly pursues its agenda and inflicts more damage on the enemy than it would like its domestic or international audience to know. There was no public approval for the so-called strategic bombing of Germany and fire-bombing of Japan in the Second World War. There was no public approval of dropping 1,75,785 tonnes of bombs in Operation Linebacker I and II in the Vietnam War, or the use of napalm, and herbicides like Agent Orange in Vietnam. But for the Pulitzer Prize winning photo of a nine-year-old girl (Phan Thi Kim Phúc at Trang Bang on June 8, 1972), running naked on a road after being severely burned on her back by a napalm attack, in one of the most haunting images of the Vietnam War, neither the Americans nor the world would have known the inhuman horrors which the Americans were unleashing upon the North Vietnamese.

The Paramount Question of Objective

A limited war would therefore be better characterized by its limited political and military objectives. It is intended more to make a point or position clear than to bring an adversary down to his knees. Defeating the adversary is not the objective, but to teach him a lesson is. That way, a limited war could be regarded as military chastisement. One could also think of a limited war as 'proportionate punishment'. Whatever be the actions which the 'punishing' nation takes, it should be clear that the 'punishing' nation knows what it is doing and its actions are 'controlled' and 'calibrated'. 'Limited' war, in this sense means a 'limited' utilization of one's capabilities for 'limited' objectives in which a general destruction or civilian casualties are assiduously sought to be minimized.

Proper Articulation of Objectives

It is the nature of the objectives and how they are politically articulated that determines the limited character of the war and ensures that it will not escalate uncontrollably. The articulation is to help shape the perception of the adversary. One must articulate his position to make it very clear that he is not consumed by an unbridled lust to subsume the other nation or grind them to dust. This means that it also depends on how well you have been articulating your objectives in the past. In general, if the signals which a country has been giving out on various forums have been confusing; if its top leaders also are given to high-voltage rhetoric; if their media has been given absolutely free reins in spewing venom; that nation, if it comes to using nukes, would find it difficult to articulate its objectives with any clarity. Viewed in this light, you will understand that a 'nuclear overhang' does not really alter the fundamental character of war. If the intents of the countries involved are 'pure' and if they have been properly articulated, they can continue to co-exist even after a small nuclear exchange. A nuclear exchange is not an irreversible cusp which, if you cross once, you can never go back. There is life beyond nukes too.

No Clash of Ideologies

The Cold War was a consequence of a clash of ideologies between the two blocs. Ideologies provided for greater determination and sustenance to fight till the end. People like Marshal Sokolovsky had argued forcefully that a full-fledged nuclear war involving exchange of strategic warheads could also be fought and eventually won, never mind the damage!

Amongst India, Pakistan and China, basically there is no clash of ideologies (even China has opened up its economy) and hence there is no desire to fight till the end. We shall stop after a brief nuclear exchange as soon as the domestic public opinion and popular bloodlust is satisfied.

FALLACY OF AN UNCONTROLLED ESCALATION

HABITUAL DOOMSDAY SOOTHSAYING

The moment one mentions the words 'nuclear exchange', it evokes the popular imagery of an uncontrolled escalation, the dreaded Armageddon. The imagery has actually been ingrained in their collective subconscious since the days of the Cold War. The world has changed since then. As I mentioned above, there is no clash of ideologies now—in fact, amongst India, Pakistan, and China, it is not even the hackneyed 'clash of civilizations'. It is therefore necessary that we stop applying the logic of the Cold War to the current context. Scratch a modern doomsday-wallah and you will find an apparition of the Cold War theorist.

Khurshid Khan, Pak army officer in the Arms Control and Disarmament Affairs Directorate, Strategic Plans Division, wrote a paper 'Limited War Under the Nuclear Umbrella and its Implications for South Asia' while working as a visiting fellow of the Stimson Center, USA. Quite understandably, he reiterates the argument that escalation is almost inevitable. Dig into his paper and you will find that in his support, he has cited Michael Krepon who, in turn, has drawn from a study of the War Plans from the Cold War!

PSYCHOLOGICAL AND SOCIOLOGICAL REASONS OF WARS

The fallacy of uncontrolled escalation believes that the nations which use nukes once will face a retaliatory strike. Then they will also respond, inviting the second retaliation, and so on. In other words, they will end up using their entire nuclear armoury till they destroy each other. No it is not so. Who said so that the nations are bound to behave so? Such a notion is based upon utter ignorance of the psychology of the act of waging war.

My fundamental argument is that nuclear weapons must not be regarded as a taboo or an inherently uncontrollable genie which once let out of the bottle would never go back into the bottle. This relies upon the psychological and sociological reasons of wars which the escalation fallacy ignores. Wars are not driven by any machine logic. Waging war is a human activity and the way the wars will be waged depends on the nature and character of the humans that are waging it. There is no good psychological, social or historical reason to even suspect that the people of India, Pakistan or China are even mentally prepared for a fight to the finish and suffer towards that end. Everything else they say on TV, in rallies and in newspapers is just plain bluster. They do have animosity; they do have a bloodlust but it is necessarily self-limiting like a simple viral infection. India and Pakistan will decide to stop the war the moment the limited bloodlust of the people is satisfied.

The difference in the fundamental nature and character of the people of India and Pakistan can be understood from several historical examples. The German people had suffered horribly in the First World War. That did not prevent them from going to war again less than three decades later. And they were fired by an indomitable spirit of 'fight to the finish' and had the moral courage to suffer immensely for that. The Americans were astonished to find in a Gallup poll conducted by the US army after the surrender of Germany that an overwhelmingly (about 95%) large number of people still reposed their faith in Adolf Hitler, the terrible devastation of Germany and its defeat notwithstanding. The Japanese would rather commit *seppuku* than surrender. The Afghans, even if they were militarily defeated by the Mughals, the Durranis, and the British, never submitted themselves to 'subjugation in spirit', something which the CIA so deftly exploited during the Mujahideen's war against the Soviets.

The use of any major weapon system in a war by a nation has to do more with the 'bloodlust' and 'pride' of the people. Once the bloodlust is satisfied, they would not clamour for more. Even a single nuke could serve that purpose. Coming to 'pride', the people of Pakistan know that the use of even a hundred nukes may not get them India surrendering before them—never mind that they themselves might not survive to see it. All that the people would want for their 'pride' to be satisfied is that their country had the courage to use nukes; that it did not go down without fighting with all it had.

HOW WARS END AND WHY FANATICISM DOES NOT LAST FOR LONG?

After all, wars do end. Whatever might have been the reasons of starting any war, after some time, nations do determine that it would not serve a useful purpose to continue it. The moment the shooting starts, both sides start claiming victory by their great armed forces. The endless stream of cooked up press releases and selective or even doctored video footage would give the impression that no side ever loses a battle, not to speak of losing a war. Wars eventually end when one or both sides are no longer able to play this charade convincingly. At times the international community intervenes as a face-saving device for both sides.

Everybody looks for a face-saving device, even the mighty US. When the US sought exit from the disastrous Vietnam War, they found a face-saving device in the form of the Paris Peace Agreement (January 1973) marking the end of the direct US military involvement in Vietnam. Fact is, even before the last American troops departed from Vietnam on March 29, the communists had violated the ceasefire and had begun their assault on the South Vietnamese—Saigon was to fall a year later on April 30, 1975. In a most telling speech, North Vietnamese Colonel Bui Tin, accepting the surrender of South Vietnam later in the day, had remarked, "You have nothing to fear; between Vietnamese there are no victors and no vanquished. Only the Americans have been defeated." Hence, dear readers do not be surprised if the jingoistic TV channels and screaming-at-the-top-of-their-voice anchors on both sides of the border start singing a different tune to suit the changed times.

So will be the case with the eventuality of a nuclear exchange too. Nuclear weapons are not nuclear chain reactions! They too will stop. If there is one thing which both nations must keep in mind is that they should not become victims of their own hype. Public posturing is one thing; real acts are quite different—this is the real art of statecraft.

Was there any race more fanatical than the Japanese in the Second World War? As the American military pressed in, Japan's war machine had turned inward, as John W Dower documented in his masterful, Pulitzer-winning history *Embracing Defeat: Japan in the Wake of World War II:* "Japanese died in hopeless suicide charges, starved to death in the field, killed their own wounded rather than let them fall into enemy hands, and murdered their civilian compatriots in places such as Saipan and Okinawa," he wrote. At home, "They watched helplessly as fire bombs destroyed their cities—all the while listening to their leaders natter on about how it might be necessary for the 'hundred million' all to die like shattered jewels." Most Japanese feared their emperor would ask them to "fight to the bitter end and die" as they'd been indoctrinated for so long, or to end the imperial mission by their own hands in ritual suicide *seppuku* rather than allow foreigners (*gaijin*) to defile them.

And yet after just two nuclear bombs, all the fanaticism evaporated in no time. More surprising than Hirohito's call for capitulation were the terms he used, which seemingly reversed the entire ideology of war and expansion that had been synonymous with his rule. It is worthwhile to have a look at some of the words of the emperor Hirohito in his just four minute long speech:

> "The enemy has begun to employ a new and most cruel bomb, the power of which to do damage is, indeed, incalculable, taking the toll of many innocent lives. Should we continue to fight, not only would it result in an ultimate collapse and obliteration of the Japanese nation, but also it would lead to the total extinction of human civilization.... To strive for the common prosperity and happiness of all nations, as well as the security and wellbeing of our subjects, is the solemn obligation which has been handed down by our imperial ancestors and which lies close to our heart."

How clever! It was the same man who, till the other day, had been pressing his citizens to carry the burdens of war and imperialism, of an ideology that demanded international primacy. He went on to advise his subjects:

> "The hardships and sufferings to which our nation is to be subjected hereafter will be certainly great. However, it is according to the dictates of time and fate that we have resolved to pave the way for a grand peace for all the generations to come by enduring the unendurable and suffering what is not sufferable."

He ended by urging his long-suffering citizens to "Cultivate the ways of rectitude, foster nobility of spirit, and work with resolution" so as to "keep pace with the progress of the world."

Take it from me, you will hear similar words from leaders of all the countries that suffer a couple of nuclear strikes and then they will manage to salvage their countries from total destruction even if they are obliged to surrender.

A little farther back in past in the USA, Chief Joseph of the Nez Perce tribe of the Red Indians was known to his people as "Thunder Travelling to the Loftier Mountain Heights." Having fought several battles with the US army, Chief Joseph, when he finally surrendered in 1877, spoke these words:

> "I am tired of fighting. Our Chiefs are killed; it is cold, and we have no blankets; the little children are freezing to death. My people, some of them, have run away to the hills, and have no blankets, no food. No one knows where they are—perhaps freezing to death. I want to have time to look for my children, and see how many of them I can find. Maybe I shall find them among the dead. Hear me, my Chiefs! I am tired; my heart is sick and sad. From where the sun now stands I will fight no more forever."

NUCLEAR WARS WILL ALSO END IN TIME

Thus I conclude that while a nuclear exchange is possible, India and Pakistan are not likely to use more than a couple of them each. After that, good sense will prevail. The people, the media and the leaders will all strive to find ingenious ways of face-saving and to explain how peace and development are more important than national pride or warmongering. Given the inherent intellectual bankruptcy of the people, they will come round in no time. Nations too develop fatigue; they too get tired. Nations too get to know what is best for them; they too know when to stop. There is no nation that would swear on God *aut vincere aut mori.*

The use of nuclear weapons is not the ejaculation of a man which once started, cannot be stopped. Nations may very well stop after inflicting and sustaining a couple of nuclear strikes, even if they are strategic weapons (read high yield) or on strategic targets. They will see to it that they let each other survive as a functional society even after they are hit by a couple of nukes each. And we have the capacity to absorb a couple of nuclear strikes. Once again, as I stressed earlier, we must remain mentally prepared for this so that we are not dazed in case of the strikes.

Hypothetical studies by self-styled experts about say 50 nuclear weapons each being used on both countries, are simply farcical and based on utterly simplistic presumptions. In 2006, climatologists Robock and Toon, for example, assumed that each country used 50 nuclear bombs, each with an explosive power of 15 kilotonnes against urban targets in the other country. They reckoned that the dust and soot kicked up would reduce surface temperatures across the planet by an average of 1.3° Celsius. That would result in an average decline of 7% in soybean production and 12% in corn production in the US and a 15% decline in rice production in China. The scientific validity of the study is eminently doubtful. You are well-advised not to get alarmed by them. (Interested readers can find a more detailed discussion on this in my treatise *Nuclear Weapons and International Security*.)

It would therefore be in the interest of all the three countries that we discourage those who speak in terms of 'complete annihilation' of the enemy. Any nation which tries doing that must be prepared to suffer crippling damages itself. Do we want that? It would not even be a proverbial Pyrrhic victory but infinitely worse than that. A Pyrrhic victory costs greatly but leaves you intact—here you would not be in one piece! If we want that then, by all means, let us go ahead and nuke the hell out of Pakistan and rejoice in a dying Pakistan and a surviving but severely crippled India. That's where the situation of Pakistan differs from China. China can expect to defeat India and may be secure surrender too. Pakistan cannot.

LIKELY POST-NUCLEAR EXCHANGE SCENARIO

Of a post-nuclear exchange scenario, I would not dare make any conjectures of my own or couch any view in my own words for fear of inviting unnecessary and avoidable reactions from certain quarters. However, for the benefit of the readers, I must quote the scenario envisaged by Michael O'Hanlon, senior fellow at the Brookings Institution in the *Newsweek* (September 5, 2015) without any comments from my side. Readers are; of course, free to have their own views on this.

> If such an Indo-Pakistani war with nuclear implications began and international negotiators became involved, it's imaginable that an international force could be proposed to help stabilize the situation for a number of years. Kashmir might be administrated under a UN mandate and protected by a UN-legitimated force, with an election eventually determining the region's future political status.

The fact that nuclear conflict might have occurred by this point would have raised the stakes enormously for both sides, making it hard for any leader to accept a simple ceasefire absent a credible political process. The mission could last a decade or more, time enough to allow for a calming of tensions, for political transitions in both countries, and for Pakistan to clamp down on terrorist groups.

India in particular would be adamantly against this idea today. But things could change fundamentally if such a settlement, and such a force, seemed the only way to reverse the momentum toward all-out nuclear war in South Asia.

American forces would likely need to play a key role, as others might not have the capacity or the political confidence to handle the mission. By my estimates, an international force numbering into the low hundreds of thousands of troops could be needed for a period.

Is such a scenario likely? Hardly. Is it crazy or implausible? I don't think so. Could we really sit it out if it happened? I fear not.

QUESTION OF THE SAFETY OF PAKISTANI NUCLEAR WEAPONS FROM A JIHADI TAKEOVER

INTRINSIC SAFING, ARMING AND FUZING SYSTEMS

This is yet another popular myth propagated by the media and in the films—that the safety of the Pakistani nuclear weapons is doubtful and that the Taliban or the ISIS could snatch them, only to be used indiscriminately against India. It is also suggested on the side that many senior officers in the Pak army are secretly in league with the terrorists and they might collude with them in this 'staged' snatching of nuclear weapons. People go to the extent of suggesting that the US, being the most responsible and powerful nation in the world, should 'take control' of the Pakistani nuclear weapons. Much of it is rooted in pitiable ignorance.

There is a whole science of safing, arming and fuzing of nuclear weapons. Most people in the media, armed forces and amongst the self-styled defence experts who are obviously not nuclear scientists have no idea of the complexity of nuclear weapons and keep on perpetrating all sorts of scary rumours and paint frightening scenarios. Sensible readers must guard against such assaults of ignorance. However, as a nuclear scientist, it is my duty to educate you about the safety systems which are built into the very design of nuclear weapons,

Pakistani or not, and how it is almost impossible for an unauthorized person to use them even if he somehow succeeds in getting physical possession of the weapon.

The first thing we must understand is that the safety standards on nuclear weapons remain the same irrespective of the explosive yield of the weapon. Thus a TNW has the same safety features as a megaton bomb. Hence the TNWs, if at all they exist and are deployed close to the border, are as safe as the bigger bombs kept somewhere else. Any apprehensions to the contrary (such as Ajai Shukla's) must be dismissed.

The second is that it is simply not possible to steal a nuclear weapon. It happens only in Hollywood or Bollywood films. No nuclear weapon is ever kept in the 'armed' state from where it could be stolen or snatched, ready to use. The arming and fuzing is done at the last moment. Nuclear weapons are seldom kept in a 'ready-to-fire' condition, and the components are usually kept at different places under great security. Terrorists may attack regular military facilities and may even defeat the soldiers—they would still not even know where nuclear weapons' components are kept. In any case, it is almost impossible to believe that the terrorists would be able to defeat entire Pak army units and force them on gunpoint to make them arm the nukes and fire the missiles. Let us not insult a professional army and its nuclear scientists this way. Subversion of Pak army officers by the terrorists is possible but once again, the entire process of safing, arming and fuzing is not in one man's hand. There is no reason to believe that the authority to launch a tactical nuclear weapon would ever vest with the local commanders. How in the world can one ever think so that the Pakistanis are so irresponsible that a Lt Gen, Maj Gen, Brigadier or Colonel would be able to launch nuclear weapons single-handedly?

LAUNCHING CODES AND PERMISSIVE ACTION LINK (PAL) DEVICES

There are elaborate security systems such as launching codes and Permissive Action Link (PAL) devices that prevent unauthorized persons from launching nuclear weapons even if they have them. Real life is different from reel life. A Permissive Action Link is essentially an electronic or electromechanical combination lock (an electronic keypad is generally used to arm the weapons) that must be set in the proper order before the weapon can be armed and either launched or dropped over its target. A PAL is intended to preclude both accidental and unauthorized detonation. By locking out critical electrical paths—regardless of any environmental effects—the PAL virtually guarantees that a nuclear warhead will not explode without proper authority. They are built into the weapon casings and are not removable without disassembly of the entire warhead. Many nuclear weapons are 'booby-trapped' to destroy critical internal components if the casing is disassembled. At present, they use Multiple-code Category-F 12-digit (or Category-D 6-digit) switch with provision for 'limited try followed by lockout'. This means that even if some James Bond-type guy, some hacker-type guy or some Smart Aleck starts showing off his skill in opening electronic locks, the device would automatically lockout after a limited number of attempts. As a further security precaution, PAL combinations are often changed at regular intervals. In addition, for some missile systems, more than one individual must co-arm the weapon with another person to avoid unintended use. SLBMs are armed by the joint actions of several key officers.

SAFETY SYSTEMS ON MISSILE WARHEADS

The safing, arming, and fuzing sub-systems of ballistic missiles are designed to 'sense' particular points in the re-entry vehicle

(RV) trajectory and then only they take steps to arm, fuze, and finally fire the warhead. An on-board computer receives signals from various pressure and temperature-sensing transducers and thermocouples mounted on the RV exterior. A baroswitch starts the arming sequence when the missile has risen to a pre-set altitude. A trajectory-sensing device determines whether or not the missile is on a correct course and completes the next step of the arming sequence. If the missile is off-course, this sensing equipment will issue a self-destruct signal to destroy the missile, RV, and warheads. If the missile is on course, the arming computer samples current environmental conditions to determine what to do next. On re-entry to the earth's atmosphere, deceleration forces of 20 to 50 times the force of gravity provide a signal to complete arming and firing of the warhead at a pre-selected burst altitude. In addition, re-entry temperatures on the order of several thousand degrees can also be used to trigger part of the arming process.

> This means that even if one steals or commandeers a missile warhead, he cannot explode it—it is designed to fire only when mounted on a missile which takes its full proper course. Now it is rather unrealistic to expect that terrorists would be able to take control of the entire missile complex and fire the missiles at will.

THE 'TWO-MAN RULE' IN USA

For the readers' elucidation, the United States has a two-man rule in place. I will explain it. National Command Authority (NCA) is a term used by the Department of Defense of the United States of America to refer to the ultimate lawful source of military orders. The NCA comprises the President of the United States (as commander-in-chief) and the Secretary of Defense jointly, or their duly deputized successors, ie the Vice President and the Deputy Secretary of Defense. While only the

President can order the release of nuclear weapons, the order must be confirmed by the Secretary of Defense (there is a hierarchy of succession in the event of the president is killed in an attack). The Secretary of Defense has the legal authority to approve the President's order, but cannot veto it. Supposing in some situation, the Secretary of Defense refuses to second the order, the President has no option but to remove him from office—he cannot force him to sign. In case he is thus removed from office, the Deputy Secretary of Defense would assume the office of Acting Secretary of Defense in accordance with the Secretarial order of succession. He may agree with the President or not agree, and risk removal. However, this cannot go on indefinitely. The Vice President and a majority of the heads of the Executive Departments could invoke Section 4 of the Twenty-Fifth Amendment to the Constitution and have the President declared incapacitated. Once the NCA has authorized a launch order under the proper procedures, the Chairman of the Joint Chiefs of Staff or the Vice Chairman of the Joint Chiefs of Staff will in turn direct a General officer on duty in the National Military Command Center (NMCC) at The Pentagon to execute the SIOP (Single Integrated Operational Plan).

CHAPTER 11

War with China

WILL THEY, WILL THEY NOT?

China has many sources of tension and rivalry with India including Nepal, Myanmar, Bangladesh and the Indian Ocean. But none of them seem to provide a casus belli strong enough to precipitate hostilities. The potential for the relationship to deteriorate is, of course, ever present. Under normal circumstances, India and China are likely to have sufficient desire and capacity to prevent any single point of friction from sparking a military crisis. As such, a pattern of border incursion, response, negotiation, and withdrawal has been developed and it has come to be accepted too. This is likely to continue.

> Yet if more than one dispute were to unfold at the same time, the risk of escalation would grow as positions taken in one conflict could complicate the management of another. Moreover, leaders on both sides will have to contend with much greater public pressure.

Arguments claiming that an Indo-China war is unlikely run as follows:

- That the war would disrupt China's remarkably successful development drive.
- That the Chinese might find it difficult to conclude the war quickly.

For the first, it should not be forgotten that wars are fought for issues higher than development. For the second, it must be kept in mind that more often than not, the result of war depends on how well it has been planned and how realistically the strategy dovetails with the objectives sought.

Arguments claiming that an Indo-China war or Chinese participation in an Indo-Pak war is likely run as follows:

- A forceful, assertive foreign policy could very well rally popular support behind an otherwise unpopular government.
- Moreover, there is always a hawkish military elite backed by a nationalist popular surge seeking wars to justify its raison d'être. Liu Yazhou, political commissar at the PLA's National Defence University, was quoted as telling the Guofang Cankao, or the Defence Reference Magazine that 'limited armed conflicts' would be a good chance to test the country's military prowess. He advocated that the PLA could emerge as a modern military power by 'seizing opportunities' for war. It may well not be the official position but does reflect what many in the establishment think and feel. Liu very rightly pointed out what I have been arguing since long (such as in my work *National Security and Global Strategic Issues*) that China has not engaged in mechanized warfare since its brief war with Vietnam in 1979, while the American army has fought several complex campaigns in recent decades, testing out everything from strategic concepts to equipment to troop capability—and that is a definite weakness in the PLA. An army which goes to war only on the strength of exercise places itself in great peril—an army can only live up to its reputation by fighting wars. There is no substitute of real experience. Bluster in the Officers' Messes, newspapers, TV debates or seminars are no substitute for real experience. That's where the Americans have a great edge over anybody else in the world.

- That a short, sharp and swift war with India would cost them say a few months of development, but would keep India in its place and dissuade it from aggressively pursuing anti-China policies. A war with the US, on the other hand, could cost them several years of development and would therefore be not acceptable. But a war against India would serve as a signal to the US that China is not just a paper tiger.
- Participating on the side of Pakistan or even aggressive posturing or mobilization will constrain India severely. This will maintain the balance of power and hopefully keep India both sober and somewhat respectful of Chinese interests in Tibet and elsewhere.
- China may decide to 'punish' India for its overly pro-USA postures in all matters that somehow relate to China, such as the South China Sea. This rests on the presumption that Japan is guaranteed US protection and Australia is too far away. A direct fight with the USA would be too risky. That leaves India as the weakest link in the chain and hence a possible target. The risk is that if the war does not end decisively, it would push India even more strongly in the fold of the USA.

LIKELY PRECIPITATING CAUSES

Possible precipitating points include situations arising from the following.

SKIRMISHES ALONG THE LAC

Perils of Multiple Simultaneous Incidents

Every year, China and India claim hundreds of incursions by the other side across the LAC. I agree with Daniel Markey that in such situations, exchange of fire could result from surprise or accident in the heat of multiple disputes. However, as long as the casualties are limited to say a few dozen at most, it should permit forces to stand down without escalating to a wider war. Still, it would always hang at the back of the minds of the respective leaders (and more so in India because the Chinese media is, for all practical purposes, controlled by the State) that the media-generated public opinion could hold them as appearing weak.

Under routine circumstances, China and India could seek various diplomatic and economic means of retaliation. For example, Beijing could curtail its plans for investment in India, and New Delhi could back away from new multilateral institutions spearheaded by China, such as the Shanghai Cooperation Organization and the Asian Infrastructure Investment Bank. However, if border clashes were to occur during a period of heightened tension, or several were to take place simultaneously at different, it is quite possible for someone, somewhere to misread the overall picture or over-react. Local level mistakes are always possible—things get complicated only when leaders of that side choose to defend them unnecessarily.

Warning Signs

Such multiple incidents could be deliberate or could be just incidental. In case, they are suspected to be deliberate, then one way of confirming our suspicions would be to look for increase in the depth of probing patrols; unilateral revision of the 'rules of the road' for tactical military operations (for instance, if one side begins firing warning shots when the past practice had been to display flag signals); new military construction projects or deployments along the border, whether of troops or hardware (such as missile sites, landing strips, or vehicles); and official use of new diplomatic formulations or visa policies that aggressively press broader territorial claims.

SIDE-EFFECT OF OR SPILL-OVER OF TIBETAN PROTESTS

China has been accusing India of supporting and instigating Tibetan insurgency. In this backdrop, a sudden increase in protest or subversive activities in Tibet could provoke China. This is what Humphrey Hawksley had also hypothesized in his novel *Dragon Fire*. But the question is, given the iron hold which the Chinese have over Tibet, is a significant protest, sabotage or terrorist action even likely? I do not think so. Chinese may be hypersensitive about Tibet and the Dalai Lama, but it is mostly public posturing and also serves as a cover for what they are doing there. It is difficult to believe outside the realms of films that the Tibetans could create such a situation which would make the Chinese really anxious. Tibet's fate seems to be sealed now what with the Han migration, strong PLA presence, greatly improved connectivity and tight internal security measures. Tibetan dissidents planning assassinations or sabotage must not waste their energy as China is perfectly capable of crushing the Tibetans or any 'misadventure' at uprising—the Chinese would have wasted all these years in Tibet if they cannot do even that. They are not going to be bothered by things like self-immolations.

MARITIME RIVALRY

While it is well-known that both sides hold important and growing interests in the waters of the Indo-Pacific as transit routes, spheres of political influence, and points of military vulnerability; maritime competition between China and India is still in a nascent stage and should not be overblown. From a strategic perspective, China's activities in the Indian Ocean are far less extensive or provocative than its moves closer to home—and India's reach into the South China Sea remains very limited.

China is very sensitive to its position on the South China Sea. India's diplomatic position on the South China Sea—supporting the principle of freedom of navigation and the peaceful resolution of disputed territory is nearly identical to that of the United States. China is irritated by that stance, along with India's investments in oil exploration off the Vietnamese coast and closer naval ties with the United States, Japan, and Vietnam. But the mere fact that India participated along with the USA and Japan in the joint naval war games called the Malabar Exercise in June 2016 near Okinawa and some 400 km from the contested Senkaku Islands, hunting for Chinese submarines and ships should not delude us into believing that we can operate independently in the South China Sea.

Warning Indicators

Warning indicators for a maritime contingency between China and India could include aggressive new Chinese harassment of other oil-exploration operations off the Vietnamese coast, a significant expansion of Chinese patrols as part of its counter-piracy mission in the Gulf of Aden, and provocative Chinese rhetoric directed against Indian oil exploration in the South China Sea. China could also react to new Indian oil-exploration investments in partnership with Vietnam.

WHAT IF THEY GO TO WAR?

CHINA'S PRIMAL DESIRE IN A WAR ON GROUND

There is a fundamental difference between the military designs of the Pakistanis and the Chinese with respect to India. The Pakistanis know it well that they cannot wrest

> Kashmir or grab any significant territory from India. Hence, for them the objective is largely psychological in character—such as redeeming or salvaging their self-respect or honour.

However, since the fundamental dispute between India and China belongs to the land, the principal object of the Chinese can be nothing but to grab land—that would be their primary object of war; any damage caused to the Indian military, industry or society would be only incidental. Rationally, the Chinese cannot have any significant psychological aspect to a war with India. When the Pakistanis fight us, they would be emotionally charged; when the Chinese fight us, they would fight like automatons.

> If they were to humiliate India by inflicting material damage on the Indian armed forces, the ground forces are not the right thing. They will have to use their missiles for that. If they are investing so much in increasing their ability to move manpower, firepower and armour, it means that they, in old fashion, want to do nothing but grab land. The PLAAF would therefore play a supportive role in that venture.

The 4,057 km long LAC between the two countries is geographically divided into three Sectors. The Western Sector is in Ladakh; the Central Sector is along the Uttarakhand-Tibet border, and the Eastern Sector is in Sikkim and Arunachal Pradesh, where China claims 90,000 square kilometres of Indian Territory. Arunachal Pradesh shares a 1,030 kilometre (650 mile) unfenced border with China. China is obsessed with Arunachal because it constitutes the vulnerable flank for Tibet.

China has got two of its so-called Military Regions opposite India. Chengdu is opposite India's North-East and part of the Central Sector; and Lanzhou is opposite the Ladakh sector. The Military Regions are further sub-divided into Military Districts (MD). But this is only of academic interest. Chengdu MR: Yunnan opposite Myanmar and Xizang (which is part of TAR) opposite Assam, Sikkim and Arunachal; Lanzhou MR: South Xinjiang opposite Uttarakhand, Himachal Pradesh and Ladakh, and East Xinjiang opposite India adjoining Ladakh.

INDIAN PREPAREDNESS FOR THE CHINESE THREAT

Intrinsic Limitations Imposed by Geography

One thing should be clear in the context of an India-China war. From a purely military point of view, the mountainous terrain, high-altitude climate, and concomitant logistic difficulties make a protracted or large-scale conflict a difficult proposition which will tax the capabilities of the respective General Staff Headquarters. Hence, whatever be the immediate reason of war, a conventional war with China would not be a long one. And, in a war of short duration, China would have the advantage of better infrastructure close to the border. The analysis is based on the current level of infrastructure and preparedness; if that changes drastically in future, the scene would change.

Troop Deployment

Mountain warfare generally calls for a ratio of nine attackers for every defender and that gives us at an advantage. The army had raised two new infantry divisions (1,260 officers and 35,000 soldiers) at Likabali and Missamari (Assam) in 2009-2010 to reduce the adverse land combat ratio with China, which hovered around 1:3. With tensions rising between China and India, by mid-2016 India deployed nearly 100 T-72 tanks to its Eastern border. The vast flat valleys along the mountain ranges allow for armoured movement. But it is still not clear as to in what strategy they would fit. And if somehow they do fit, how was the obvious not seen for so many years?

On July 17, 2013, the Cabinet Committee on Security (CCS) had approved the Army's proposal for raising a Mountain Strike Corps (XVII) for the mountains for 'swift counter-offensive capabilities'. The new corps will have two high-altitude infantry divisions (59 Division at Panagarh and 72 Division at Pathankot) with their integral units, two independent infantry brigades, two armoured brigades and the like. It will include 30 new infantry battalions and two Para-Special Forces battalions. While the new corps will be based in Panagarh, West Bengal, the force will be deployed from Ladakh to Arunachal Pradesh. On 13 January 2016, army chief Gen Dalbir Singh told the media that the strike corps was on course and would be raised by 2021. The 59 Mountain Division with 16,000 soldiers had been raised in Panagarh, West Bengal, but the proposed 72 Mountain Division in Pathankot was stalled.

Air Power

The Indian ground forces are supported by two squadrons of Su-30MKI at Tezpur—the deployment had begun in 2009. Tezpur and Chabua districts were regarded as vulnerable. In addition, as reported in the media (Rezaul H Laskar) in August 2016, the Cabinet Committee on Security cleared the raising of a new missile regiment to be equipped with an advanced version of the BrahMos developed for mountain warfare at a cost of more than ₹4,300 crore. The new regiment for the north-east will have some 90-100 missiles, five mobile autonomous launchers on heavy-duty trucks and a mobile command post. This really rattled China and the PLA Daily immediately spoke of this having 'a negative influence' on stability along the border as it threatened China's Tibet and Yunnan provinces.

According to Arthur Dominic Villasanta, India has operationalized IAF airfields (or ALGs—Advanced Landing Grounds) at Mechuka, Ziro, Along, Wallong and Pasighat within the past one-and-a-half years. The ALGs have hard-surface runways; aprons for ground manoeuvring; air traffic control towers and perimeter roads, but not repair and maintenance facilities. Work is underway on upgrading ALGs at Tuting and Tawang. Reconstruction of the ALG at Vijaynagar will be undertaken after the road between Miao and Vijaynagar is restored—ALGs. Some of them are 100 km or less from its border with China in Arunachal Pradesh. They are capable of supporting all our aircrafts including the Su-30MKI.

CHINESE PREPARATIONS AND THEIR ADVANTAGES/DISADVANTAGES

Troop Deployment

Sheer numbers (being a relic of the hardcore communist era) have never been a problem with the Chinese; the problem is how they are going to fit the numbers (or in their post-modernization *avtar*, the more proficient and technologically better-equipped troops) into their war-fighting strategy. This is neither the Korean War nor 1962—sheer numbers on the ground are not going to achieve strategic objectives. Even if we grant that mountain warfare demands more numbers amongst the attackers, the era of 'human wave' attacks is passé. Hence, as such, there is no need to unnecessarily hype the so-called 3 lakh Chinese troops on our border.

For getting information on Chinese forces, usually analysts depend on Western sources like the US Congressional Report. While such reports are conservatively reliable, their primary focus is on China's preparations against Taiwan and Japan and as such cannot help Indian planners much.

According to other sources in the public domain (such as Vivekanand International Foundation), 13 and 14 Group

Armies (a Group Army is roughly our corps level) from Chengdu Military Region and 47 and 21 Group Armies from Lanzhou military region can be deployed in the TAR (Tibet Autonomous Region). 13 Group Army is designated as a Rapid Reaction Force and 21 Group Army as an offensive mobile force. They can concentrate up to seven divisions in TAR within one week; 12 divisions in 20-30 days because of the QTR (Qinghai Tibet Railway, Golmud to Lhasa—1,142 km and passes over 16,640 feet at Tanggula pass in Kunlun mountain range). It is believed that they can mobilize a 'Rapid Reaction Division' into Lhasa within 24-36 hrs and deploy up to two to three heli-lift battalions.

> We should be more concerned about the strategy which they could employ. So far, at least from their own publications, there is little information about the strategy which they might adopt in their next war with India. Most analysts are so obsessed with Chinese attack in Ladakh and the North-East that the possibility of other novel methods of attack, such as through Nepal, has not crossed their minds.

In this connection, reference is often made to a rather unusual paper by a high level military analyst, entitled 'Tibet Military District is Fully Prepared to Deal with a Possible Sino-Indian Border Clash' (bbs.news.sina.com.cn, November 17, 2008) which gives out enormous data on the ORBAT (Order of Battle) in Tibet Military District. While expressing satisfaction over the facilities for communications and transport through the newly built Qinghai-Tibet Railway, new highways in the Ali region and the latest building of airports like Linzhi, it notes that the PLA Air Force is not permanently stationed in Tibet. Further, since Indian troops may try to enter and attack China's Yunnan province, it suggests that the 14th Army of Chengdu Military Region should be stationed in Kunming, Yunnan's capital. It also says that the position that 80% of China's strategic bomber force is in Lanzhou Military Region, is not ideal. The analysts further argue that should this 'partial war' get escalated, China should make Pakistan as its ally and help the latter in recovering Kashmir. Such critical details could not have seen the light of day without official patronage.

Rapid Reaction Forces (RRFs) of China

People often highlight the raising of the Rapid Reaction Forces (RRFs) by China. They are believed to have been raised after the so-called modernization. The RRFs are self-contained and have airborne assets too. The basic idea is quick (overnight) mobilization, great mobility and an attempt to overrun Arunachal in say 48-72 hours.

But I do not think that the Chinese could have based all their strategy on the RRFs. Possession of airborne assets by a land force is not the same thing as support by a regular air force. The claim that the RRFs would be used for attack on Arunachal Pradesh does not factor in their air force, particularly in view of the fact that we have now a sizeable air force presence there. They can counter our air force only by a proper air force and their ground forces will have to be protected from our air force. They cannot be left to defend themselves with nothing but anti-aircraft fire. Thus, I do not think that the RRF alone can do the job.

Chinese Attention to Communication Links and Logistics

The lay of Tibetan plateau is such that Chinese can build road or rail link almost parallel to the LAC whereas, the Indian side, it is interspersed with valleys running north-south—making laying of a road parallel to LAC is very difficult. As such, there are technical doubts over the feasibility of execution of the 1,800 km long highway project in Arunachal Pradesh intended to connect Tawang, East Kameng, Upper Subansiri, West Siang, Upper Siang, Dibang Valley, Desali, Chaglagam, Kibithu, Dong, Hawai and Vijayanagar border areas of the state. Similar situation exists in the central sector in the state of Uttarakhand.

With geography helping the Chinese, India must be seriously concerned about the logistics infrastructure and road network that they have built up in the Tibet Autonomous Region (TAR) and opposite other disputed areas giving appreciable strategic mobility to the PLA and Logistics, as I have explained at length earlier, is the cornerstone of victories. Good Chinese road network means that they can keep their forces adequately furnished with supplies and ammunition, irrespective of the strategy used.

Journalist Sandeep Unnithan claimed in late 2011 that over the past decade the Chinese Army had built a road-rail network of over 58,000 km and nine new military airfields on the Tibetan plateau. In contrast, nearly one-fourth of India's strategic border roads totalling 600 km remain unfinished. These roads were identified by the China Study Group as vital for the army to rush troops to the border in case of war. Delays in environment clearances and slow work mean they will be complete only by 2017. It is said that from Demchok sector, 300 km from Leh, Chinese armoured and infantry columns can drive up to Leh in a day. In Tawang, the PLA has built a two-lane highway for its military to drive up to the border. The Chinese roads nearly reach the line of actual control (LAC) or in some cases go beyond, while on the other hand most Indian roads stop well before the Indian side of the LAC. Long stretches of Tawang's sole link to India, a 320-km road from Chariduar town in Assam, remain a muddy track. It reportedly takes about 20 hours to drive 500 km from Guwahati to Tawang—you can judge the severe condition of the road network in the region yourself.

The Official History of the 1962 war (SN Prasad, chief ed) had stated: "Strategically, Walong, Tawang and the forward areas in Ladakh were indefensible in 1962 against a major attack. But, regarding Eastern Ladakh in particular, it is difficult to think up any viable strategy to save it once the Chinese have stolen a march in logistics by quietly building the road through Aksai Chin." Incidentally, this is what the Chinese did all these years—stealing a march over us in logistic support.

Possible Chinese Use of Paratroopers

A war is to be fought with a clear objective, not for fun. If the Chinese do intend to capture territory in Arunachal, it would not be easy with regular infantry attacks, particularly in view of the fact that, in terms of numbers, equipment and preparedness, the Indian Army is no longer in that bad a situation vis-a-vis the PLA in which they were in 1962. This means that the Chinese will adopt unconventional tactics like the using paratroopers or para commandos, and we will have to be prepared for that. If the primary objective of the Chinese is to quickly capture some territory and establish control, the first thing they might do is to seize key personnel, offices, institutions, or installations including airfields. For that, they will have to drop paratroopers and we must factor that in our planning. Besides this they may also deposit ultra-lightweight field howitzers slung under helicopters. Thus China's transport aircraft capability will be a critical issue here. Paratroopers with small arms alone are good for surprise only—not for serious fighting. As I have mentioned earlier, they do not have heavy-lift choppers like the Merlin or the Chinook. They have developed technology for excellent transport aircrafts including an equivalent of even the venerable Globemaster, though they have yet to make them in sufficient numbers. But once they acquire it, we will have to be careful.

In case they are using paratroopers, a lot will depend on the intelligence they have regarding the targets which they have to capture. We will have to deny them this intelligence and make our counterintelligence very rigorous. The security of key personnel, offices, institutions, or installations including airfields is generally limited to rifles and machineguns only. Chinese paratroopers can overcome these defences, if they are armed with belt-fed light machineguns; automatic grenade launchers; commando mortars; demolition charges; and incapacitating gases like fentanyl derivatives, etc. The Russians had used this gas very effectively in the Moscow Theatre Siege. For greater mobility, they might drop ATVs (all terrain vehicles) also. In 1989 during the US invasion of Panama, M551 Sheridan tanks (designed to be landed by parachute and to swim across rivers) were also dropped by air. The Chinese might very well do something like this. Vulnerability of key personnel, offices, institutions, or installations including airfields may prove costly and India must keep that in mind.

Seizing buildings, airfields and strategically important has been commonplace for paratroopers all over the world. In Operation Storm 333 on December 27, 1979, Soviet forces had stormed the Tajbeg Palace in Afghanistan and had captured the then Afghan President Hafizullah Amin. On October 19, 2001 an element of the US 75th Ranger Regiment had secured an airfield in Kandahar. On March 26, 2003 the US 173rd Airborne Brigade had seized an airfield in northern Iraq. In 2009, Pakistan Army's paratroopers had seized control of strategic mountain areas during Operation Black Thunderstorm and Operation Rah-e-Nijat against the Pakistani Taliban in north-west Pakistan to support Special Forces and infantry troops. In January 2013, French paratroopers jumped into northern Mali to support an offensive to capture the city of Timbuktu.

> If there is one job that is best suited for commando action, it is this—that is, behind enemy lines. Commandos get chewed up in front of the enemy lines, and it is only the regular infantry

and armour that has any chance! We should never forget that once key offices, institutions, installations or airfields are taken, and key people taken hostages, the battle is effectively lost. The Indian Army could remain in control of the remaining territory and manage to mount attacks too but that would not help much—once again, the psychological advantage goes to one who takes control of key points and personnel.

THE AIR WAR

Strategic Objectives of the PLAAF

The principal object of the PLAAF in the next war would be to support the operations of the PLA. This would translate into air superiority battles and ground attacks. To hurt Indian ground forces and to hamper supplies, the next logical target would be key railway bridges on rivers, rail junctions, and critical roads. Vital industrial targets like refineries would come next. All these would demand precision bombing because, unlike the US bombers in Vietnam, their aircrafts cannot expect to have an unhindered bombing run in India. Thus the availability of PGM or smart bombs will be a critical factor. The missions will have to be carried by their fighter bombers as the H-6K (based basically on the Tu-16 Badger) may find it difficult to penetrate Indian air space—however, the H-6 can use their ALCMs.

The Chinese have a strategic weakness. The Chengdu Aircraft Industry Group is within the strike range of the Su-30MKI without requirement for mid-air refuelling.

Air Power

Reliable information regarding Chinese airpower pitted against India in the concerned region is not available in public domain.

Older references like Manish Girdhar (2010) present a rather questionable picture. A claim that in the Chengdu Military Region, the PLAAF has two fighter divisions of J-6, J-7, J-10 and Su-27 aircrafts besides one transport division; and two fighter divisions of J-6, J-7G, J-7II, J-8I, J-8F and J-11 aircrafts and one bomber division of H-6 in the Lanzhou Military Region, does not fit into the scheme of a sensible air force with aggressive designs—in fact, it would reflect extremely poor planning and preparedness by the PLAAF. The J-6 is a copy of the MiG-19; the J-7 is a copy of the MiG-21; and the J-8 too is an interceptor of MiG-21 technology. Only the J-10, Su-27 and J-11 are modern aircrafts. Still, there is a gap of more than one generation with the Su-30MKI and Rafale. They cannot hope to fight these aircrafts with 1960s aircrafts—no way! Something is obviously amiss here as it is difficult to believe that they could be so dumb. Either we are in the dark or their strategy places more emphasis on missiles.

It can be reasonably expected that by the time of the next war, the Chinese will have a substantial number of new generation aircraft. Since they are producing frontline aircrafts indigenously in sufficient numbers, this gives them an advantage. The IAF is practically entirely based on imported stuff and that is a disadvantage.

There are 14 airbases in these two regions from where PLAAF can launch air operations. We are told of airbases at Hoping, Bangda, Shiquanhe, Bayixincun (in central Tibet opposite Arunachal Pradesh) and Kongka. These airbases support six airfields in the Tibetan Autonomous Region that can handle fighter jets and heavy transport aircraft.

Air Defence and Electronic Warfare

The Chinese ground forces are believed to have a huge network of radar and point defence air defence system—how effective they are, is anyone's guess. According to the US Defence Department's 2015 report to Congress, "PLA EW strategy focuses on radio, radar, optical, infrared and microwave frequencies in addition to adversarial computer and information systems." It is difficult to predict what will be its effect on us.

Combat Record

Combat record of both air forces is poor. The IAF had a very limited exposure during the Kargil war. And since the very technology of aircrafts has changed materially since 1971, that experience can be consigned to the archives. So is the case with the Chinese who saw action last in a brief war with Vietnam in 1979.

CHAPTER 12

The War at Sea

INDIA'S STRATEGIC PERSPECTIVE IN THE INDIAN OCEAN

ECONOMIC IMPORTANCE

The Indian Ocean Region is a transit zone for much of the world's energy resources. Since most of the trade of the Indian Ocean littorals and the South Asian States is seaborne, SLOCs form the lifeline of these countries. A large volume of international long haul maritime cargo from the Persian Gulf, Africa and Europe transits through this ocean. Some of the primary items transported are energy products, mainly oil and gas. Given the spiralling demand for energy from India, China and Japan, it is inevitable that the SLOCs and choke points of the region have become strategically important for these countries and that they are extremely sensitive to their security.

For example, the closure of the Straits of Malacca, through which a great quantity of oil passes every day, can seriously threaten the economies of South-east Asia and the energy intensive economies of China and Japan. India imports some 70% of its oil and gas, and some two-thirds of it moves through the Indian Ocean. Crude oil is India's largest import—nearly one-third of all imports; and refined oil is its largest export—all passing through the Indian Ocean. Any disruptions in the choke points such as the Strait of Hormuz, the Gulf of Aden, the Suez Canal and the Strait of Malacca, can lead to serious consequences for the Indian economy.

India is assisting Iran in upgrading the deep-sea port of

Chahbahar, which is close to the Strait of Hormuz and which could provide future access to Central Asia and Eastern Europe via a planned highway and railway system.

TASKS FOR THE NAVY FOR DOMINATING THE IOR

India has therefore no option but to secure the IOR. It is in context of defending India's economic and maritime interests that the Indian Navy has to gear up its capabilities. In addition to a defensive role of guarding the coastline, the ports and offshore assets like drilling rigs, the Indian Navy will need to play an active blue water role in ensuring that SLOCs are kept open. This role shall include surveillance, monitoring, interdiction, capture, and confrontation (if necessary). The surveillance capabilities should stretch well beyond India's EEZ, and well into the Gulf Region on one hand and the Indian Ocean and the Malacca Strait on the other. Obviously, this would require space-based satellite assets dedicated to naval use.

REQUISITES FOR A BLUE WATER NAVY

The Indian Navy shall need the capability to project force well beyond India's shores or EEZ for extended periods of time if an adversary's efforts to intimidate India's neighbours are to be stymied. The ability to project power throughout the huge Indian Ocean region would, first of all, require a 'Blue Water Navy' built around aircraft carriers. The Indian Navy needs to have at least two functional carrier-based task forces at all times. This means that India would have to look forward to creating three aircraft carrier battle groups.

For vessels that may operate for long from the base, the only option is nuclear powered submarines. A submarine support base with all facilities as well as a VLF communications centre in the vicinity of the Ten Degree Channel, perhaps on Little

Andaman in the South Andaman Islands may be of help to diesel-electric submarines.

A 'Blue Water Navy' also depends on forward support sites for logistical and intelligence support. If some foreign bases allow us berthing, refuelling, victualling, communication and other support facilities, it would be of great help. Possible places include Gan of Maldives; Bandar Abbas or Kish of Iran; some place in Singapore or Malaysia.

India has already established a number of strategic support sites throughout the Indian Ocean, including on the Lakshadweep islands to the west of the mainland, the Andaman and Nicobar Islands to the east of the mainland, and monitoring stations in Madagascar. India has also signalled an interest to lease the Agalega Islands from Mauritius. But would that be enough, is open to debate.

CAN THEY DO IT AFTER ALL?

> Can India, even with its increased spending and naval purchases, dominate the necessary part of the IOR on its own? It is a difficult question to answer. The organizational interests of the Indian Navy would compel them to claim that they can indeed do it. Others argue that India cannot dominate the region on its own, and must come to regard the US presence as neutral or even beneficial to India's interests.

INDIAN OCEAN IN CHINESE STRATEGIC PERSPECTIVE

CRITICAL OIL SUPPLY ISSUES

China now imports approximately 60% of its oil from the Middle East. Of this, about 80% is carried in Very Large Crude Carriers (VLCC or supertankers) for obvious reasons of economy—each carrying about two million barrels of oil. The supertankers are very costly (about $120 million each, compared to $43 million of a medium range tanker), take longer routes and are obliged to stay at sea for much longer periods of time. In other words, they are more vulnerable in a war or warlike situation. Chinese oil imports are expected increase two times and become about 15 MBD (million barrels per day) by 2020. By 2035, China is likely to import between 70 to 80% of its oil from the Middle East.

The greatest geographical impediment to expedient oil supply to China is the Strait of Malacca. It is described it as a 'World Oil Choke Point' moving approximately 15 million barrels of oil through the strait each day. Chinese President Hu Jintao stated in November 2003 that China faces a 'Malacca dilemma', in a reference to the vulnerability to disruption of its oil supply lines from the Middle East and Africa.

FORWARD BASES

China is also supposed to be investing in forward bases and infrastructure in the region, including listening posts in Coco Island and Mawlamyaing in Myanmar, the Hambantota port project in Sri Lanka, Chittagong in Bangladesh and Gwadar in Pakistan. The Chinese are supposed to be sounding Seychelles and Djibouti for hub-and-spoke logistics support agreements. Hub-and-spoke refers to a system of air transportation in which local airports offer air transportation to a central airport where long-distance flights are available.

THE SIGNIFICANCE OF GWADAR AND HAMBANTOTA PORTS

The port of Gwadar, re-vitalised so as to make it a deepwater port and naval base is a mere 200 nautical miles from the mouth of the Arabian Gulf. China has provided a substantial part of the $1.16 billion total cost of the project. The Gwadar deep-sea port in Pakistan can be seen as a rival to Chahbahar in Iran, which is heavily financed by India. Gwadar makes strategic sense for Pakistan as it will provide economical access to the sea for cargo generated in the northern and southern parts of Pakistan.

Gwadar makes strategic sense for China as currently, transportation of oil takes place from the Persian Gulf to Shanghai—an obvious vulnerability. Gwadar will eventually provide direct access to Xinjiang in Western China, assuming the Pakistani initiative of the Sino-Pakistani railway system comes to fruition. With rail links through Pakistan/POK/Gilgit and Baltistan, Gwadar is an alternative route for trade with Europe, although they are building long-distance rail connections through Central Asia anyway. More importantly, Gwadar would avoid the risk of a choke-point in the Straits of Malacca for their trade, especially their oil supplies, if they can instead ship the stuff through Pakistan, thus negating India's overwhelming geopolitical presence in the Indian Ocean. Thus, at one stroke, they are making themselves less vulnerable, and at the same vastly increasing their 'String of Pearls' capability to surround and contain India. The Americans call it the 'Chinese Gibraltar'. China might also have a long-term plan of eventually establishing a new oil and gas pipeline to Central Asia, provided the cost is not prohibitive and the Hindu Kush/Karakoram mountain ranges can be surmounted.

China is funding about $1.4 billion for the Hambantota Port Development Project near Dondra Head in the southern part of Sri Lanka. It will be Sri Lanka's largest port after Colombo. The first of the three phases of the Port opened in 2010. Upon completion, the port will cover 4,000 acres of land and accommodate 33 vessels at any given time, making it the largest port in South Asia replete with four terminals (12 berths), bunkering and refuelling facilities, an LNG refinery, aviation fuel storage facilities and dry docks.

The strategic advantage of the new port is that it is only six nautical miles from major SLOCs between the Bay of Bengal and Arabian Sea. Hitherto, the oil tankers bound to China, Japan and Korea had to make a detour of three-and-a-half days to Singapore and also to India, Thailand, and Malaysian harbours for refuelling, buying provisions, medical supplies and other essentials. The Colombo Port was never on the map of those tankers and other ships which sail close to Sri Lanka due to its location and limited capacity. The Hambantota Port would save nearly three days sailing time for them—a great saving for maritime operations.

It is not yet clear whether China plans to set up a naval base there. But if they could, or if they could obtain assurances regarding basic support in case of hostilities, it will be a formidable asset and could give Diego Garcia a run for its money. Once again, it should be kept in mind that the Chinese would not simply sink their money for altruistic reasons. Hambantota has the potential to become an island fortress analogous to that of Hainan Dao, guarding Chinese oil supply movements through the South China Sea.

CHINESE-FUNDED DEVELOPMENTS LOCATED ELSEWHERE IN THE INDIAN OCEAN

In November 2014, a Namibian paper had cited a Chinese media report to the effect that China planned to set up 18 naval bases in several places including Sri Lanka. All these development fit into what many experts make out of China's long-term naval strategy. The Namibian report had said that Walvis Bay of Namibia would be one of 18 naval bases to be established by Chinese in various countries including Pakistan, Sri Lanka and Myanmar in the northern Indian Ocean, Djibouti, Yemen, Oman, Kenya, Tanzania and Mozambique in the Western Indian Ocean and Seychelles and Madagascar in the central South Indian Ocean.

'STRING OF PEARLS' OR THE MARITIME SILK ROAD?

Officially, China maintains that it has only economic and commercial interests in the Indian Ocean Region (IOR). In fact, in late 2013, the Chinese President had spoken of the MSR (Maritime Silk Road) concept to convey that their interests were only economic. Some people say that the MSR and the 'String of Pearls' are essentially the same thing presented differently.

According to the 'String of Pearls' concept, China is seeking to expand its influence aggressively by consolidating its presence through the acquisition and construction of military and naval facilities and by improving relations with Indian Ocean island and littoral States, thus isolating India and reducing the role of the United States in the region. The idea is that in a war situation, the land-based operational logistics and command and control infrastructure could provide logistics support to the Chinese maritime forces. However, this makes sense only in the context of harassing shipping to and from Indian ports, or for a conventional naval war. Imposing a naval blockade is well-nigh impossible.

CONFLICT BETWEEN CHINESE ASPIRATIONS AND NAVAL CAPABILITIES

The Chinese say, "We can no longer accept the Indian Ocean as only an Ocean of the Indians." But they will have to first make it clear to themselves as to what exactly they want to do in the IOR? A 'Look West' strategy in response to India's 'Look East' strategy sounds good but unless they are able to define as to what exactly it means, it will be only rhetoric. The desire to "play a more pro-active role in affairs of the region" also needs elaboration. Desiring a 'Blue Water Navy' is fine but they should be clear as to what they expect the Blue Water Navy to do? Supposing the US chokes them in the Malacca Straits?

How exactly would they retaliate? Would they go nuclear? Can they afford to go nuclear?

Building a chain of forward bases and having access to several ports is good for maritime trade—they could help non-nuclear surface ships too. That, in turn, could help them undertake overseas military missions of expeditionary nature. However, non-nuclear surface ships can, at best, fire surface-to-air missiles, cruise missiles, anti-ship missiles or anti-submarine missiles. What can be achieved by this? They should not even think of fighting with the US Navy this way. The US Navy, with its great combat experience and resources, would simply decimate the Chinese who have no naval combat experience. And what could China possibly gain by indulging in a desultory exchange of missiles with India which is equally inexperienced, is not clear?

As we saw earlier, the PLA Navy has to cover a lot of ground. We have discussed the issues with their aircraft carriers. They are better off with their submarines, though. There is no real substitute for the power packed in a nuclear aircraft carrier based Carrier Strike Group/Carrier Battle Group. Even SSBNs would be of use only when they have to fire nuclear-armed missiles in a decisive strike. Though they can use their SSBN to fire nukes on India too, their real utility lies against the USA in attacking which China would fall short of ICBMs—Indian targets, on the other hand, are within the range of their other missiles also; why waste ICBMs on India?

It is this lack of conceptual clarity that is sought to be hidden under the cover of mysterious and vague or even contradictory terms. On one hand, the Blue Book of June 2013 claims that China will deepen its economic engagements with the Indian Ocean Region's (IOR) littoral States, and stresses that Beijing's interests will be driven by commercial objectives [that is, to protect the Sea Lanes of Communications (SLOCs) along the Indian Ocean, vital for the country's energy imports]—rather than military objectives. On the other hand, it warns that the Indian Ocean could end up "as an ocean of conflict and trouble" if countries like India, the US and China failed to engage with each other more constructively as their interests begin to overlap. What they have left unexplained is what they are prepared to do in case of a conflict and how?

CAN A NAVAL BLOCKADE STRATEGY WORK?

In view of the fact that the PLA Navy's capabilities are not commensurate with the massive dependence of the country on oil imports, several so-called experts have been arguing that India can impose a naval blockade of China. People have gone to the extent of saying that "a couple of submarines and a fighter squadron at Car Nicobar could easily enforce a declared blockade." Once again, the perils of compartmentalized thinking must be obvious. Even if we invest ₹60,000 crore or so on building up India's naval interdiction capability, it is childish to think that India can hold the entire Himalayan border to hostage. Moreover, it cannot be believed that the Chinese are not aware of the natural vulnerabilities of oil tankers and other merchant ships to attacks from the sea, underwater, or air. They have been applying a great deal of mind to a possible blockade by the USA.

A blockade is regarded an act of war. Above all, imposing a naval blockade is a complicated and rather slow operation. You cannot do it quickly and certainly not in the time frame in which a land offensive could produce tangible results. The TV-wallahs might erupt in glee over the sinking of some Chinese warships or some oil tanker going up in flames. But, unfortunately, it would have no bearing on what could possibly be going on in the land war. In fact, a maritime venture in isolation cannot be thought of.

There are three types of blockades. A close blockade is probably what most people think of, a fleet within weapons-range and probably in direct sight of the enemy. This works better for the TV or films. A loose blockade is a close blockade where the blockading ships are withdrawn out of sight from the coast (behind the horizon) but no farther. The object of loose blockade is to lure the enemy into venturing out but to stay close enough to strike. A distant blockade is beyond the defenders' weapons-range and probably beyond their direct sight as well. A distant blockade will take place on the open sea, such as the one imposed by the Royal Navy in the English Channel and North Sea in both World Wars.

The greater the volume of traffic to be prevented, the greater the blockade—and the greater the resources needed to maintain it. An ideal blockade would have to use multiple layers, with each layer having a different purpose. These layers should include (1) a distant conventional blockade focused on chokepoints of sea lines of communications to China; (2) a close, unconventional maritime engagement zone, and (3) diplomatic engagement to embargo points of embarkation. A blockade is, by its very nature, an effective strategy only for a protracted conventional war. The Chinese have no intention of fighting a protracted war even if the intensity of the exchanges is not high.

Those who are given to making sweeping jingoistic statements do not understand some complexities. The focal point of a blockade would be the Strait of Malacca and nearby archipelagic straits through Indonesia. These locations derive the protection of international law and the UN Convention of the Law of the Sea, which states that belligerents cannot operate in neutral waters. Consequently, to make the blockade legal, the countries bordering the Strait of Malacca must explicitly support a blockade, becoming belligerents themselves. While failing to gain Malaysia's support would be a surmountable challenge—it might simply move the blockade 12 miles outside the straits into international waters—Indonesia's support will make or break a blockade. Its archipelagic sea lanes (at least four basic routes) provide several corridors for blockade runners exploiting innocent passage. Without Indonesian support, only a United Nations Security Council Resolution allows closure of these sea lanes, and China's Security Council veto would never allow that.

As Jason Glab rightly points out,

> "even setting legalities aside, a blockade of the Strait of Malacca would be a complicated undertaking. Given the vast quantity of traffic that transits these chokepoints—much of it bound for allied or neutral countries—traditional methods of visit and search are challenging. Approximately 165 ships of all types transit the Strait of Malacca each day, of which 52 are oil tankers. A blockader would need to investigate all appropriate ships, evaluate whether they were blockade runners, and seize those that were. As many as thirteen warships would be required to enforce an oil blockade using traditional methods of visit and search. This number does not allow for force protection, replacements for material failures or prize crews. Additional ships would have to guard other passages such as the Lombok/Makassar straits. Increased insurance rates and risk-averse shippers would reduce that number of tankers destined for China; however, China's large national fleet and other Chinese owned merchants would still sail, and China's significant cash reserves could supplant traditional insurers. As such, the operational commander would still need to dedicate a squadron of significant size to blockade, revealing a major opportunity cost."

A close blockade focusing on Hong Kong, Shanghai and other major shipping hubs would be easier. This would demand submarines, mine warfare, and long range aircraft that would attack blockade runners that slipped through or around the chokepoints and entered a Maritime Exclusion Zone (MEZ).

> Even if the Indian Navy expands to say 50 capital ships by 2030 or so, it would still not be enough to impose a blockade successfully. At present, both the navies can only look forward to some occasional interdiction and nothing more.

In any case, China recognizes its reliance on foreign oil and has taken steps to reduce its vulnerability to supply disruptions. Specifically, China has established a robust strategic oil reserve. China's 2011 strategic oil reserve was sufficient to supply 100% of domestic consumption (factoring in domestic production) for 25 days without rationing. Improvements to this reserve are planned to more than double its duration by 2020, even factoring in an increase in Chinese oil demand. Then in a crisis, Russia could decide to support China with oil over land routes. Never forget that a naval blockade against a country with inferior naval power could work for a small island nation or a virtually landlocked nation like Germany with few ports. It cannot work for a huge country like China with many other means of transport.

CHAPTER 13

Two-Front and Two-and-a-Half-Front War

POSSIBILITY OF INDIA FIGHTING A TWO-FRONT WAR

CHINA INTERVENING IN INDIA-PAKISTAN WAR

When?

An India-Pakistan crisis can take place under numerous circumstances that we have already discussed at length. China is not so irresponsible as to be drawn into these compulsively. Past experience shows that they have behaved maturely. For over a decade, China has worked behind the scenes with the United States to manage crises between India and Pakistan, mainly by urging caution and restraint in conversations with top Pakistani leaders. That remains Beijing's preference. However, they would have a different perception if, perchance, the problems with Pakistan were to occur at the same time when they have their own irritations with India.

It is beyond dispute and debate that, being a strategic ally, China would, in a crisis, side with Pakistan. When they would intervene, depends on how they assess the situation and whether it really constitutes a crisis for Pakistan or not. It will be a proper military assessment. Experience suggests that unless the balance of power was to appear drastically tilted against Pakistan as a result of some categorical defeat, China would refrain from intervening. In the triangular power balance game, they would do everything to ensure that the South Asian military balance of power is neither pro-India nor pro-Pakistan, but pro-China. A

Chinese South Asia analyst at Fudan University in Shanghai, Shen Dingli, told *The Wall Street Journal* clearly: "China needs to send a message: For my own security, I will intervene." China's geopolitical imperatives demand that it must come to Pakistan's defence if the latter's very existence as a viable nation-state is threatened by India. The 'all-weather friend' and strategic partner cannot afford to remain a mute spectator. China cannot let Pakistan down now.

How?

The next million-dollar question is to what extent it would get involved if it decides to get involved at all. Some people cite the example of 1971 when it did not really do anything. But the China of the second decade of the 21st century is materially different from the China of 1971. It was a bipolar world then and China, in spite of having exploded its hydrogen bomb in 1967, was nobody before them as it lacked proper delivery vehicles. Now it is a uni-polar world and the Chinese have made great advances since then. This is not 1971—the world has changed; it is no longer the backyard of the NATO and the Warsaw Pact forces. China in 2016 is far stronger than what it was in 1971. Now China cannot back out of its long-term commitments to Pakistan. China has 'guaranteed Pakistan's territorial integrity' and in the words of the leaders of the two countries, their friendship is "higher than the mountains and deeper than the oceans."

Moreover, China's economic interests are far more spread out and intertwined than they were in 1971. It is imperative for them to aggressively protect those interests now—and it is not limited to just the economic corridor in Pakistan through Balochistan. Chinese covert assistance to Pakistan's nuclear and missile programme apart, Pakistan and China have now joint ventures for many important battlefield machines including tanks and planes. Besides the investments, their relationship with Pakistan runs deeper than economic interests. According to the Kanwa News, the Chinese leaders had clearly conveyed the following message to Gen Musharraf in 2002: "If a war does break out between India and Pakistan, Beijing will firmly stand on the side of Islamabad." Never mind what their leaders say when they visit India. Further, in my opinion, we cannot scare China by playing the 'Taiwan and Tibet cards'. If they had to be so scared, they would not risk provoking India so often for a direct conflict—and here we are talking of an indirect conflict!

Logically, the Chinese intervention should be in the form of war. However, depending on the gravity of the situation, even Chinese aggressive posturing during an India-Pakistan war would have to be viewed seriously because we cannot afford to lower our guard for a moment. Prudence demands that posturing be regarded as pregnant with the possibility of imminent attack.

Warning Signs to Look For

India should always view joint Chinese-Pakistan military exercises with suspicion, particularly with reference to their timing and place. They could also include increased Chinese arms sales to Pakistan. At diplomatic level also, warning signs could be felt in any sudden change in China's official diplomatic stance on Kashmir—shifting back to full support for Pakistan's favoured position—or action to support that position at the United Nations must be viewed with suspicion.

Readers may recall how in October 2016, days after India reviewed its use of water under the Indus Waters Treaty with Pakistan in the wake of the Uri attack, China announced that it had blocked a tributary of the Brahmaputra to facilitate work on one of its 'most expensive' hydropower projects in Tibet. The Lalho project on the Xiabuqu river, a Brahmaputra tributary, at

Xigaze in Tibet entails an investment of $740 million. While this announcement might be intended to only give India a scare, the timing of the development needs to be taken note of. It would be naive to argue that it has nothing to do with India's stance on the Indus Water Treaty. Moreover, a diversion of Brahmaputra waters remains an emotive, volatile issue in India's northeast, particularly Assam and Arunachal Pradesh.

PAKISTAN INTERVENING IN INDIA-CHINA WAR

If there is a crisis between India and China, Pakistan may decide to fish in troubled waters and add to the woes of India by opening up another front. China does not need their help but Pakistan would gain by the adventure. Superficially, it could appear that a two-front war is a two-front war and militarily it would be the same thing for India, whether China jumps in or Pakistan jumps in. But there is a difference. While China can rattle India merely by posturing, Pakistan will have to do more substantial things. This means that if Pakistan intervenes to take advantage of an India-China war, they would go whole hog, the purpose being to really choke India. They could also supplement China's efforts by making diversionary moves in Kargil or Siachen, so as to force our formations in Ladakh to 'look' both ways.

PURPOSEFUL TWO-FRONT WAR

There is a third possibility also. In this, China and Pakistan could, by prior design, attack India simultaneously. This would obviously be the worst-case scenario.

COMPLEXITIES OF A TWO-FRONT WAR

Indian Army officers may claim that now 'a proportionate focus towards the Western and North-Eastern fronts' has been accorded so as to 'strategically counter the stark military asymmetry with China in the Eastern sector.' It's very fine in sentiments but in a professional work like this it is my duty to apprise the readers of the complexities of two-front war.

Militarily, a two-front war is an extremely difficult proposition by any standards. The complexity of the challenges of two-front war is often lost sight of in bluster aimed at popular appeal for the hoi polloi. Any claim that we will hold off China, while we finish off Pakistan, and then turn to mop up China is not even juvenile bluster—it is outright infantile. The military history of the world stands witness, some of the greatest generals in history have floundered, have bitten dust in conducting two-front wars. The nation cannot afford the luxury of the so-called experts speaking in terms of generalities. Merely saying that we must improve our military capacity (can one be more vague than this); have greater focus on cyber, space, C4I and special operations capabilities (wars are not won by Special Forces—one must learn to distinguish between wars and skirmishes); have better rail, road infrastructure development on both fronts, which would enable force mobilisation with minimum delay (by God, are we waking up to this now? What have we done all these 70 years?); and better intelligence collection (Oh, oh. Are we realizing the importance of intelligence now?); would not help. We must have specifics to inspire confidence in the minds of the people—no operational secrets but certainly more than sweeping statements.

On the ground, the fact is the Indian armed forces do not have any recent combat experience of even a single-front war. It is preposterous to claim that we can, by working out on paper alone, acquire the capability to deal simultaneously with two fronts, and that too against two nuclear powers. That would be a reckless translation of rhetoric into doctrine. However, since we cannot wish away a two-front war, we will have to address this worst-case scenario in all the seriousness it deserves. Let no one lose sight of the fact that even if we have configured our forces in such a manner that the two theatres may operate independently of each other so as not to drain on each other's resources, the nation and national resources remains one—the psychological pressure of having been caught between two armies would be great on the Indian public.

AN UN-INTENDED POSITIVE SIDE-EFFECT OF A TWO-FRONT WAR

I foresee an unintended positive side-effect of a two-front war. As we saw above, China is likely to open the second front only when Pakistan is getting a serious drubbing at our hands. Opening another front would ease the pressure on Pakistan and thus actually help in raising their nuclear threshold. Thus, in a way, the second front would avert a nuclear exchange.

TWO-AND-A-HALF FRONT WAR

This term has been given to a hypothetical situation in which India might have to engage both Pakistan and China simultaneously besides conducting a serious counterinsurgency campaign inside. Though we have been conducting counter-insurgency operations since long, insurgencies would become important if the insurgents or terrorists launch on a systematic campaign of fifth-columnist action by way of disrupting communications and attacking Indian Army logistics.

The trouble-potential of the additional half front would depend on how skilled the terrorists are. If they know their job, they would employ their energy and resources in sabotaging the lines of communication and not waste time in attacking security forces (except attacks on convoys). All-time favourite targets of sabotage (even in hinterland) are power sub-stations; transformers; high voltage pylons (they would not bother to attack power stations, as they have security anyway); derailing rolling stock (particularly those connected with army efforts); passenger trains to spread panic; steel bridges; fuel dumps;

runways; grain godowns; mobile switching centres; and spreading rumours of biological/radiological and chemical warfare.

Most people do not know that modern society presents a million targets which the fifth-columnists can attack and which will directly or indirectly have an effect on the operations of the armed forces. And they do not really require a sympathetic population, even as it helps. Sabotage can be carried out by small groups. As I mentioned earlier, elementary techniques to destroy bridges are very much available in public domain and terrorists do not need any special ISI course for that. I had mentioned about a US Army Manual Explosives and Demolition, FM 3-34.214 (FM 5-250). Then there are numerous other sources also in public domain. There was a celebrated work called *Total Resistance*, originally published in German as *Der totale Widerstand: Eine Kleinkriegsanleitung für Jedermann* (*Total Resistance: A Guerrilla Warfare Manual for Everyone*). It was written in 1957 by a Swiss army officer Hans von Dach and was published by the Swiss Non-Commissioned Officers' Association (Schweizer Unteroffiziersverband, SUOV) to prepare the Swiss population for an occupation of Switzerland by Warsaw Pact forces, an eventuality then considered possible in the context of the Cold War. So popular was the book that it was reprinted five times. The book has been republished as pirated translations in dozens of languages in numerous countries. *TM 31-210 Improvised Munitions Handbook* is a United States Army technical manual available in public domain (for example, http://gunfreezone.net/wp-content/uploads/2016/03/improvised-munitions-handbook.pdf) and intended for the United States Special Forces describing manufacture of improvised weapons and explosives from readily available materials, from junk piles, common household chemicals and supplies purchased from regular stores. I mentioned only sort of 'official' sources. Much more stuff is available but I am refraining from mentioning them for obvious reasons. The purpose of telling you this is to inform you that creating a dedicated team of saboteurs is not at all difficult and we must be prepared to face that eventuality.

How we will fare in a two-and-a-half front war will depend on how skilled the saboteurs are. The ball is in their court. But if they are skilled, we are in for serious trouble. Being the large country that we are, we have so many assets to protect that even if we close down every single police station and pull out every single paramilitary man from internal security duties, even then we would find it nearly impossible to protect all of them.

CHAPTER 14

Chinese Nuclear Arsenal

WHY INDIA SHOULD BE WARY OF CHINESE NUKES AND MISSILES?

HOW MANY WARHEADS AND ICBMS THEY HAVE?

The Chinese may not have as many nukes as the Americans or the Russians. Even though they were able to explode their first hydrogen bomb way back in 1967 itself and that too in their sixth nuclear test, just 32 months after the test of their first fission device, they are still believed to have only 260-263 strategic nuclear warheads besides about 150 tactical nuclear warheads. Given the fact that the USA has 2,200 strategic warheads, this is pitifully small. It has remained a mystery as to why, with all the resources and determination at their command, did not go for making nuclear weapons on a large scale. If countries like India and Pakistan could make more than 100 warheads each or so, what prevented this giant from making warheads at least commensurate with the status it seeks? The Chinese are also poor in missiles. Once again, even as they have made excellent missiles—may be, some of the best in the world, including MIRV equipped missiles—they are very few in number. According to Nuclear threat Initiative they have just about 50-60 ICBMs; the US Department of Defense report "The Military and Security Developments Involving the People's Republic of China 2016" for the US Congress, puts this number at 75-100.

HOW DO THEY FIT INTO CHINESE STRATEGY?

With Respect to USA

Now the question is what they could have planned to do with these few missiles and warheads. The Americans are quite far from China. If the Chinese have to attack the US mainland, they have only two options: ICBMs or SLBMs. But given the very few ICBMs that they have, they do know that if they start a slugfest, the USA can decimate the country easily and reduce their second-strike capability seriously. A massive nuclear retaliation by the USA is a frightening prospect. ICBMs are also susceptible to being destroyed on the ground itself. SLBMs are safe but they have rather few of them. Hence, except for the threat of destruction of some cities (we cannot say how many), the USA ought not to be seriously worried by China. However, if they feel that the destruction of those cities is just not acceptable to the American people, then they have a lot to worry about.

With Respect to India

However, the situation with respect to India is materially different. We are close to China. They do not have to expend their ICBMs on us and they also know that we do not have as many nukes to retaliate as the Americans have. Moreover, since we have not been baptized by blood and fire, we are not as likely to sustain damage as the USA can. Remember, approximately 55% of China's missiles are in the medium range category, targeted at regional theatre targets. Even the smallest of their missiles, the DF-11 would almost touch Delhi, besides the entire North-East, parts of Uttar Pradesh and Bihar, and almost complete J&K, Himachal Pradesh and Punjab. The DF-15 would cover Delhi, Rajasthan, parts of Madhya Pradesh, Bihar and West Bengal in addition. The DH-10 would cover entire north, central and Eastern India—only

Bombay and south India will be spared. The DF-21 would cover Bombay also—parts of south India will remain. The DF-3 and all the missiles having range more than them would cover every inch of India. Hence the Indians should be more concerned about them.

They have up to 750 of the short-range missiles, that is, the DF-11, DF-15 and DF-10. They could have up to 200 of the DF-21. This means that they will have about 950 missiles which can cover almost entire India except parts of Karnataka, Kerala and Tamil Nadu. Hence the fact that they have very few ICBMs is no great solace to the Indians. It may be of some solace to the Americans—they have 450 land-based ICBMs carrying some 550 warheads; 288 SLBMs carrying as many as 1,152 warheads; and 500 warheads on their strategic bombers to give them comfort.

Chinese Technical Sophistication in Nuclear Weapons

Warhead Design

There are other reasons why we must be wary of the Chinese nuclear arsenal. They are far ahead of us in technical sophistication, miniaturization and design perfection of the nuclear devices. The Chinese thermonuclear warheads are so good that it left the Americans shocked, astounded, dumbfounded—in fact, the very prosecution and trial of the Taiwanese-born nuclear scientist Dr Wen Ho Lee working at Los Alamos National Laboratory in the USA was based on the false allegation of espionage of the design of the greatest American thermonuclear warhead W-88—the prosecution, of course, did not succeed, and in 2006 the federal government and five media organizations paid him $1.6 million in damages. The Americans could not simply digest the fact that what (that is, the design of the W-88 warhead) took them full five years (1984-89) and that too 32 years from the date they exploded their first thermonuclear bomb, the Chinese could do within 25 years of their first thermonuclear bomb by 1992 and in a total of just 21 tests or so till then.

Yields of Warheads

Most of their warheads are in the now world-standard state-of-the-art 200-300 kilotonne, 3.3 megatonne, and 4-5 megatonne categories whereas if our test explosions are any guide, we are still in the 10-40 kilotonne range. They have conducted 45 tests; we have conducted only two. They have also successfully made variable yield and enhanced radiation ('neutron bomb') devices. China's nuclear tests in the late-1980s and 1990s were geared toward further modernizing its nuclear forces. Although China officially declared in 1994 that these tests were for improving safety features on existing warheads, these tests were also intended for the development of new, smaller warheads for China's next-generation solid-fuel ICBMs (for example, DF-31 and DF-41) and also possibly to develop a multiple warhead (MRV or MIRV) capability.

Neutron Bomb

The subject of China's neutron bomb capability has been the subject of considerable public attention over the last several years. On September 29, 1988 China conducted a test of what is believed to have been a neutron bomb. It was a 1-5 kilotonne nuclear device with an enhanced radiation yield, advancing the country's development of a very low yield neutron weapon and laying the foundation for the creation of nuclear artillery. In fact, China publicly admitted in 1999—in response to the release of the Cox Report—that in the 1970s and 1980s China had "mastered in succession the neutron bomb design technology." In March 2000 a Chinese military newspaper threatened to use neutron bombs to capture Taiwan if it declared independence.

Comparison with India

They developed their first thermonuclear device in 1967 itself—just 32 months after they developed their first fission-based nuclear device; our so-called thermonuclear device in 1998 was doubtful. There is huge controversy about the claimed yields of the Indian devices of 1998 as the claims are not well supported by available scientific evidence. Scientists from all over the world had refused to accept them. They say that as far as the thermonuclear device is concerned, the boosted primary had performed correctly, but that the secondary stage had failed. Indian scientists, of course, refute it. In the photographs of the test site on nuclearweaponarchive.org, there is no crater seen for the Whiskey shaft of the thermonuclear device, whereas a subsidence crater 80 m across and 15 m deep is seen for the Tango shaft. There is no crater for the Kumbhkaran shaft. According to them, this device was apparently an experimental fission device using 'non-weapon grade' (reportedly reactor-grade) plutonium. It was probably a test of fusion-boosted device without the deuterium-tritium boost gas to prove the ability to use lower grade plutonium from India's large power reactor plutonium stockpile. The NT1 and NT2 craters are about 3.5-4 m across.

Just for the information of the readers, from information which is already in public domain, I may mention that 11 years after the tests, K Santhanam himself, the DRDO's Chief Adviser (Technologies), DRDO and a key figure in the Pokhran-II team, also called the thermonuclear test a 'fizzle'. [See, Manoj Joshi in *India Today*, August 27, 2009; Praful Bidwai in *Frontline*, Volume 26, Issue 19, September 12-25; and K Santhanam and Ashok Parthasarathi in *The Hindu*, September 17, 2009]. That led to further controversy. I am not discussing the subject further here for obvious reasons.

The point being made is that the Chinese had perfected their thermonuclear weapons (hydrogen bomb) in 1996 itself and were so confident of having perfected the design that they stopped testing thereafter. No one should lose sight of the fact that the Chinese have developed their nukes real fast and really well. The Americans had needed test of 1,151 devices over 47 years to achieve that level of perfection; the Soviets had needed 969 devices in 41 years. The Chinese needed just 45 tests in 29 years to reach the same level in technical sophistication as the Americans and the Soviets.

Hence, as far as India is concerned, the Chinese nuclear arsenal and their delivery platforms are a far more serious threat than what the Pakistanis pose.

ASSESSMENT OF CHINESE MISSILES

CHINA'S STRATEGIC MISSILE FORCE (SMF)

The Strategic Missile Force, also known as the Second Artillery Corps in a throwback to Soviet-style unglamorous nomenclature, is the strategic missile branch of the People's Liberation Army (PLA), controlling all of PRC's land-based strategic missile assets as well as the majority of its conventional theatre missile assets. Orders are passed down to operational units via a four-level chain of command: CMC, missile bases, missile brigades, and launch battalions. Currently the SMF has six operational missile bases, which are numbered from 51st to 56th.

In 2005, the DOD believed that China had some 793 to 916 ballistic missiles of various types. Of these, some 83 to 126 were thought to have ranges of 1,770 km to over 8,460 km. The JL-1 SLBM had a range of 1,770 km; the DF-21 (CSS-5) MRBM had a range of 1,770 km; the DF-3 (CSS-2) IRBM had a range of 2,790 km; the DF-4 (CSS-3) ICBM had a range of 5,470 km; and the DF-5 (CSS-4) ICBM had a range of 8,460 km. DF stands for Dong Feng which means 'East Wave'. The US designation CSS stands for Chinese Surface-to-Surface. This does not include the DF-15 (600 km) and DF-11 (300 km) which are in large numbers. At the time of the DOD report, some other missiles were under development. That included the DF-31 ICBM with a range of 7,250 km and the DF-31A ICBM with a range of 11,270 km.

Why is China modernizing its nuclear arsenal when it signed the CTBT in 1996 itself? Three primary explanations exist. First, China may simply wish to update their aging weapons systems and replace them with more modern systems. Second, China may be seeking a stronger fighting capacity to increase the survivability of its nuclear deterrent. As other countries (particularly the United States) continue to increase their military capabilities, China feels more vulnerable. From Desert Storm through the 2003 war in Iraq, the United States has continuously demonstrated its ability to use conventional forces to destroy fixed targets with tremendous accuracy. US efforts to develop a ballistic missile defence system also threaten the deterrence capability of China's nuclear forces. China's leaders fear that their older nuclear forces are vulnerable or ineffective as a deterrent, and should be replaced by newer, more mobile, more survivable nuclear forces and ICBMs such as the DF-31 and DF-41 missiles. Finally, China's efforts to increase its nuclear capabilities may indicate an important, yet undeclared, shift toward a more aggressive nuclear policy.

HOW CAPABLE THEY ARE IN MIRVS?

It is believed that some of the missiles will indeed have MIRVs. According to the Pentagon, China has started to place multiple independently targetable re-entry vehicles, or MIRVs, on its

DF-5B missile. It might place MIRVs on the DF-41 as well. China's smallest warhead weighs about 500 kg. The silo-based, liquid-fuelled DF-5B—the only multiple-warhead missile Beijing has deployed thus far—has an estimated throw-weight—or lifting power of 3,000 kg. It would be hard for China to fit more than three 500-kg warheads plus a 1,500-kg post-boost vehicle on the DF-5B. To add more warheads to this missile, China would need to develop smaller warheads, a challenging feat as long as Beijing adheres to the CTBT and refrains from testing new warhead designs.

The DF-41 is a Chinese nuclear solid-fuelled road-mobile intercontinental ballistic missile in the flight-test stage of development. It has an operational range between 12,000 km to 15,000 km. This would make the DF-41 the world's longest range missile, surpassing the range of the US LGM-30 Minuteman which has a reported range of 13,000 km. The claims will have to be viewed in the backdrop of the fact that other modern mobile missiles—such as the Russian SS-25 (Topol) and SS-27 (Topol-M)—have throw-weights in the 1,000-1,200-kg range only. Hence how could the DF-41 carry more than 3 warheads is difficult to believe. The Federation of American Scientists asserts that despite having the theoretical ability to develop MIRV payloads, China has not deployed or even flight tested MIRV buses or MRV delivery payloads due to the high cost of development and deployment. As a scientist, I too have doubts for the same reasons.

QUALITATIVE EDGE: MARV AND SUPER-CARRIER KILLER MISSILE

The Americans take great pride in their carrier groups—the most visible and fascinating projection of American military might across the high seas. The carriers maintain the dominant American influence in the East Asian waters and counterbalance the threat of the globally emerging China. The carrier groups, based on 95,000 tonne super-carriers, pack so much fighting force that they were thought to be invincible. Any attacking aircraft or cruise missile could be shot down by its aircrafts or point defence systems. Well, no longer so. The US Department of Defense has confirmed the existence of the DF-21D land-based ASBM system (Anti-Ship Ballistic Missile), which is the world's first and only of its kind. This will be a 'smart missile'. By combining Manoeuvrable Re-Entry Vehicles (MaRVs) with a terminal guidance system, the DF-21C is capable of targeting a slow-moving aircraft carrier battle group from a land-based mobile launcher and has earned the soubriquet of Super-Carrier Killer. The missile can be launched from land and strike an aircraft carrier 900 miles away. China has 11,200 miles of coastline. That fact coupled with the range and accuracy of the new missile could spell doom for any US or allied carrier fleet.

THE KT SERIES ANTI-BALLISTIC MISSILE/ANTI-SATELLITE MISSILE

In March 2006, China tested an interceptor system comparable to the US Patriot missiles. In January 2007, they tested their first anti-satellite (ASAT) weapon based on a kinetic kill vehicle (KKV). In January 2010, it announced a successful mid-flight ABM test. In addition to ABM capability, China's missiles also possess ASAT capabilities. On January 11, 2010, China has officially announced a successful land-based high-altitude anti-ballistic missile test. If the test was truly successful, this brings China the second country in the world after the United States of America to achieve such a test, therefore closing the gap quicker than anticipated in ABM development in comparison.

KT series anti-ballistic/anti-satellite missiles is reportedly a series of highly classified and thus little known missiles based on DF-21. Four models of KT series have been developed so far, including KT-1 and KT-1A (designed to engage sub-orbital targets), KT-2 [designed to engage low earth orbit (LEO) targets at altitude up to 600 km], KT-2A (designed to engage polar orbital targets) and KT-III (designed to engage targets at altitude 1,000 km or higher).

CHINA'S CRUISE MISSILES

The oldest and domestically developed Chang Feng series of land attack cruise missiles are rather large and heavy, necessitating their deployment on land-based platforms only. Since it was desirable to develop air-launched cruise missiles, they developed the Hong Niao (HN, meaning Red Bird) family of cruise missiles which are turbofan powered and the latter two of them are based on the variants of the Russian Kh-SD/65. The HN-1 has a range of 600 km, the HN-2 has a range of 1,800 km, and the HN-3 has a range of 3,000 km.

The Chang Jian-10 (meaning Long Sword) is a cruise missile developed by China, based on the Hong Niao missile family. It has a range of 2,200 km. Although not confirmed, it is suspected that the CJ-10 could carry nuclear warheads. An air-launched variant (named CJ-20) has also been developed. It made its first public appearance during the military parade on the 60th Anniversary of the People's Republic of China. A similar naval cruise missile, the YJ-62, was also revealed during the parade.

The Dong Hai 10 (DH-10, meaning East Sea) is a second-generation land-attack cruise missile (LACM), with over 4,000 km range, integrated inertial navigation system, GPS, terrain contour mapping system, and digital scene-matching terminal-homing system.

At least some of the cruise missiles can indeed be expected to be armed with tactical nuclear warheads.

A stealthy, supersonic cruise/anti-ship missile called HN-2000 has been reported to be under development. It is reported to be equipped with a millimetre wave radar, infrared image mapping, synthetic aperture radar (SAR), and Beidou satellite guidance. It will have an accuracy of up to 1-3 metres and a range of 4,000 km.

A qualitative difference, particularly with regard to the USA, would arise if China is able to develop nuclear-armed submarine launched cruise missiles.

CHINA'S RATIONALE OF KEEPING TACTICAL NUCLEAR WEAPONS

According to the 'Nuclear Threat Initiative', they are believed to have about 150 tactical nuclear warheads on their short-range ballistic missiles and cruise missiles. We have discussed Pakistan's rationale of keeping TNWs. What makes China keep them when they are not inferior in conventional forces? The Lexington Institute says there is evidence the PLA considers tactical nuclear weapons to be a useful element of an anti-access strategy, particularly with regard to its navy which, admittedly, has to operate from a position of inferiority vis-a-vis much bigger and experienced Western navies. In addition to the nuclear-capable ballistic missiles, China is reported to have nuclear mines for use at sea and nuclear anti-ship missiles. At the very least, China would expect the presence of these weapons and the threat to use them to be a significant deterrent to any rash American action.

But there is evidence that they intend to use it elsewhere too. In June 1982, a joint service exercise included a simulated tactical nuclear detonation. The DIA believes that they might have proof-tested a tactical nuclear weapon delivered by an old F-9 [Q-5] ground attack aircraft.

CHAPTER 15

Nuclear War with China

INDIA'S NUCLEAR CONCERNS WITH CHINA

CHINA'S NUCLEAR DOCTRINE

There is not much informed public debate in India regarding India's strategic position with respect to China. Most people would agree that China, with its vast arsenal of both conventional and nuclear weapons and its great strategic depth, presents a formidable military problem—something even the US would be vary of fiddling with without a great deal of thought and preparation.

Moreover, the Chinese maintain such great secrecy about their doctrines that nobody is sure of their expected responses to various situations. The whole world knew how the US and the USSR thought; the whole world does not know how the Chinese think. The Chinese may react in rather strange or unexpected ways, and the lessons derived from the Cold War may not be of any help in dealing with them. In fact, fighting even a conventional war with China is a daunting and disquieting task.

REAL OBJECTIVE OF CHINA'S NUCLEAR STRATEGY

Little is known about China's real nuclear strategy. They are adept at speaking in confusing, poetical, and almost mystical terms. However, from their often aggressive posturing over several contentious issues and frenetic missile developments it is clear that China is developing and building capabilities to have impact much beyond Asia. In fact, their Dong Feng 41 (NATO designation CSS-X-10, tested on December 13, 2014), has a range of 12,000-15,000 km, much more than that of the famous Minuteman ICBM of the USA. The DF-5A (CSS-4) also had a range of 13,000 km. This can only mean that China is preparing a force meant to challenge and deter the United States itself. Because the US has the largest nuclear arsenal in the world and continues to pursue the nuclear strategy based on the policy of 'first-use' of nuclear weapons, China says that it feels compelled to maintain the minimum nuclear deterrence capability. If the US increases the number of interceptors of its missile defence system, China has to raise its nuclear warhead count.

From this it would appear that they seek global superpower status and their problems with India assume a secondary place in their overall scheme of things. As far as India is concerned, it would be prudent not to waste time deciphering the real intentions of the Chinese. They are known to have behaved in an unpredictable manner. But we would do well to take note of the Chinese ability to survive a first strike. I have discussed it a little later.

Officially, they have gone through several phases: from the 1964 'No First Use' policy to 'Doctrine of Assured Retaliation' (as against the Doctrine of Assured Destruction practised by the USA and the USSR) to laying emphasis on 'Surviving Nuclear Strikes', the current concept of 'Minimum Deterrence', the 'self-defensive nuclear strategy' (supposedly involving 'counterattack in self-defence' and 'limited development' of nuclear weapons), and developing the 'Integrated Nuclear War-Fighting System'.

Within the framework of assured retaliation, an implicit assumption was that China could absorb a first strike. From that point on, China began to establish air-raid shelters, some of which could withstand nuclear attack, on a big scale throughout the country. In 1972, Chairman Mao put forward the concept of "Digging deep shelters, accumulating food in big stockpile, and not seeking hegemony." That became the national strategy of China.

In 1979, the Central Committee of Chinese Communist Party had made the decision to build the 'The Underground Great Wall Project' comprising over 3,000 miles of tunnels, the purpose of which was to make China's land-based strategic nuclear force have the capability to survive and retaliate after suffering from a first nuclear strike by other countries. The Project, under the Second Artillery, was completed in 1995. Since then, the Chinese land-based strategic nuclear force has had underground positions for fighting, defending, being deposited, commanding and living. Even if struck by nuclear warheads launched from other countries, China's land-based strategic nuclear force can retaliate in 10 minutes, after a few days, or even one month of living in the underground bunkers.

NUCLEAR EXCHANGE WITH CHINA

POSSIBLE TARGETS FOR CHINESE NUCLEAR STRIKES

If the Chinese attack India with nukes, it would, in all probability, be by a megatonne range thermonuclear warhead (their 3 MT warhead). It does not make any sense for the Chinese to use kilotonne range warheads on India as they would not achieve any worthwhile purpose. Moreover, it is very likely that they would restrict the use to just one bomb. In that case, the ideal target would be Delhi. The idea would be to obliterate the Indian command structure in one go and force India to immediately terminate hostilities and surrender outright. It makes eminent sense for them—settle the issue by one heavy nuclear punch on the Indian nerve/command centre. They do not have any good reason to indulge in a nuclear slugfest with India. They would like the issue to be decided in one go with some finality.

Pakistan does not have megatonne hydrogen bombs. Hence they cannot, even if they wish to, take out Indian command structure in one strike—and they would be reluctant to use multiple strikes for fear of even more serious retaliation. China can sustain considerable nuclear damage and hence they can afford to be more 'adventurous' in nuclear strikes. But militarily, the safest option for them is to take out the command structure in one strike (so that they are not accused of having used more than one nuke) and end the war for a long time.

The second possibility, albeit remote, is what we have discussed for Pakistan. That is, to keep it demonstrative in character so that the Indian leadership survives and is forced to negotiate from a position of disadvantage. Who will negotiate from how much position of disadvantage, will depend on how well he has been able to sustain that damage and how much public pressure has been built upon the leadership by the people and the media. The Chinese, by the very nature of their society, have a distinct advantage over India in this regard.

POSSIBLE TARGETS FOR INDIA AGAINST CHINA

Since India does not have megatonne range devices, it can only damage a huge city like Shanghai or Beijing but not obliterate them. India can think of multiple strikes on a single city but China may react to it vehemently. India must clearly understand that given the huge size of China and the nature of the political system and the society, Indian can theoretically exhaust all its nuclear warheads on China and even then China would be able to survive. On the other hand, the Indian public would not be willing to or capable of sustaining the damage by multiple strikes. As indulging in a nuclear slugfest with China is therefore not a viable option. The best option is to avoid a nuclear showdown with China.

CHINESE OBSESSION WITH SURVIVABILITY

EMPHASIS ON ROAD-MOBILE MISSILES

Historically, and for quite understandable reasons, the Chinese leaders knew it too well in the early years that if their tiny nuclear force had to count at all in front of the superpowers; survivability had to be a major concern for them. Accordingly, China's ballistic missile force has been made predominantly mobile since the 1960s, and more than half of China's long-range missile force is mobile even today. We hear rumours of Chinese road-mobile missiles being hidden in caves. Several Chinese airbases that have been examined with satellite images also have large underground facilities that may be used to hide aircraft and weapons, but could potentially also serve as shelters for mobile missile launchers. The Second Artillery Corps is learnt to conduct 'Red vs Blue confrontation exercises' where missile launchers disperse from their bases to pre-designated launch points hundreds of miles away. In one such exercise in January 2005, they moved as much as 620 miles or a 1,000 km.

We must keep in mind that the deployment of mobile missile units comes with considerable operational and logistical challenges—there are also special Communication, Command and Control (C3) complications that come with operating mobile forces. The vehicles must constantly remain in touch with each other; breakdowns, if any, must be very quickly repaired or might come under enemy attack. If, in spite of these complexities, the Chinese still persist with road-mobile missiles, it would mean that they have found ways to overcome these problems.

UNDERGROUND FACILITIES FOR AIRCRAFTS

The US intelligence community believes China has a large number of underground facilities. They may not all be 'hard and deeply buried', but placing important assets underground in some form seems to be a common element of China's military planning. One example of this is the Feidong Airbase which includes a long taxiway that connects the main base and runway with a large underground facility inside a nearby mountain. To me it seems a rather primitive way to protect aircrafts. If the adversary can identify and locate these facilities accurately enough, a couple of precision weapons can seal the entrances or exits to a tunnel trapping all the aircraft inside.

THE THIRD LINE: A WHOLE COUNTRY UNDER THE GROUND?

Between 1964 and the mid- to late-1970s, China carried out a massive construction programme, in effect building a duplicate industrial base in the remote regions of China to serve as a strategic reserve in the event of war, initially foreseen with the United States and later with the Soviet Union. This project, called the 'Third Line', encompassed mining, energy production, railways, hydroelectric power, steel factories, and machine building. Many of the new sites were concentrated in the Western and South-Western provinces of Sichuan, Yunnan, Guizhou, Gansu, Ningxia and Qinghai, as well as parts of Shaanxi, Henan, Hubei and Hunan, away from the more vulnerable coastal cities and provinces. In general, the Chinese tried to use topography for protection, building in narrow valleys or near mountains. The scale of the undertaking was enormous, much larger than Roosevelt's New Deal or Stalin's Five-Year Plan. The Third Line was accomplished in great secrecy and even today it is not well-known or discussed.

NAVAL BASES UNDER THE SEA

China is learnt to have built underground facilities at naval bases. DIA estimates that the facilities have two purposes: storage of missiles, ammunition and logistics; and protection against a pre-emptive nuclear strike. One of these underground facilities is located at the Jianggezhuang base approximately 15 miles east of Qingdao on the Yellow Sea—sort of a gigantic artificial sea cave, camouflaged and hardened against attack. The base comprises multiple shelters, each of which has a number of facilities to load and unload nuclear fuel roads, move supplies, monitor the performance of various subsystems, repair breakdowns, and conduct demagnetization. The cavernous shelter where the boats are docked is believed to be as high as a 12-storey building. Large-sized cranes in this shelter can load or off-load the SLBMs. The base appears to be the homeport for China's solitary Type 092 Xia-class SSBN. The base is probably used by Han-class nuclear-powered attack submarines also.

LIKELY US POSITION IN THE EVENT OF AN INDIA-CHINA CONFLICT

THEIR BUSINESS INTERESTS PARAMOUNT

The US has, by itself, assumed the role of an international arbiter and one who pretends to be the most responsible nation in the world. It is a different thing that Russia and China do not care about this attempt of theirs at domineering. Let us look at it this way. What is the interest of the US in the affairs of India and China? Why should they bother even if India and China decide to nuke each other to their hearts' content and reduce each other to rubble? The radioactive fallout would not reach the American mainland. And, by God, they do not have any right to invoke the 'Butterfly effect' (that something small happening somewhere on the planet could have a larger effect somewhere else)—by that logic, all that they have been doing since the Second World War should have had profound impact all over the world. Then what is their concern?

By all means, their concern is and could be nothing but economic. Their main concern would be that an India-China war could roil international markets and exacerbate fears in other Asian capitals about Chinese assertiveness. Then the setbacks resulting to the Chinese and Indian economies as a result of the war could potentially harm US investors, retailers, manufacturers, and service providers. That is their major concern because they are the 'nation of industrialists and businessmen' in much the same way as England was the 'nation of shopkeepers'. Everything else about the desire to maintain peace etc is pure rhetoric for the consumption of the intellectually challenged people and the sycophants of the US—they do not think of peace when they bombard other nations to Stone Age.

EVENTUAL PRO-INDIA TILT

But the dilemma of the US is that both countries are important trading partners for the US. They would not like to lose the money on either side. Beijing would likely perceive any US support to India as part of an unwelcome US strategy to contain China. The US would certainly want to avoid worsening of relations with China to such an extent that swords might have to be drawn. But if Washington were to remain neutral or favour China's position, India could perceive US policies as abandonment. That could jeopardize prospects for US-India strategic partnership (read massive arms sale by American companies or sales of other cost-intensive items). The Americans are certainly more interested in selling things to India—China is not going to place such heavy orders which would make even the mighty USA salivate! China may be a great trading partner but India is a great buyer! Moreover, the US also knows that a humiliating Indian retreat from a crisis with China (for example, pulling back from Indian claims along the LAC) would undercut US efforts to support India's rise as a regional and international power and a counterweight to China—it is only to such an entity to which it can sell things of billions upon billions of dollars. A US failure to back India in the face of Chinese military intimidation would also weaken the US government's ability to reassure its East Asian allies elsewhere, including those along the South China Sea.

Further, in such a difficult situation, their ultimate decision would also be guided by their assessment of post-war behaviour of these two countries. If the USA analyses the behaviour of India and China over the decades, it will have no option but to conclude that India will be a more manageable, more malleable, more accommodative, and more docile 'customer' than even a 'defeated' or 'crushed' China. In the end, the USA is more likely to lend its weight in support of India—after that it is only a matter of finding some diplomatic jargon to couch it—such as resolving the crisis on terms that would promote a closer US partnership with India.

WHAT THE US COULD POSSIBLY DO?

In international diplomacy, short of providing active military aid, everything else is just different shades of posturing, verbose rhetoric, or dissimulation. There is nothing radical or innovative that seems possible for the US in this delicate game which seeks to preserve and maximize their long-term economic interests. The US could encourage, facilitate or perhaps even arbitrate a China-India dialogue on territorial disputes. Theoretically, the US could engineer trilateral dialogues or even quadrilateral dialogues involving Pakistan too. The option of leveraging Track II and shuttle diplomacy is always there. The Americans are good at offering the bogey of technical services too. For example, they could try to buy time by offering its satellite imagery of the LAC for help in dispute resolution talks.

In the world of realpolitik, one must clearly understand that the basic role of the US would be to somehow provide a face-saving device to any party that is prepared to back out of its pre-war posture but is reluctant to do for fear of losing out on domestic public opinion. The US efforts may be given any name, 'honest broker' or whatever, their purpose remains unchanged.

A military posturing does not appear likely. It is not 1971 and sending a carrier group would not be a wise idea. That could actually provoke China into doing something rash on India. That time, we must not forget, the Americans were deterred by the mere announcement of the movement of a Soviet nuclear sub. The Chinese do not have that patience. And there is good reason for it. Let us not forget that there is still hell of a difference in their military might and that of the Soviet Union in 1971. The PLA Navy has no chance before the US Navy—the Russians had a credible chance. This means that if the US intends to threaten China by its naval might, the Chinese might hasten to end the conflict by nuking Delhi with a megatonne blast.

> Pakistan they can arm-twist; China they cannot. It would be impolitic at the time of India-China tension to announce some major arms sales (or imminent deliveries) to India, though the trick might well work in the case of India-Pakistan tension.

CHAPTER 16

Why India as a Nation Might not Win a War even as Its Armed Forces Could Win?

ARMIES WIN BATTLES; NATIONS WIN WARS

HISTORICAL APATHY OF THE PEOPLE TOWARDS A 'NATIONAL' CAUSE

For all practical purposes, a nation means, primarily, its people—it's the people who 'create' the nation. Now, the popular refrain amongst the people, the media and the TV studios is that Pakistan and China need to be 'taught a lesson'. Incidentally, mutual contempt and hatred can go to any length and subjugate reason. In July 1914, the German Kaiser had famously declared that he "hated the Slavs, even though one should not hate anyone." The nation of Pakistan is perhaps the last thing that the Indians hate and vice versa. But the question is do we have the resolve and the strength of character as people to carry our bluster to its logical end?

Throughout the course of history, Indians are one of those few races that have learnt to live with utter ignominy. That's how we were repeatedly subjugated—whether by Muhammad Ghauri, the Mughals, the Portuguese, the French or the British. From the Second Battle of Tarain in 1192 AD (which Prithviraj Chauhan lost to Muhammad Ghauri) to the end of the Mutiny in 1858, they suffered continuous subjugation. Yet, even as there were isolated pockets and episodes of glorious resistance (such as by Maharana Pratap), the Indians never revolted en masse. Why? There are two reasons for it.

The first is political. Indians were never fired as a nation or as a large group for the simple reason that they were never a nation in the sense the word is used in modern European political theory—when we speak of Indians, basically for convenience, it refers only to a socio-religio-cultural construct bound by fate to have been born in the same geographical entity—otherwise, there was nothing called an Indian. It was only the genius Chanakya who first understood this fundamental weakness and tried to enforce the semblance of nationalism by invoking the concept of 'rashtra'. However, it lasted only as long as the imperial sceptre was wielded strongly enough. The people never participated in this experiment of nationhood willingly.

The second reason is psychological. It is not that the Indians were cowards by nature or that some of them did not know how to wield weapons. On an individual level, we have always had highly valiant people and great fighters. Yet we never revolted en masse against the conquerors because we did not care. We did not care because we were absolutely apathetic. That's how the Indians made it into a habit to endure ignominy—the lot of the people at large was going to remain the same irrespective of who ruled them. They were more bothered about their immediate surroundings and their own survival than what was happening thousands of kilometres away. Who cared what happened in the distant capital (the rajdhani) which they had only heard about; what happened in their village and nearby was more important. The fortunes of the capital would not have any bearing on their own fortunes. When their own honour and well-being was worthless, when nobody gave a damn whether they ate or starved, how could they ever bother about the abstract concept of the honour of something called a nation or State?

For the vast multitudes, there was never any nation or State—only rulers, and they could not care less who the ruler was. That made them into materialists, fatalists and above all, disinterested, disenchanted and apathetic to the affairs of those in power. We never wanted the house that we have built with a lifetime's savings to be reduced to a heap of rubble for the cause of the ruler—the nation could be laid waste by an invader, who cared?

The people knew that wealth has had traditionally been cantered in few hands—they were, in any case, going to sleep on at most a single meal a day only. Most readers would not know that till the food grain production in India became respectable following the introduction of hybrid wheat, the availability of food grains was so low that millions upon millions of people in the rural areas ate only one square meal a day—the other meal even for the not-so-poor was just jaggery and water or something like sweet potatoes, etc. Hence having a ruler of their own religion or racial stock did not make any difference to anybody. Precisely for this reason, the masses refused to take part in any movement, however inspired it might have been. Had the people of this geographical entity called India risen as a whole against the British, they could have butchered the last of them with ease. They did not need any great generalship for that; after all there were not more than 44,000 of the British soldiers in India at that time and they would have run out of bullets had we simply swamped them. But we did not do it because there was no motivation for it. On the contrary, hundreds of thousands of Indian soldiers in the employ of the British fought against their own people—many rulers happily, openly colluded with the British and reaped rich rewards after that.

The same thing happened in 1942 also. Have you ever seriously thought how could the British control it effectively by March 1943 itself? In 1942, the British were extremely hard pressed in the Second World War and were suffering military reverses everywhere since September 1939. On a military plane, the Second World War presented them with the most dangerous prospect everywhere—from Dunkirk to the Battle of Britain, everything seemed to be sounding the death knell for the Empire; everywhere the Empire managed to hang by the skin of their teeth. Their first battlefield victory came at El Alamein in December 1942 only. In spite of all these difficulties, they, with a notional British army presence left in India and largely with the help of the Indians in the bureaucracy and the police, still managed to effectively contain the movement. If you read the accounts of British administrators and police officers of that period, you will find that they were always supplied with abundant intelligence against the movement—all from 'informers' within our own people—which helped them make arrests on a large scale.

I am myself the son of noted freedom fighters; both of my parents carried huge cash rewards on their heads, remained underground for full five years and could never be arrested by the British, in spite of all their hectic efforts. The 1942 movement has been discussed in my family every day till they lived. But we will have to face reality and this should not be misconstrued as an attempt to belittle the significance and the contribution of the Quit India Movement in the history of our freedom struggle. Still, no one can deny that had the people really risen en masse; had there really been massive unrest across the country; had there really been an uprising; had the British police not been supplied with abundant intelligence by the informers; a beleaguered Empire would have been forced to pack off. On their own, the British race did not have enough resources to contain such a huge restive population.

What made a very large number of Indians continue to support the British? It was the same phenomenon which we have witnessed throughout the course of history. I have reasons to believe that, as far as the psyche of the average Indian is concerned, nothing has changed even now. This will have a profound impact on the ability of the nation to withstand the horrors of a war. Because the modern Indians are so materialistic; because they attach so much significance to their lives, possessions and status quo; they will make themselves believe that defeat is better than destruction of whatever they have. Indians are so used to living under subjugation that we would not be surprised that they agree to even surrender. What Humphrey Hawksley wrote in his fiction *Dragon Fire* about India surrendering after China nukes Delhi, could well become reality because that fits excellently into the Indian mind-set.

DEARTH OF A STRONG NATIONAL CHARACTER

Wars are fought as much by the national character of a nation as they are fought with military hardware. Indian people will crack much before the Indian military ever cracks or does not crack at all. (For a full analysis of the subject, interested readers must refer to our treatise *Indian Defence: Crisis and Challenges*.) The stoic character of the British people was more important than the underground Cabinet War Rooms in London. The faith of the German people in their Fuhrer and the faith of the Japanese in the 'divinity' of the emperor was the most critical factor in enabling them to endure the terrible destruction unleashed upon them in the strategic bombing campaign of the Allies than the war-fighting capacity of the respective nations. The lack of a strong national character is the Achilles Heel of India. We have never exhibited any trace of such character—how else can we explain centuries of subjugation?

HOW MEDIA AND OTHER OPINION-BUILDERS HAVE EMASCULATED THE NATION?

The aforementioned sense of apathy has been bolstered, albeit indirectly by the media. They have taken pains to promote consumerism, materialism, hedonism, and selfishness—all in the name of dreams like 'success', 'good times', 'progress', 'your signature of having arrived', and so on. The average Indian of this age clings ever so desperately to his possessions, his 'achievements' in life, and his 'way of life', that there is nothing more horrifying to him than the merest hint of some such cataclysmic events that could upset his status quo. And what could be more cataclysmic than a war—when bombs could fall on factories, businesses, railways, airports, and markets, and in which you could lose your 'assets', job, limbs or even life? No, no, war is not for them!

In times of peace, the media works overtime to project, protect and perpetuate the interests of the upper class people, the business houses and the industrialists. Where does the common man fit in this? Why do they bombard him with those dreams? It is a simple matter of perception management. The common man, even if his purchasing power be not that high at an individual level, still presents a massive market by virtue of their sheer numbers. To him shall be sold what the business houses and industrialists make. To cite just one example, the media teaches you to 'work hard and party hard'—by working hard you serve your industrialist/businessman employer better; by partying hard, you spend in hotels, restaurants, shopping malls and generally consume what the industries produce, and more than what you really need.

Now consumerism is diametrically opposed to the very concept of sacrifice and suffering for a cause other than your personal matters. The media and their 'hired' opinion-builders work assiduously to inject a pathological fear of suffering in the minds of the people. By instilling consumerism in the collective subconscious of the people, the Indian media and their 'hired' opinion-builders have weakened, enfeebled and emasculated the entire nation. In fact, the Indian media has not even tried to 'inform' the people about the horrors of a total war. If at all they do, it is to scare, not to prepare the people.

And they are clever people. Lest they ever be accused of not being patriotic enough, they take great care to bombard you with patriotic songs and films also on certain occasions like August 15 and January 26. Films like 'Border' (based on the Battle of Longewala in 1971) and 'LOC' (based on the Kargil war) were repeatedly televised even before the India-Pakistan cricket match in the semi-finals of the Cricket World Cup 2011—the purpose: to build a mania so that more and more people buy tickets to watch the match and a much larger number watches it on TV, all to the benefit of the organizers, the channels and the sponsors. For the rest of the year, they want you to concentrate on business and pleasure—that is, things that have a more direct bearing on their profits.

The combined effect of all this onslaught of 'perception management' has been to turn Indians into a people who are not prepared to sacrifice or endure suffering for the nation. The army of India could perhaps be very well prepared for fighting battles and winning them; India as a nation is mentally absolutely unprepared for fighting a war and endure all its horrors to such an extent that it finally emerges victorious.

WHAT WE LACK AS A 'PEOPLE' TO WIN A WAR?

INDIANS JUST LOVE A WAR, BUT ON TV

It's our traditional 'Indian subcontinent' culture—we do love to make a lot of noise, threatening postures and hurl abuses—when it comes to hurling punches, we think otherwise. We have great desire to fight, but not a great will to fight. We would love to beat the shit out of each other, but cannot bring ourselves easily to actually do it. Our verbal tirades are sort of masturbatory activity, a way of letting off stream.

Supposing both sides somehow muster the will to fight, what will happen next? For the first few days or hours of a war the media will go ballistic. Embedded journalists will provide you a blow-by-blow account of the battles with graphics and animated battle scenes. You will have a bevy of all the be-medalled, be-whiskered retired officers of the armed forces swarming the TV studios for expert comments and debates. There will be repeated visuals of the Bofors howitzers booming; the T-90 tanks rumbling across the desert amidst clouds of dust; and some lusty bayonet charges with familiar battle cries. Footage of our Su-30s, Mirage-2000s, MiG-29s and Rafales streaking across the skies at supersonic speeds and firing their rockets will be played continuously. That's standard stuff and we have seen it in an era when the newsreel of Films Division was played in cinema halls.

Emotions sell fast in such times—hence tales of the heroic deeds of young, fair, good-looking and recently-married officers and *jawans* will flood the channels. There will be emotionally charged 'human stories' on 'heroes in making' and interviews with their family members, girlfriends, primary school teachers and buddies. With martial music playing in the background, highly excited anchors in tight business suits will tell you that our forces have advanced so many miles inside enemy territory and how the Pakistani or the Chinese army is in full retreat leaving thousands of their dead behind. Kids all across the country will welcome it with lusty hoorays. The question is, what will happen afterwards? Supposing, the war runs into rough waters? Anything can happen in a war. How will the Indian people react then? Before we discuss that, we must understand one of the fundamental weaknesses in the character of the Indian people.

MORBID FEAR OF CASUALTIES IN THE COLLECTIVE INDIAN PSYCHE

Indians have a morbid fear of suffering casualties—this is what makes the nation weak at its core. It is so because in the wars in this country, we have not had casualties on the same scale as the European nations have faced since the Middle Ages in spite of their small populations. Historically, we have never had our baptism by fire and blood. The bloodiest battle in ancient India was that of Kalinga but it resulted in only a few thousand casualties. This alone was enough to shake Ashok so much that he denounced violence and became a Buddhist! India had to wait long for the battle in which casualties took place on a large scale. This was the Third Battle of Panipat in 1761 in which the Afghans under Ahmed Shah Abdali killed about a hundred thousand Marathas. All the battles of the Mughals and others before and after them, have not had involved casualties on a large scale. In Europe small principalities fought brutal wars regularly with each other; at other times, countries after countries were reduced to waste by invaders like the Mongols.

Even if we do not go far into history, other nations of the world have suffered frightening casualties in numerous wars of the 20th century. The total casualties in the Second World War are estimated between 62 to 78 million! Of these the Soviet Union alone contributed about 10.7 million in soldiers and 14.15 million in civilians. The total casualties in the First World War are estimated at about 20 million. In the Vietnam War, the American casualties were 3,61,911. The North Vietnamese casualties were 1.1 million soldiers and 1.522 million civilians. The South Vietnamese military casualties were 0.54 million. In the Korean War, nearly 2 million civilians perished and the military casualties were about 0.9 million. In the two Iraq Wars against the American forces, the Iraqi casualties were about 4,00,000 and 1,51,000 respectively. The civil wars in the African nations have taken a tremendous toll. Because usually the Indians do not even read of them, they have no idea of this. In the Second Congo civil war involving Rwanda and Uganda against Zimbabwe, Angola and Namibia, the casualties were 3.8 million. In the Rwandan civil war it was 0.9 million; in the Burundi civil war it was 0.2 million. In the first Congo civil war the casualties were 0.9 million. In the Yugoslavian civil war, the total casualties were 2,60,000. In the Chechnya war, the casualties were 2,00,000. Going a little back, the Soviet Revolution took a toll of 5 million people. Then about 13 million people were killed in the purges of Stalin. Casualties were nearly half a million in the Japanese invasion of China and about 1.2 million in the Chinese civil war.

The Indian people have, in comparison, not seen enough bloodshed and destruction through the ages. The net result has been that the collective Indian psyche developed a morbid fear of casualties.

How the Rich, the Beautiful and the Powerful will React to a War?

The euphoria on TV mentioned above will last till the war takes place in some distant land, some unseen border that the people see on the map kept in the TV studio. The situation will change instantaneously the war touches the urban Indian, the upper classes, the business houses, and the industrialists. The moment the bombs start dropping in their comfort zone, however, sheer panic would engulf them. Panic is actually a mild word; the urban Indians will be outraged, perplexed, bewildered, disorientated, petrified, horrified, and scandalized—there will be confusion worse confounded and utter stupefaction all around. Any of the following things will quickly end the euphoria generated by the war. The list is obviously only illustrative:

- A bomb drops say in the Connaught Place.
- A Delhi Metro train derails and falls down from its flyover track somewhere.
- Some local train in Bombay derails and blocks traffic.
- Delhi or some other major airport is shut down.
- Vehicles damaged in bombing lead to interminable traffic jams in Bombay.
- Rumour floats in that an air force base deep inside the country, such as in Agra has been attacked by enemy air force.

- The mobile phone network breaks down in a couple of major cities.
- Bombs fall near some posh markets or malls where rich and smart girls go shopping.
- Internet is disrupted.
- Some petrol dump catches fire somewhere. All they need is the visual of flames leaping and thick black smoke billowing.
- The Sensex crashes 1,000 points in a day.
- The Bombay Stock Exchange starts fluctuating.
- Relatives of patients start screaming hysterically at hospitals because there is no blood in the blood bank and not enough doctors.
- A blackout or power outage in a major town.
- An announcement by a MNC that it is cancelling its FDI (foreign direct investment) in India because of the war.

I tell you; the yuppies, the techies, the smart professionals, the media persons, the corporate honchos, the film actors, the theatre personalities, the fashion designers, the classical dancers, the Page-Three people and the socialites will all be lost and crying inconsolably the moment any of these things happen. And you will have the TV channels descending upon them in droves—how are you feeling; how horrible it all is; will you now reschedule the Fashion Week; what is the view of the industrialists' body on the carnage, and the like. Urban India will cry the loudest.

Our armies could be winning gloriously; however, the moment the war touches the Indians who matter (that is, the rich, the beautiful and the powerful), the Indian people who matter would start buckling—never bother about the common man—his opinion or feelings do not matter in such times.

Eventually, their materialism will soon get the better of their jingoism. The next day you will have:

- Peace marches by social activists, intelligentsia, academics, and film actors demanding an immediate end to hostilities.
- Candlelight vigil by young boys, girls and bored housewives.
- Seminars denouncing war per se and exalting the values of international peace.
- Endless TV debates condemning war per se and also the USA for not putting enough pressure on Pakistan or China.
- Statements by the Big Business houses that 'let bygones, be bygones'; India must move forward and how we must create conditions conducive for attracting foreign investment.
- Blood donation camps organized by cricketers and film actors.
- TV debates inviting a cross-section of the 'civil society' regarding the terms on which the Government of India must negotiate.
- Mass emails to the US President with fervent appeals to act fast. (I am serious. This happens. Indians do look up to the POTUS as a demigod—the ultimate *Taaranhaar* of this century. In September 2016 after the Uri attack, it was reported that a petition on the White House website asking for Pakistan to be declared as a State sponsor of terrorism has gathered massive support from netizens. Created with a goal of 1,00,000 signatures on September 21, there had been over 82,000 signatories in under five days. You see, you do not have to do anything—just pray to the POTUS. Any problem under the sun, POTUS will solve it.
- Some 'Run for Peace' by way of a Marathon or Half Marathon—voluptuous actresses in tight shorts and even tighter T-shirts will lead.
- The channels would find some 'guru' who would be

suggested to be sent across as emissary of universal peace.

The rich, the beautiful and the powerful will remind you endlessly of your commitment to world peace, prosperity and sustained development. They will convince you that if the US is asking us to stop fighting, we must. America is always right, you see—when they fight, it's the right thing to do; when they ask you not to fight, it's the right thing to do. Do as the Americans tell you to do and you will be the happiest people on the planet. Thank God for having created America!

Once the post-war negotiations are over, the rich, the beautiful and the powerful will explain you everything. Historically, rulers and the rich, the beautiful and the powerful have been intimately entwined, if not synonymous with each other. We speak of regal beauty, isn't it? Have we not been calling a beautiful girl a 'princess'? Have we not been describing large businesses as business or industrial 'empires'? Have we not been speaking of movie or media Moguls? [The very word Mogul traces its immediate origin to the Mughal emperors (who, in turn, traced their lineage to the Mongols), fabled for their riches and, of course, absolute power.]

Throughout the centuries, rulers and those people whose interests the rulers catered for (that is, the rich, the beautiful and the powerful) across the world have been able to convince their people of anything and everything they did or did not—the masses have essentially been so indifferent that they would accept any logic, however absurd it be. That actually is the secret of the art of ruling. One need not rule by sheer might all the time—that is very crude and passé. As business is the art of making a fool of the customer, ruling is the art of making a fool of the ruled. The industrialists hire beautiful girls for their ads and make the people believe that if they used their product, they would also become as beautiful and desirable as that enticing girl in the ad—or that they would get the 'approval' of a beautiful girl like that. In the end, it is he who laughs all the way to the bank—the customers do not get any benefit at all but that does not stop them from purchasing that product or trying out another product of somebody else being sold by an equally beautiful girl. Similarly, clever rulers throughout history have manipulated the minds of their people—if they are really clever, their people would genuinely believe that they were the best things that could have happened to them. After the surrender of Germany in the Second World War, the Americans did conduct a Gallup poll and found that 95% of the German people still believed in Hitler and all that he had done the terrible devastation of the country and the horrible sufferings of the people notwithstanding.

European history is replete with examples of how the rulers manipulated the minds of their people throughout the ages. If the rulers of some European nation, State or principality decided to go to war and invite destruction, it was, of course, for the sake of 'national pride' and an eloquent manifestation of the nation's manly spirit—nothing was too costly for the honour of the nation. If the same rulers decided not to go to war, it was described as an act of highly responsible and astute statesmanship; here were men who cared more for peace and prosperity. If the rulers decided to do something and yet did not do something substantial, it was described as an act of strategic restraint.

The spin doctors of the rulers could always, hire or 'purchase' a battery of self-styled experts on everything under the sun to give an 'academic explanation' of everything. And what they could not do was done by poets, singers, film actors and sportspersons. Remember the famous poem 'The Charge of the Light Brigade' written by Alfred Tennyson, which was basically an extremely clever attempt to first window dress and then whitewash the terrible professional mistake committed by the British Generals in that disastrous cavalry charge on Russian artillery in the Battle of Balaclava in which hundreds of them had perished? The common man suffers from a deep inferiority complex—whenever something is said by those whose beauty, physical prowess, wit, success, or wealth he secretly envies and admires at the same time, he does listen to them—it is precisely for this reason that they are hired as 'brand ambassadors' for all sorts of things.

In short, there is every reason to believe that the rich, the beautiful and the powerful would be infinitely more interested in protecting their vested interests over 'national interests'. They need not bother about something called public opinion either because it is they who create, shape and mould public opinion in the first place. In effect, in the event of a war, we are not likely to have a majority which will place 'national interest' above their vested interests.

WHAT WE NEED AS PEOPLE TO COPE WITH NUCLEAR STRIKES OR OTHER DEVASTATIONS OF WAR?

The people of the country have hitherto refused to even think along these lines—as if it is unthinkable. Preparations of military targets to withstand nuclear attacks can be expected to be secret and I cannot comment on that. But there are no preparations at all by any industry whatsoever, private or public; no city; no residents' associations; and no infrastructure owners/operators to cope with nuclear strikes or with other devastations of war.

You may recall that following the terrorist bomb blasts in Jaipur some years ago, the situation was so bad in the hospitals of that city that blood had to air-lifted from as far as Jodhpur. For years now, Delhi has been coming under the seasonal grip of vector-borne diseases like dengue, chikungunya and swine flu. The medical system simply cracks under the pressure—thousands of patients are either obliged to sleep on floor or are turned out. What do we expect do during wars with bombs falling?

Huge critical infrastructures like railways have a disaster management plan for accidents only. (For details, interested readers may see my treatise *Disaster Management*.) That plan does not contemplate even a 1 kilotonne nuclear strike at a critical railway junction and how to cope with it. The country has one railway junction of 7 routes, namely, Mathura; 4 junctions of 6 routes each, namely, Rewari, Bhatinda, Sabaramati and Muzaffarpur; 22 junctions of 5 routes each; 101 junctions of 4 routes each; and a still larger number of junctions of 3 routes each. How many could they protect? So far the railways have prepared only for railway accidents—that is, some trains derailing or colliding. Even for that, they presume that at least one set of tracks would be left intact at the place to send in the relief trains and cranes etc. For a nuclear strike, the destruction would be enormous, depriving the railways of any track whatsoever in a very large area and there would be the additional problem of contamination. The railways do not have any system for decontamination. Critical infrastructure like the railways in a large area will simply collapse as a result of the domino effect of a strike at any important junction. By a careful selection of the junctions to be struck keeping the extent and nature of rail traffic in mind, the railway network in most of the important parts of the country can be paralysed. This will, by itself, be catastrophic for the people as well as military effort.

Airports are sought to be kept beyond public scrutiny in the name of security. But it does not require any imagination to figure out that the civilian airports do not have any mechanism to save the runways and the critical systems like air traffic control etc from even conventional bomb strikes, not to speak of a nuclear strike. In effect, this means that this part of our critical infrastructure would not survive any nuclear strike. Once again, please note that damage to civilian airports might not have any effect on the war-fighting capability of the IAF, but it would generate such panic, such despair amongst the upper classes that the morale of the entire nation would go down.

Similarly, communication systems and Internet would be knocked out instantly. They are so fragile anyway—mobile communication collapses in cyclones also. When a group of labourers digging road for a sewer line happen to break the optical fibre cable of Internet, it takes days for the company to restore it, readers can imagine what would happen for a nuclear strike.

Take it from me, the preparedness of the Indian people to absorb the shocks of any kind of war (not to speak of a nuclear war) is simply zero. This should not be misconstrued to mean that only India is vulnerable. Yes, Pakistan too has almost similar vulnerabilities. China's case is different. They have prepared for surviving nuclear strikes since long as a matter of policy and have built elaborate systems for that.

In the end, surviving nuclear strikes or other horrors of war boils down to the will power of the nation as a whole. It is like professional boxing. There have been certain great boxers who were very good in attack but could not take 'punishment'. On the other hand, there have been great boxers who can take any degree, any amount of punishment. One could throw everything, every single punch known in the book on them and yet they could take it—the so-called 'iron chin' or 'granite chin', as Muhammad Ali and George Chuvalo had. Similarly, you can inflict the same damage on two nations by nuclear strikes; one would survive it, the other would not. It will have to be seen which of the two, India or Pakistan, can produce the necessary mental toughness when it is needed the most.

The bottom line is that, if India wants to emerge victorious in a nuclear war, it must develop the national character to face human sufferings and, of course, civilian casualties—exactly the way in which other nations of the world have done in numerous wars of the past centuries. India needs its baptism by blood and fire. If they can do that, we can emerge victorious in any war. We have the military potential to win any battle, let's develop the 'national character potential' to win any war.

LET'S GO WIN THE NEXT WAR

Armies win battles; nations win wars. Strong armies do not win wars; strong nations do. Conversely, weak nations lose wars even before their armies have lost battles. And victories do not come cheap. You must expect fierce resistance by the enemy and, of course, losses to us as people. Modern wars are total wars. No nation in the history of wars has got victory cheap—it is purchased at the cost of sheer blood.

A nation must therefore prepare itself mentally for the sufferings, deprivations, devastations, and destruction of a war. Then only they can ever hope to endure wars. War in general and total war in particular is not surgery in an operation theatre; you make a few nice cuts here and there, a few snips, a few knots and you are done. No, it's not like that. War is a dirty grind. Study history and reflect upon it. Then you will realize what war entails. War is not what you saw on TV when America invaded Iraq. The American media had fooled the whole world. They made you believe that it was just the precision-guided bombs that were released miles away by the fighters, flew quietly, entered through ventilators and took the bad guys out. So simple, so clinically precise, so clean a way to kill. Nothing happened to the guy living in the next room. You did not have to even see the bad guy! No shooting, no fighting, no blood, no gore. That was a massive exercise in deception. You were not shown what the carpet bombing by the B-52s did. You were not shown what the waves upon waves of rockets unleashed by the MRLS did? The media had you believe that the Gulf War was no different from the video games your kids played. No my dears, this is not what makes a nation capitulate. That's the difference between battles and wars.

A nation capitulates when the will of the people to fight is broken. Iraq's will to fight was broken by the 88,500 tonnes of high explosive unleashed upon it that killed people by the hundreds of thousands, and destroyed homes and industries. As revealed by Paul Walker, of this tonnage, 93.6% consisted of traditional unguided 'dumb' bombs (meaning they damaged indiscriminately) and only 6.4% were the much-touted, much-hyped 'smart' or 'precision' bombs.

India has never had any experience of long destructive wars of the types other nations of the world have endured. The Indian experience of devastation is limited to that by droughts, famines, floods and pestilences—all of which were dismissed and accepted as scourge of God.

Wars are not fought in battlefields alone. A military tradition of a nation is not about just armies winning wars, but fighting them efficiently as a nation. The Indian people would run into trouble when the fighting would cross the battlefields and starts impinging upon the people as a whole.

You must recall what the British went through in the Battle of Britain when German planes were pounding London mercilessly—V-2 and V-1 rockets fell on London by the thousands. Hundreds of thousands of Britons use to sleep underground in the tunnels of London Metro. But the British did not buckle. The courage, the grit, the resolve did not come from the famous "we shall fight on the beaches" speech of

Churchill—famous speeches were made elsewhere also. The Brits had that resolve within them, borne out of a military tradition centuries old.

Even the Americans, their awesome military industrial might notwithstanding, did not wince at taking 5,86,628 casualties in Europe and 1,69,635 casualties in the Pacific Theatre. Sadly, that brave, resolute generation is gone now. I miss General Patton, really! Now things have come to a sorry pass. US commanders in the Gulf were clearly told during the summer of 1990 that keeping US casualties low was to be accorded a very high priority. As a result, operations likely to result in high casualties were avoided, which was why there were no amphibious or airborne assaults. One comment heard from several senior officers in the wake of the US Gulf War victory was that no one wanted to be in charge in a future war where more than 200 Americans were killed. No one relished having to explain to Congress why this was so, and why the Gulf War was an exceptional situation that could not be expected to occur in future wars.

The real crisis of Indian defence is not on account of ours or theirs military hardware; it is on account of what we as a people are. We must therefore strive hard to become a nation of strong people and victory shall always be ours.

Bibliography

Abhishek Saksena, '6 Things that could Happen if India, Pakistan or China Decided to Resort to Nuclear Warfare', Indiatimes, April 14, 2015.

Adrian R Lewis, *The American Culture of War: A History of US Military Force from World War II to Operation Enduring Freedom*, Abingdon: Routledge, 2007.

Afsir Karim, 'Needed a New Military Doctrine to Deter Pakistan Permanently', October 30, 2014, *Indian Defence Review*, also at http://www.sunday-guardian.com/investigation/needed-a-new-military-doctrine-to-deter-pakistan-permanently.

Agha Shahi, 'Zulfiqar Ali Khan and Abdul Sattar: Securing Nuclear Peace', *The News*, October 5, 1999.

Agha Umer Farooq, 'Deterrence Stability, Security Doctrines and Escalation Control in South Asia' (paper presented at the US-Pakistan Strategic Partnership: A Track II Dialogue', Phuket, Thailand, 18-19 Sept 2011).

Ahsan I Butt, Do Nuclear Weapons Affect the Guns-Butter Trade-off? Evidence on Nuclear Substitution from Pakistan and Beyond, *Conflict, Security and Development*, 229-257, 2015.

Ajai Shukla, 'As Pakistan's Army Chief Heads to US: Is a Tactical Nuke Deal Possible?', Rediff.com, Nov 16, 2015.

Alexei Arbatov, Vladimir Dvorkin and Sergey Oznobishchev, 'Contemporary Nuclear Doctrines', Institute of World Economy and International Relations, Russian Academy of Sciences, Moscow, Imemo Ran, 2010.

Ali Ahmed, Limiting War in South Asia, Routledge, New Delhi, 2015.

Ankit Panda, 'Pakistan Clarifies Conditions for Tactical Nuclear Weapon Use Against India', *The Diplomat*, October 20, 2015.

http://thediplomat.com/2015/10/pakistan-clarifies-conditions-for-tactical-nuclear-weapon-use-against-india/.

Antoine J Bousquet, *The Scientific Way of Warfare: Order and Chaos on the Battlefields of Modernity*, Chichester, NY: Columbia University Press, 2009.

Anwar Iqbal, 'Pakistan's Response to Attack will be Intense', Says Report, *Dawn*, Jan 21, 2010.

Arpit Rajain, *Nuclear Deterrence in Southern Asia: China, India and Pakistan*, Sage Publications, New Delhi, 2005.

Arthur Dominic Villasanta, 'Battle of the Airfields' being Waged by India and China along Volatile Arunachal Pradesh Border', *Yibada*, September 10, 2016.
http://en.yibada.com/articles/158893/20160910/battle-airfields-being-waged-india-china-along-volatile-arunachal-pradesh.htm.

Arunabh Saikia, 'PM for review of Indus Water Usage by India', *Live Mint*, September 27 2016.
http://www.livemint.com/Politics/y9G510Zv3bFV7foP5xhxaL/Narendra-Modi-chairs-meeting-to-review-Indus-Waters-Treaty.html.

Arzan Tarapore, 'Holocaust or Hollow Victory: Limited War in Nuclear South Asia', IPCS Research Papers, No 6, New Delhi: Institute of Peace and Conflict Studies, Feb 2005.

Ashley J Tellis, *Stability in South Asia*, Santa Monica, CA: RAND, 1997.

BBC News, 'Russian-Built Nuclear Submarine joins Indian Navy', 4 April 2012.
http://www.bbc.com/news/world-asia-india-17606829.

Benjamin Lambeth, Peter Lavoy and Ashley Tellis, 'Airpower at 18,000': The Indian Air Force in the Kargil War', Carnegie Endowment for International Peace, September 20, 2012.
http://carnegieendowment.org/2012/09/19/airpower-at-18-000-indian-air-force-in-kargil-war-event-3777.

Benjamin S Lambeth, 'Combat Pair: The Evolution of Air Force-Navy Integration in Strike Warfare', RAND Project Air Force, RAND Corporation, 2007.

Bharat Karnad, *Nuclear Weapons and Indian Security: The Realist Foundations of Strategy* (New Delhi: Macmillan, 2002), p 558.

Bill Fawcet (ed), *How to Lose a War: More Foolish Plans and Great Military Blunders*, Harper, New York, 2009.

Brian McAllister Linn, *The Echo of Battle: The Army's Way of War*, Cambridge, MA: Harvard University Press, 2007.

Bruce D Berkowitz, *The New Face of War: How War will be Fought in the 21st Century*, New York, NY: Simon and Schuster, 2003.

Charles Townshend (ed), *The Oxford Illustrated History of Modern War*, Oxford: Oxford University Press, 1997.

'China Military Strength'. http://www.globalfirepower.com/country-military-strength-detail.asp?country_id=china.

Christine Fair, 'Explaining Support for Sectarian Terrorism in Pakistan: Piety, Maslak and Sharia', *Religions*, 1137-1167, July 20, 2015.

Christopher Clary and Vipin Narang, 'Doctrine, Capabilities, and (In)Stability in South Asia', in Michael Krepon and Julia Thompson (eds), *Deterrence Stability and Escalation Control in South Asia*, Washington DC: The Stimson Center, 2013.

Christopher Clary, 'Deterrence Stability and the Conventional Balance of Forces in South Asia', in Krepon and Thompson, *Deterrence Stability and Escalation Control in South Asia*, 143-5.

Christopher Clary, 'What Might an India-Pakistan War Look Like?', MIT Center for International Studies, Spring, 2012.

Chuan han Wong, 'China Begins Building Second Aircraft Carrier', *Wall Street Journal*, December 31, 2015.

CLAWS Research Team, 'Strategic Reserves of Pakistan', *Scholar Warrior*, Autumn 2011.

CLAWS, 'Pakistan Army: Modernization, Arms Procurement and Capacity Building', New Delhi, India, 21 Feb 2011.

Colin Gray, *Another Bloody Century: Future War*, London: Weidenfeld and Nicolson, 2005.

Colin McInnes, *Men, Machines and the Emergence of Modern Warfare, 1914-1945*, Camberley: Strategic and Combat Studies Institute, 1992.

Colin S Gray, *Modern Strategy*, Oxford: Oxford University Press, 1999.

Colin S Gray, 'Nuclear Weapons and the Revolution in Military Affairs' in TV Paul, Richard J Harknett, and James J Wirtz (eds), *The Absolute*

Weapon Revisited: Nuclear Arms and the Emerging International Order, Ann Arbor: University of Michigan Press, 1998.

Colin S Gray, *Strategy for Chaos: Revolutions in Military Affairs and the Evidence of History*, London: Frank Cass, 2002.

Commander Muhammad Azam Khan (retd), 'India's Cold Start is too Hot', *Proceedings Magazine*, March 2011, Vol 137/3/1, 297.

Comptroller and Auditor General, Report No 24: 'Union Government (Defence Services) Army and Ordnance Factories', Dec 2011.

Corey Charlton and Imogen Calderwood, 'Pentagon say Reason most Expensive Fighter Jet ever the F35 Lost a Dogfight with an F16 from 40 Years Ago was because it did not have a Special Coat of Stealth Paint, *The Daily Mail*, July 3, 2015, http://www.dailymail.co.uk/news/article-3148585/Pentagon-say-reason-expensive-fighter-jet-F35-lost-dogfight-F16-40-years-ago-did-not-special-coat-stealth-paint.html.

DM Jones and MLR Smith, 'Whose Hearts and Whose Minds? The Curious Case of Global Counterinsurgency', *The Journal of Strategic Studies*, Vol 33, No 1 (February 2010).

Daniel Markey, 'Armed Confrontation Between China and India', Contingency Planning Memorandum No 27, Center for Preventive Action, Council on Foreign Relations, New York, November 2015.

Daniel Markey, 'Terrorism and Indo-Pakistani Escalation', Contingency Planning Memorandum No 6, Washington DC: Council on Foreign Relations, Jan 2010.

Daniel S Geller and J David Singer, *Nations at War: A Scientific Study of International Conflict*, Cambridge: Cambridge University Press, 1998.

David E Johnson, *Military Capabilities for Hybrid Warfare: Insights from the Israeli Defense Forces in Lebanon and Gaza*, Santa Monica, CA: RAND, 2010.

David J Lonsdale, *The Nature of War in the Information Age: Clausewitzian Future*, New York, NY: Frank Cass, 2005.

David Jordan, James D Kiras, David J Lonsdale, Ian Speller, Christopher Tuck and C Dale Walton, *Understanding Modern Warfare*, Cambridge: Cambridge University Press, 2008.

Declan Walsh and Ismail Khan, 'US Drone Strike Kills 6 in Pakistan, Fueling Anger', *New York Times*, September 6, 2013. http://www.nytimes.com/2013/09/07/world/asia/us-drone-strike-kills-6-in-pakistan-fueling-anger.html?_r=0

Edward C Mann, III, *Thunder and Lightning: Desert Storm and the Airpower Debates*, Maxwell, AL: Air University Press, 1995.

Emily O Goldman, and Leslie C Eliason, *The Diffusion of Military Technology and Ideas*, Stanford, CA: Stanford University Press, 2003.

Express Tribune, 'Islamabad, Kabul Look Inwards as Tehran Blames US', *Express Tribune*, June 26, 2011. http://tribune.com.pk/story/196587/islamabad-kabul-look-inwards-as-tehran-blames-us/.

Express Tribune, 'Pakistan Army to preempt India's Cold Start Doctrine', *Express Tribune*, June 16, 2013. http://tribune.com.pk/story/564136/pakistan-army-to-preempt-indias-cold-start-doctrine/.

Farhat Taj, 'Drone Attacks: Pakistan's Policy and the Tribesmen's Perspective', The Jamestown Foundation, *Terrorism Monitor*, Volume 8, Issue 10, March 11, 2010.

Feroz Hasan Khan, 'Going Tactical: Pakistan's Nuclear Posture and Implications for Stability', IFRI Security Studies Center, Brussels, September 2015.

Feroz Hasan Khan, 'Nuclear Security in Pakistan: Separating Myth from Reality', Arms Control Association. http://www.armscontrol.org/act/2009_07-08/khan.

Feroz Khan, 'Minimum Deterrence: Pakistan's Dilemma', *RUSI Journal*, 156/5 (Oct 2011), 44-51.

Francisco Aguilar, Randy Bell, Natalie Black, Sayce Falk, Sasha Rogers, and Aki Peritz, *An Introduction to Pakistan's Military*, Belfer Center for Science and International Affairs, Harvard Kennedy School, Massachusetts, July 2011.

Frank Hoffman, *Conflict in the 21st Century: The Rise of Hybrid Wars* (Arlington, VA: Potomac Institute for Policy Studies, 2007.

Gary Schmitt and Sadanand Dhume, 'Can India's Military be Fixed?', *Weekly Standard*, 19/40, June 2014.

Gen VP Malik (retd), 'A Comprehensive Response Strategy to a Collusive and Collaborative Threat from China and Pakistan', 30th USI National Security Lecture.

George C Marshall and Claremont Institute, 'Indo-Pak Tactical Missiles Risk Dangerous Miscalculation, US Intel Officer, Missile Threat', A Project of the George C Marshall and Claremont Institute, June 18, 2013.

http://missilethreat.com/indo-pak-tactical-missiles-risk-dangerous-miscalculation-u-s-intel-officer/

George Perkovich and Toby Dalton, 'Modi's Strategic Choice: How to Respond to Terrorism from Pakistan', The Elliott School of International Affairs, *The Washington Quarterly*, 38:1 pp 23-45, Spring 2015.

Globalsecurity.org, 'XVII Corps Mountain Strike Corps'.

Goldstein, Lyle, 'Chinese Naval Strategy in the South China Sea: An Abundance of Noise and Smoke, but Little Fire', Contemporary Southeast Asia Institute of Southeast Asian Studies, 33 (3): 324, December 2011.

Gregory Koblentz, *Strategic Stability in the Second Nuclear Age*, Washington DC: Council on Foreign Relations, 2014.

Griffiths, *Forward into Battle: Fighting Tactics from Waterloo to the Near Future*, Chichester: Anthony Bird Publications, 1981.

Hans M Kristensen and Robert S Norris, 'Pakistani Nuclear Forces, 2015', Nuclear Notebook, Bulletin of the Atomic Scientists. 'World Nuclear Forces', *SIPRI Yearbook*, 2015.

Harlan K Ullman and James P Wade, *Shock and Awe: Achieving Rapid Dominance*, Washington, DC: National Defense University, 1996.

Herman Kahn, *Thinking About the Unthinkable*, Horizon Press New York, 1962.

http://aermech.in/ins-chakra-nuclear-powered-attack-submarine indian-navy/

http://www.dia.mil/News/Speeches-and-Testimonies/Article/13225/worldwide-threat-assessment/

http://www.globalsecurity.org/military/world/india/corps-xvii.htm

http://www.ndtv.com/wikileak/wikileaks-us-on-indian-armys-cold-start-doctrine-440802

http://www.npr.org/sections/thetwo-way/2015/08/27/435189782/report-in-a-decade-or-sooner-pakistan-could-be-no-3-nuclear-power
http://www.nti.org/learn/countries/china/nuclear/
https://en.wikipedia.org/wiki/List_of_terrorist_incidents_in_Pakistan_since_2001
https://www.strategypage.com/htmw/htart/articles/20101024.aspx?comments=Y

'India and Pakistan, Agreement on Advance Notice on Military Exercises, Manoeuvres and Troop Movements', 6 April 1991, UNTS No 31420. http://treaties.un.org/doc/publication/unts/volumeper cent201843/volume-1843-i-31420-english.pdf

'India Helping Terrorists in Pakistan: Pak Defence Minister', *Indian Express*, 13 Jan 2015. http://indianexpress.com/article/world/neighbours/india-helping-terrorists-in-pakistan-pak-defence-minister/

'India Sponsoring Terrorism in Pakistan, Alleges Rehman Malik', *Hindustan Times*, 23 Sep 2009. http://www.hindustantimes.com/world/india-sponsoring-terrorism-in-pakistan-alleges-rehman-malik/story-MlpWbn3VJ7JTTnSczy253I.html

'Indian Military's Cold Start Doctrine and its Implications for Strategic Stability in South Asia', Conference Report, South Asian Strategic Stability Institute, Islamabad, Pakistan: 20-22 July 2010.

Iskander Rehman, 'Sino-Indian Border Skirmishes Towards a Limited Confrontation?', *IPCS*. Issue Brief, No 117, September 2009.

Iskander Rehman, 'The Indian Navy has a Big Problem: The Subsurface Dilemma', *The National Interest*, 4 Nov 2014. http://nationalinterest.org/feature/the-indian-navy-has-big-problem-thesubsurface-dilemma-11598

JP Kiszely, 'The Contribution of Originality to Military Success' in Brian Holden Reid (ed), *The Science of War: Back to First Principles*, London: Routledge, 1993.

Jack S Levy, 'Quantitative Studies of Deterrence Success and Failure' in Paul C Stern et al (eds), *Perspectives on Deterrence*, New York: Oxford Uuniversity Press, 1989, 98-133.

Jacqui Goddard, 'Pearl Harbour Memo Shows US Warned of Japanese Attack', *The Telegraph*, December 4, 2011.
http://www.telegraph.co.uk/news/worldnews/northamerica/usa/8932197/Pearl-Harbour-memo-shows-US-warned-of-Japanese-attack.html

Jaganath Sankaran, 'Pakistan's Battlefield Nuclear Policy: A Risky Solution to an Exaggerated Threat', *International Security*, Winter 2014/15, Vol 39, No 3, pp 118-151.

James Holmes et al, *Indian Naval Strategy in the Twenty-First Century*, London: Routledge, 2009.

James J Wirtz and Surinder Rana, 'Surprise at the Top of the World: India's Systemic and Intelligence Failure' in Lavoy, *Asymmetric Warfare in South Asia*, 207-30.

James Jay Carafano, 'Measuring Military Power', *Strategic Studies Quarterly*, 8/3 (Fall 2014), 11-18.

Jason Glab, 'Blockading China—A Guide', War on the Rocks, October 1, 2013.
http://warontherocks.com/2013/10/blockading-china-a-guide/#

Jeffrey Lewis, 'Pakistan's Nuclear Artillery', *Arms Control Wonk*, December 12, 2011.
http://www.armscontrolwonk.com/archive/204866/pakistans-nuclear-artillery/
https://qzprod.files.wordpress.com/2015/12/43e77-pakistanhave createdsmallestnuclearbomboftheworld.jpg?quality=80&strip=all

Jeffrey R Cooper, *Another View of the Revolution in Military Affairs* (Carlisle, PA: Strategic Studies Institute, 1994.

John Andreas Olsen and Martin van Creveld (eds), *The Evolution of Operational Art: From Napoleon to the Present*, Oxford: Oxford University Press, 2011.

John Arquilla, 'Nuclear Weapons in South Asia: More may Be Manageable', *Comparative Strategy*, 16/1 (Jan-March 1997), 13-31.

John E Peters et al, *War and Escalation in South Asia*, Santa Monica, CA: RAND Corporation, 2006.

John H Gill, 'India and Pakistan: A Shift in the Military Calculus?', in Ashley J Tellis and Michael Wills (eds), *Strategic Asia, 2005-06: Military*

Modernization in an Era of Uncertainty, Seattle, WA: National Bureau of Asian Research 2005, 237-68.

John H Gill, 'Military Operations in the Kargil Conflict' in Peter R Lavoy (ed), *Asymmetric Warfare in South Asia: The Causes and Consequences of the Kargil Conflict*, Cambridge: Cambridge University Press, 2009, 92-129.

John J Mearsheimer, 'Assessing the Conventional Balance: The 3:1 Rule and Its Critics', *International Security*, 13/4 (Spring 1989), 54-89.

John J Mearsheimer, *Conventional Deterrence*, Ithaca, NY: Cornell University Press, 1983.

John Lancaster, 'Kashmir Crisis was Defused on Brink of War; As US Reviews Showdown, Nuclear Danger Looms Large', *Washington Post*, July 26, 1999.

John Mazach, USN (retd), 'The 21st-Century Triad: Unconventional Thinking About the New Realities of Conventional Warfare', *Sea Power*, March 2002, p 53.

John W Garver, 1962, 'Once More?', *Outlook*, October 22, 2012. http://www.outlookindia.com/magazine/story/1962-once-more/282572

Jonathan M House, *Combined Arms Warfare in the Twentieth Century*, Lawrence, KS: University Press of Kansas, 2001.

Jonathan Marcus, Analysis: 'The World's Most Dangerous Place?', BBC News, March 23, 2000.
http://news.bbc.co.uk/2/hi/south_asia/687021.stm

Joseph Wylie, *Military Strategy: A General Theory of Power Control*, Annapolis, MD: Naval Institute Press, 2014.

Josy Joseph, 'Army's Demand for Attack Choppers Triggers Fresh Turf War with IAF', *Times of India*, July 14, 2012.
https://timesofindia.indiatimes.com/india/Armys-demand-for-attack-choppers-triggers-fresh-turf-war-with-IAF/articleshow/14871959.cms

Justin Kelly and Mike Brennan, *Alien: How Operational Art Devoured Strategy*, Carlisle, PA: Strategic Studies Institute, September 2009.

K Santhanam and Ashok Parthasarathi, 'Pokhran-II Thermonuclear Test, a Failure', *The Hindu*, September 17, 2009.

http://www.thehindu.com/opinion/op-ed/pokhranii-thermonuclear-test-a-failure/article21311.ece

Kapil Patil, 'India's New Mountain Strike Corps: Conventional Deterrence', *The Diplomat*, August 8, 2013. http://thediplomat.com/2013/08/indias-new-mountain-strike-corps-conventional-deterrence/

Kartikeya Sharma and Gautam Datt, 'Parliamentary Standing Committee on Defence Admits Shortage of Ammunition', *India Today*, April 23, 2012. http://indiatoday.intoday.in/story/parliamentary-panel-to-ensure-ammunition-supply-for-army/1/185610.html

Kelsey Davenport, 'China Expands Missile Arsenal, Arms Control Association', June 2016. https://www.armscontrol.org/ACT/2016_06/News/China-Expands-Missile-Arsenal/

Khurshid Khan, 'Limited War under the Nuclear Umbrella and Its Implications for South Asia', Washington DC: Henry L Stimson Center, June 14, 2012. http://www.stimson.org/content/limited-war-under-nuclear-umbrella-and-its-implications-south-asia

Lawrence Sondhaus, *Strategic Culture and Ways of War*, London: Routledge, 2006.

Lt Gen BS Pawar, 'Indian Army Aviation Corps: Today and Tomorrow', *Defence and Security Alert*, Oct 2012.

Lt Gen Khalid Masood Khan (retd), 'Cold Start Doctrine—An Analytical Study', *The Nation*, Sept 19, 2015.

Lukas Milevski, 'Fortissimus Inter Pares: The Utility of Landpower in Grand Strategy', *Parameters*, Summer 2012.

Mainichi, 'Going Nuclear: Plutonium and Uranium Bombs' (Pt. 6), *Mainichi*, August 12, 2014.

Maleeha Lodhi, 'Pakistan's Nuclear Compulsions', *The News*, 6 Nov 2012.

Malik Qasim Mustafa, 'Pakistan's Military Security and Conventional Balance of Power', *Strategic Studies*, 29/1 (Spring 2009), 35-44.

Manish Girdhar, 'PLAAF Deployments in Tibet', CLAWS, April 09, 2010.

http://www.claws.in/347/plaaf-deployments-in-tibet-manish-girdhar.html

Manjeet S Pardesi, 'The Impact of RMA on Conventional Deterrence: A Theoretical Analysis', Institute of Defense and Strategic Studies, Singapore, Dec 2005.

Manoj Joshi, 'Indian Hydrogen Bomb was a Dud', *India Today*, August 27, 2009.
http://indiatoday.intoday.in/story/'Indian+hydrogen+bomb+was+a+dud'/1/58655.html

Mansoor Ahmed, 'Security Doctrines, Technologies and Escalation Ladders: A Pakistani Perspective' (paper presented at the US-Pakistan Strategic Partnership: A Track II Dialogue, Phuket, Thailand, 18-19 Sept 2011.

'Mapping Militant Organizations, Tehreek-e-Taliban Pakistan', Stanford.edu. 13 Dec 2007.
http://web.stanford.edu/group/mappingmilitants/cgi-bin/groups/view/105

Mark A Ryan, Finkelstein, David M and McDevitt, Michael A (eds), *Chinese Warfighting: The PLA Experience Since 1949*, London: ME Sharpe, 2003.

Mark Thompson, 'The True Cost of the Afghanistan War may Surprise You', *Time*, Jan 1, 2015.
http://time.com/3651697/afghanistan-war-cost/

Martin van Creveld, *Technology and War: From 2000 BC to the Present*, London, Brassey's, 1991.

Michael Evans, Alan Ryan and Russell Parkin (eds), *Future Armies, Future Challenges: Land Warfare in the Information Age*, Allen & Unwin, Australia, 2004.

Michael Krepon, 'Pakistan's Nuclear Strategy and Deterrence Stability' in Michael Krepon and Julia Thompson (eds), *Deterrence Stability and Escalation Control in South Asia*, Stimson Center, 2013.

Michael Krepon, 'Command and Control in South Asia', Arms Control Wonk.com, December 7, 2009.
http://krepon.armscontrolwonk.com/archive/2558/command-control-in-south-asia

Michael Krepon, Rodney W Jones and Ziad Haider (eds.), *Escalation Control and the Nuclear Option in South Asia*, 164-166.

Michael Krepon, 'Tac Nukes in South Asia', Arms Control Wonk, 18 April 2012.
http://www.armscontrolwonk.com/archive/403419/tac-nukes-in-south-asia/

Michael O'Hanlon, 'What If a War Between Pakistan and India Went Nuclear?', *Newsweek*, September 5, 2015.
http://www.newsweek.com/what-if-war-between-pakistan-and-india-went-nuclear-368799

Milan Vego, *Joint Operational Warfare: Theory and Practice* (Newport, RI: US Naval War College, 2009.

Military Balance, International Institute for Strategic Studies, London, 2011, 239.

Minemura, Kenji, 'China to Start Construction of 1st Aircraft Carrier Next Year', *Asahi Shimbun*, December 31, 2008.

Mohan Malik, 'The China Factor in the India-Pakistan Conflict', Occasional Paper Series, Asia-Pacific Center for Security Studies, November 2002.

Muhammad Ashiq Khan and Syed Mussawar Hussain Bhukhari, 'Nuclearisation in South Asia with Special Reference to Cold Start Doctrine a Limited War Option: An Analysis', *European Academic Research*, Vol II, Issue 1/April 2014.

Munir Akram, 'Gambling Against Armageddon', *Dawn*, 26 Oct 2014.

'Musharraf Promulgates Ordinance to Establish NCA', *Daily Times*, December 14, 2007.
http://www.dailytimes.com.pk/default.asp?page=2007\12\14\story_14-12-2007_pg7_3.

Nasr: 'Tactical Ballistic Missile'.
http://www.military-today.com/missiles/nasr.htm.

'NCA Takes Serious Note of Indian Statements', *The International News*, January 14, 2010.
http://thenews.jang.com.pk/TodaysPrintDetail.aspx?ID=26663&Cat=13&dt=1/14/2010.

Nitin Gokhale, 'India's Doctrinal Shift?', *The Diplomat*, January 25, 2011.

http://thediplomat.com/2011/01/indias-doctrinal-shift/

'Pak's Conventional Deterrence Averted War: Musharraf', Rediff, 22 June 2002.

'Pakistan Has Quality Army, India Has Quantity, Say Experts', Agence France-Presse, 22 May 2002.

'Pakistan's Leader Cedes Nuclear Office', *The New York Times*, November 29, 2009.
http://www.nytimes.com/2009/11/29/world/asia/29pstan.html
pakistanbodycount.org

Paolo Cotta-Ramusino and Maurizio Martellini, 'Nuclear Safety, Nuclear Stability, and Nuclear Strategy in Pakistan', A Concise Report by Landau Network—Centro Volta, Pugwash Conferences on Science and World Affairs (January 14, 2002).
http://www.pugwash.org/september11/pakistan-nuclear.htm

Patrick O'Sullivan, *Terrain and Tactics*, London: Greenwood, 1991.

Paul Bracken, 'The Problem from Hell: South Asia's Arms Race', *The Diplomat*, 29 Nov 2012.

Paul K Davis, *Aggregation, Disaggregation and the 3:1 Rule in Ground Combat*, Santa Monica, CA: RAND 1995.

Paul K Kerr and Mary Beth Nikitin, 'Pakistan's Nuclear Weapons: Proliferation and Security Issues', Washington DC: Congressional Research Service, 10 May 2012.

Paul Walker, 'US Bombing: The Myth of Surgical Bombing in the Gulf War'.
http://deoxy.org/wc/wc-myth.htm

Peter Paret (ed), *Makers of Modern Strategy: From Machiavelli to the Nuclear Age*, Princeton, NJ: Princeton University Press, 1986.

Peter R Lavoy, 'Islamabad's Nuclear Posture: Its Premises and Implementation', in Henry D Sokolski (ed), *Pakistan's Nuclear Future: Worries Beyond War*, Carlisle, PA: US Army War College, Jan 2008, 129-65.

Polly M Holdorf, 'Limited Nuclear War in the 21st Century'.
https://csis-prod.s3.amazonaws.com/s3fs-public/110916_Holdorf.pdf

Polly Nayak and Michael Krepon, 'The Unfinished Crisis: US Crisis

Management after the 2008 Mumbai Attacks', Washington, DC: The Henry L Stimson Center, February 2012.

Polly Nayak and Michael Krepon, 'US Crisis Management in South Asia's Twin Peaks Crisis', Report No 57, Washington, DC: The Henry L Stimson Center, September 2006.

Praful Bidwai, 'India Sharpens Nuclear Claws', *Asia Times*, January 31, 2002,
http://atimes.com/ind-pak/DA31Df03.html.

Praful Bidwai, 'H-Bomb or a Fizzle', *Frontline*, Volume 26, Issue 19, September 12-25, 2009.
http://www.frontline.in/static/html/fl2619/stories/20090925261908000.htm

Pranav Kulkarni, 'Indian Army Ammunition won't even last 10 Days in Event of a War, Suggests CAG Reports', *Indian Express*, May 9, 2015.
http://indianexpress.com/article/india/india-others/3-years-on-armys-plan-to-fill-ammo-stock-yet-to-take-off-cag/

Praveen Swami, 'India and the Hidden Hand', *The Indian Express*, August 24, 2015.
http://indianexpress.com/article/opinion/columns/india-and-the-hidden-hand/

Praveen Swami, 'New Pakistan Army Green Book Voices Fear of India-US Axis', *The Hindu*, December 6, 2013.
http://www.thehindu.com/news/national/new-pakistan-army-green-book-voices-fear-of-indiaus-axis/article5426665.ece

Praveen Swami, 'Pakistan Army Warns of 'Disproportionate Response' in Future Wars', *The Hindu*, December 5, 2013.

Pravin Sawhney, 'Ruse and Reality on the Border', *Indian Defence News*, November 19, 2015.
http://www.indiandefensenews.in/2015/11/ruse-and-reality-on-border.html

Priyanka Mogul, 'Are India and Pakistan on the Brink of a Water War? The Indus Waters Treaty Explained', *International Business Times*, September 30, 2016.
http://www.ibtimes.co.uk/are-india-pakistan-brink-water-war-indus-waters-treaty-explained-1584218

Qiao Liang and Wang Xiangsui (senior colonels of the PLA), *Unrestricted Warfare*, 1999, China.

Rajat Pandit, 'Army's Ammunition won't Last 20 Days of War', *Times of India*.
http://timesofindia.indiatimes.com/india/Armys-ammunition-wont-last-20-days-of-war/articleshow/40862131.cms

Rajat Pandit, 'Response to Strike from Pak will be Very Heavy: IAF Chief, *Times of India*, Jul 26, 2011.
http://timesofindia.indiatimes.com/india/Response-to-strike-from-Pak-will-be-very-heavy-IAF-chief/articleshow/9370406.cms

Reshmi Kazi, 'Nasr: A Disadvantage for Pakistan', IDSA comment, August 19, 2011.
http://www.idsa.in/idsacomments/NASRADisadvantageforPakistan_ebhearne_140711.

Rezaul H Laskar, 'China Warns India Against Deploying BrahMos Missile in Arunachal Pradesh, *Hindustan Times*, August 23, 2016.
http://www.hindustantimes.com/india-news/china-warns-india-against-deploying-brahmos-missile-in-arunachal-pradesh/story-ui0psBJZ3WOvn3aJzLCqiJ.html

Richard Holmes, *Acts of War: The Behaviour of Men in Battle*, London: Cassell, 2004.

Richard Weitz, 'South Asia's Nuclear Arms Racing', *The Diplomat*, 1 Oct 2011.

Rob Johnson, Michael Whitby and John France, *How to Win on the Battlefield: The 25 Key Tactics of All Time*, London: Thames and Hudson, 2013.

Robert M Citino, *Blitzkrieg to Desert Storm: The Evolution of Operational Warfare*, Lawrence, KS: University Press of Kansas, 2004.

Robert Pape, *Bombing to Win: Air Power and Coercion in War*, Ithaca, NY: Cornell University Press, 1996.

Rodney W Jones, 'Pakistan's Answer to Cold Start?', *The Friday Times*, May 13-19, 2011.
http://www.thefridaytimes.com/13052011/page7.shtml

Rodney W Jones, 'Conventional Military Imbalance and Strategic Stability in South Asia', University of Bradford: South Asian Strategic Stability Unit, March 2005.

S Kaliski, *Journal of Technical Physics*, Warsaw, Vol 19, 4, 1968.

SN Prasad (chief ed), *History of the Conflict With China, 1962*, History Division, Ministry of Defence, Government of India, New Delhi, 1992.
https://chinaindiaborderdispute.files.wordpress.com/2010/07/1962 classifiedhistory.pdf

Sachin Parashar, 'Pak's Friend China Blocks Brahmaputra Tributary', *Times of India*, October 2, 2016.
http://timesofindia.indiatimes.com/world/china/Paks-friend-China-blocks-Brahmaputra-tributary/articleshow/54635283.cms

Saira Bano, 'Pakistan is Learning the Wrong Lesson: Tactical Nuclear Weapons in South Asia', *International Policy Digest*, Dec 27, 2014.
http://intpolicydigest.org/2014/12/27/pakistan-s-nuke-plan-in-south-asia-is-dumb-policy/.

Sandeep Unnithan, 'Not Ready for War', *India Today*, 29 Oct 2011.
http://indiatoday.intoday.in/story/indian-army-war-readiness-against-china/1/157763.html

Scott D Sagan, 'Why Do States Build Nuclear Weapons? Three Models in Search of a Bomb', *International Security*, 21/3 (Winter 1996-1997), 54-86.

Shahid Javed Daskavi, 'If Nuclear Program were Under Supervision of Political Governments, God Knows What would Have Happened: Samar Mubarakmand', *Jehan Pakistan*, February 5, 2016.

Shambaugh, David, *Modernizing China's Military: Progress, Problems, and Prospects*, Berkeley, CA: University of California, 2004.

Shashank Joshi, 'Pakistan's Tactical Nuclear: Nightmare Déjà Vu?, *Washington Quarterly*, 36/3 (Summer 2013), 159-72.

Shubhodeep Chakravarty, Declare Pakistan a Terrorist State: Online Petition to White House Gets Massive Response', *Times of India*, September 26, 2016.
http://timesofindia.indiatimes.com/world/pakistan/Declare-Pakistan -a-terrorist-state-Online-petition-to-White-House-gets-massive response/articleshow/54523330.cms

Siddharth Srivastava, 'Indian Army "Backed Out" of Pakistan Attack', *Asia Times*, 21 Jan 2009.

Sir Julian Stafford Corbett, *Some Principles of Maritime Strategy*, (new ed), New York: Longmans, Green, and Co, 1918, 11-12.

Stephen Biddle, *Afghanistan and the Future of Warfare: Implications for Army and Defense Policy*, Carlisle, PA: US Army War College, Nov 2002.

Stephen Biddle, *Military Power: Explaining Victory and Defeat in Modern Battle*, Princeton, NJ: Princeton University Press, 2004.

Stephen P Cohen and Sunil Dasgupta, *Arming without Aiming: India's Military Modernization*, Washington DC: Brookings Institution Press 2010.

Sudhi Ranjan Sen, 'INS Chakra: Top 10 Must-Know Facts', NDTV, April 6, 2012.
http://www.ndtv.com/india-news/ins-chakra-top-10-must-know-facts-475108

Sumit Ganguly and S Paul Kapur, *India, Pakistan and the Bomb: Debating Nuclear Stability in South Asia*, Columbia University Press, 2010.

Sunil Dasgupta and Stephen P Cohen, 'Is India Ending its Strategic Restraint Doctrine?', Center for Strategic and International Studies, *The Washington Quarterly*, 34:2, pp 163-177, Spring 2011.

The Dawn, 'US Drone Strikes Fail to Mobilise Pakistan Masses', October 30, 2011.
http://www.dawn.com/news/670080/us-drone-strikes-fail-to-mobilise-pakistan-masses

The Express Tribune, "India Accuses Pakistan of Maintaining 'Militant Camps' Along Border", Pakistan, 4 Dec 2012.

Theo Farrell and Terry Terriff (eds), *The Sources of Military Change: Culture, Politics, Technology*, Boulder, CO: Lynne Rienner, 2002.

Theo Farrell, *The Norms of War: Cultural Beliefs and Modern Conflict*, Boulder, CO: Lynne Rienner, 2005.

Thomas G Mahnken, *Fighting a Nuclear War in the 21st Century: Future Scenarios of Limited Nuclear Conflict*, Chapter 6, Programme on Strategic Stability Evaluation, Georgia Tech.

Thomas X Hammes, *The Sling and the Stone: On War in the 21st Century*, St Paul, MN: Zenith, 2004.

Toby Dalton and Jaclyn Tandler, *Understanding the Arms 'Race' in South Asia*, Washington DC: Carnegie Endowment for International Peace, Sept 2012.

Tom Hundley, 'Pakistan and India: Race to the End', *Foreign Policy*, 5 Sept 2012.
www.foreignpolicy.com/articles/2012/09/05/race_to_the_end

Tom Thounaojam, 'Indian Air Force vs People's Liberation Army Air Force, Hypothetical Air Aarfare', *Defenceaviation*, April 9, 2013.
http://www.defenceaviation.com/2013/04/old-hatred-indian-air-force-vs-peoples-liberation-army-air-force-hypothetical-air-warfare.html.

Travis Wheeler, 'China's MIRVs: Separating Fact from Fiction', May 18, 2016, *The Diplomat*.
http://thediplomat.com/2016/05/chinas-mirvs-separating-fact-from-fiction/.

Trevor N Dupuy, 'Combat Data and the 3:1 Rule', *International Security*, 14/1 (Summer 1989), 195-201.

Usman Ansari, 'Experts: Missile Test Firing Shows Development Complete', defensenews.com, November 6, 2013.

VP Malik, 'Asia—Limited Wars in South Asia: Against the Nuclear Backdrop', GlobalDefence.Net, 2012.

VR Raghavan, 'Limited War and Nuclear Escalation in South Asia', *The Nonproliferation Review*, Fall-Winter 2001.

Vinod Anand, 'Review of the Indian Army Doctrine: Dealing with Two Fronts', *CLAWS Journal*, Summer 2010.

Vivekanand International Foundation, *Strategic Posture of China in Tibet Autonomous Region and its Implications: Is India Prepared?*, October 2012, New Delhi.

Walter C Ladwig III, 'A Cold Start for Hot Wars?: The Indian Army's New Limited War Doctrine', *International Security*, Vol 32, No 3 (Winter 2007/08), pp 158-190.

Walter C Ladwig III, 'Drivers of Indian Naval Expansion' in Harsh V Pant (ed), *The Rise of the Indian Navy: Internal Vulnerabilities, External Challenges*, Farnham, UK, Ashgate 2012), 19-40.

Walter C Ladwig III, 'Indian Military Modernization and Conventional Deterrence in South Asia', *The Journal of Strategic Studies*, 2015.

Wikileaks, 'Subject: Cold Start—A Mixture of Myth and Reality Ref: IIR 6 844 0101 10 (Cold Start—A Dao Perspective)', Classified By: Ambassador Tim Roemer. Reason: 1.4 (b,d). https://wikileaks.org/plusd/cables/10NEWDELHI295_a.html

William A Owens, *Lifting the Fog of War*, Baltimore, MD: Johns Hopkins University Press, 2001.

William Johnson, *Redefining Land Power for the 21st Century*, Carlisle, PA: Strategic Studies Institute, 1991.

William S Lind, *Maneuvre Warfare Handbook*, Boulder, CO: Westview, 1985.

Williamson Murray, *Military Adaptation in War: With Fear of Change*, Cambridge: Cambridge University Press, 2011.

WS-2: Multiple Launch Rocket System. http://www.military-today.com/artillery/ws2.htm.

Yatish Yadav, '"Green Book" Reveals Sinister Pak Design, *The New Indian Express*, December 22, 2013. http://www.newindianexpress.com/magazine/Green-Book-Reveals-Sinister-Pak-Design/2013/12/22/article1954317.ece.

Zachary Keck, 'Pakistan wants "Battlefield" Nukes to Use Against Indian Troops', February 6, 2015, *The National Interest*. http://nationalinterest.org/blog/the-buzz/pakistan-wants-battlefield-nukes-use-against-indian-troops-12200.

Zeenews Bureau, 'Only Ten Days of Ammunition Left?', 6 April 2012. http://zeenews.india.com/news/nation/only-ten-days-of-ammunition-left_768543.html.

Zulfqar Khan, 'India-Pakistan Nuclear Rivalry: Perceptions, Misperceptions and Mutual Deterrence', Islamabad Policy Research Institute, Islamabad, Jan 2005.

Index